Quotations of Courage and Vision

OTHER BOOKS BY CARL HERMANN VOSS

THE UNIVERSAL GOD: An Interfaith Anthology of Man's Search for God

THE PALESTINE PROBLEM TODAY: Israel and Its Neighbors

THIS IS ISRAEL: A Cultural Reader (with Theodore Huebener)

RABBI AND MINISTER: The Friendship of Stephen S. Wise and John Haynes Holmes

IN SEARCH OF MEANING: Living Religions of the World

STEPHEN S. WISE—SERVANT OF THE PEOPLE: Selected Letters

A SUMMONS UNTO MEN: An Anthology of the Writings of John Haynes Holmes

QUOTATIONS OF COURAGE AND VISION

A Source Book for Speaking, Writing, and Meditation

Selected by

Carl Hermann Voss

ASSOCIATION PRESS   New York

International Standard Book Number: 0-8096-1849-4
Library of Congress Catalog Card Number: 72-7319

Library of Congress Cataloging in Publication Data

Voss, Carl Hermann, comp.
    Quotations of courage and vision.

    1. Quotations, English. I. Title.
PN6081.V6   808.88'2   72-7319
ISBN 0-8096-1849-4

PRINTED IN THE UNITED STATES OF AMERICA

To the memory of
my father and mother

CARL AUGUST VOSS   LUCY WILMS VOSS
(1876-1943)   (1877-1961)

A certain awkwardness marks the use of borrrowing thoughts. but as soon as we have learned what to do with them, they become our own.

RALPH WALDO EMERSON

PREFACE

The purpose of this volume is clearly stated in its title and subtitle: here is a source book of quotations of courage and vision, designed to aid people in speaking, writing, and meditation. It will help a speaker illumine exposition and buttress arguments; enable a writer to avoid dullness and tedium, and guide the troubled in their hours of anxiety, sorrow, or doubt.

I have tried to bar the trite and the maudlin; focus on quality, not quantity; choose from many centuries and cultures, rather than center on the contemporary; and to rely on beauty, nobility of thought, and durability as criteria for the choices.

There are 117 categories, beginning with "Achievement, Adversity, Affliction, Age" and concluding with "Wonder, Worship, Youth." The categories are in alphabetical order and each is listed in the Contents. An Index of Authors follows the text and includes brief biographical items concerning the vocations or roles in history of these men and women.

It was deemed unnecessary to list paragraphs, pages, chapters, and titles of the works from which these quotations were excerpted, for libraries are full of reference books to which readers may turn for more precise identification.

This collection had its inception almost fifty years ago during school days in my native Pittsburgh; it slowly grew during years of study in college, abroad, and in theological seminary and throughout all the varied activities of my professional life. The conscious effort to bring into one book the most valued and significant selections began to take shape seven years ago at the request of the editors of Association Press. Initially, I gathered 3,500 quotations, and then winnowed them to the 1,500 in these pages.

Because the selections are the result of a personal quest, they are a very personal choice. The large number of quotations by Ralph Waldo Emerson and William Ellery Channing may be traced to my interest aroused in these men's writings by the two people to whom this book is dedicated: my father and mother. Similarly, the writings of such men as my teachers—Reinhold Niebuhr, Paul Tillich, and Harry Emerson Fosdick—or my ideals in the ministry—Stephen S. Wise and John Haynes Holmes—or friends and mentors like Lewis Mumford, David Ben-Gurion, Martin Buber, and Abraham Joshua Heschel reflect another kind of indebtedness, that of having looked to these men as exemplars and inspirers of my own work as minister, teacher, and author. Furthermore, many selections in this book were of enormous help to

7

me in sermons and lectures, articles and books, in my own meditations, and in services of public worship.

I hope they will convey something of the Meaning behind all other meanings in this life of ours. I trust this distillation of the wisdom of great men and women will be as helpful to others, and as enjoyable a search, as it has been to me.

I am indebted to the following friends for their gracious consent to help gather quotations and publish them in this book:

Margaret T. Applegarth	John F. Hayward
W. Waldemar Argow	Abraham Joshua Heschel
Stringfellow Barr	Roger Wellington Holmes
David Ben-Gurion	Robert Maynard Hutchins
Frances Holmes Brown	Robert C. Kimball
Roland Burdick	Sidney M. Lefkowitz
Elizabeth Stuart Calvert	Israel Herbert Levinthal
Yu-Kuang Chu	Rollo May
Gypsy da Sylva	Charles White McGehee
Elinor Fosdick Down	Lewis Mumford
Robert A. Elfers	Gunnar Myrdal
Dov Peretz Elkins	Tamar Pool
Emil Fackenheim	Justine Wise Polier
Rose Fackenheim	Nathan M. Pusey
Sophia Lyon Fahs	Maurice Samuel (deceased)
Dorothy Fosdick	Edward S. Skillin
Raymond B. Fosdick	Howard Thurman
Viktor E. Frankl	Hannah Werner Tillich
Horace Friess	Robert A. Ward
Roland B. Gittelsohn	James Waterman Wise
Author Graham	Robert Roy Wright
Donald Szantho Harrington	Lesser Zussman

My greatest debt is to my wife, Phyllis Gierlotka Voss, who gave constant encouragement and wise counsel. She provided the domestic felicity without which such painstaking work could not have been carried on and assisted me in every way possible during the years devoted to this project. The book should really be dedicated to her, too, not just to my father and mother. She knows how grateful I am to her for her help and her guidance.

Autumn, 1972   CARL HERMANN VOSS
Jacksonville, Florida

8

CONTENTS

QUOTATIONS OF
COURAGE AND VISION

❧

Achievement

It is not faith and works; it is not faith or works; it is faith that works.

ANONYMOUS

The six basic mistakes of man are:
(1) The delusion that individual advancement is made by crushing others.
(2) The tendency to worry about things that can not be changed or corrected.
(3) Insisting that a thing is impossible because *we* cannot accomplish it.
(4) Refusing to set aside trivial preferences.
(5) Neglecting development and refinement of the mind and not acquiring the habit of reading and study.
(6) Attempting to compel other persons to believe as we do.   CICERO

To accomplish great things, we must not only act but also dream, not only plan but also believe.   ANATOLE FRANCE

The pessimist sees the difficulty in every opportunity; the optimist, the opportunity in every difficulty.   L. P. JACKS

Every man feels instinctively that all the beautiful sentiments in the world weigh less than a single lovely action.   JAMES RUSSELL LOWELL

For of all sad words of tongue or pen,
The saddest are these: "It might have been!"
JOHN GREENLEAF WHITTIER

11

I'm living in a house and I know I built it. I work in a workshop which was constructed by me. I speak a language which I developed. And I know I shape my life according to my desires by my own ability. I feel I am safe. I can defend myself. I am not afraid. This is the greatest happiness a man can feel—that he could be a partner with the Lord in creation. This is the real happiness of man—creative life, conquest of nature, and a great purpose.
DAVID BEN-GURION

> In future days men will become so powerful
> That they seem to control the heavens and the earth,
> They seem to understand the stars and all science.
> Let them beware. Something is lurking hidden.
> There is always a knife in the flowers.
> There is always a lion just beyond the firelight.
> EURIPIDES

Greater than an army with banners is an idea whose time has come.
VICTOR HUGO

Only when you have worked alone—when you have felt around you a black gulf of solitude more isolating than that which surrounds the dying man, and in hope and in despair have trusted to your own unshaken will—then only can you gain the secret isolated joy of the thinker, who knows that, a hundred years after he is dead and forgotten, men who had never heard of him will be moving to the measure of his thought, the subtle rapture of a postponed power, which the world knows not because it has no external trappings, but which to his prophetic vision is more real than that which commands an army. And if this joy should not be yours, still it is only thus that you can know that you have done what lay in you to do, can say that you have lived, and be ready for the end.   OLIVER WENDELL HOLMES, JR.

Wisdom is knowing what to do next, skill is knowing how to do it, and virtue is doing it.   DAVID STARR JORDAN

Did you ever hear of a man who had striven all his life faithfully and singly toward an object and in no measure obtained it? If a man constantly aspires, is he not elevated? Did ever a man try heroism, magnanimity, truth, sincerity, and find that there was no advantage in them, that it was a vain endeavor?   HENRY DAVID THOREAU

Hope deferred maketh the heart sick; but when the desire cometh, it is a tree of life.   THE BIBLE

Do not be too timid and squeamish about your actions. All life is an experiment. The more experiments you make the better. What if they are a little coarse, and you may get your coat soiled or torn? What if you do fail, and get fairly rolled in the dirt once or twice? Up again; you shall never be so afraid of a tumble. RALPH WALDO EMERSON

If you would not be forgotten as soon as you are dead, either write things worth reading or do things worth writing. BENJAMIN FRANKLIN

It is better to light one small candle than to curse the darkness.
CONFUCIUS

The keen spirit
Seizes the prompt occasion—makes the thought
Start into instant action, and at once
Plans and performs, resolves and executes.
HANNAH MORE

See also: ADVERSITY; AMBITION; ASPIRATION; CHARACTER; DEDICATION; EXAMPLE; FAITH; INSPIRATION; MATURITY; PERSEVERANCE; PURPOSE; RESPONSIBILITY.

Adversity

Never fancy you could be something if only you had a different lot and sphere assigned you. The very things that you most deprecate, as fatal limitations or obstructions, are probably what you most want. What you call hindrances, obstacles, discouragements, are probably God's opportunities.
HORACE BUSHNELL

Prosperity is a great teacher; adversity is a greater. Possession pampers the mind; privation trains and strengthens it. WILLIAM HAZLITT

God of our life, there are days when the burdens we carry chafe our shoulders and weigh us down; when the road seems dreary and endless, the skies grey and threatening; when our lives have no music in them, and our hearts are lonely, and our souls have lost their courage. Flood the path with light, we beseech Thee; turn our eyes to where the skies are full of promise; tune our hearts to brave music; give us the sense of comradeship with heroes and saints of every age; and so quicken our spirits that we may be able to encourage the souls of all who journey with us on the road of life, to Thy honor and glory.   SAINT AUGUSTINE

Has any man ever attained inner harmony by pondering the experience of others? Not since the world began. He must pass through the fire.

NORMAN DOUGLAS

A wise man struggling with adversity is said by some heathen writer to be a spectacle on which the gods might look down with pleasure.

SYDNEY SMITH

Almighty Father, Source of all blessings, we thank Thee for the preservation of our life and for the joy of living, for the powers of mind and heart and for the wisdom that comes to us from seers and sages filled with Thy spirit.

Teach us to use wisely the blessings Thou hast bestowed upon us. May prosperity not enfeeble our spirit or harden our heart. May it never so master us as to dull our desire for life's higher ideals.

And should adversity come, may it not embitter us or cause us to despair, but may we accept it as a mark of Thy chastening love which purifies and strengthens. Let every obstacle become an incentive to greater effort, and let every defeat teach us anew the lesson of patience and perseverance.

Gird us with strength to bear our trials with courage. Let not the loss of anything, however dear to our hearts or precious in our sight, rob us of our faith in Thee. In light as in darkness, in joy as in sorrow, help us to put our trust in Thy providence, that even through our tears we may discern Thy divine blessing.   UNION PRAYER BOOK

Adversity introduces a man to himself.   ANONYMOUS

> And these vicissitudes come best in youth;
>   For when they happen at a riper age,
> People are apt to blame the Fates, forsooth,
>   And wonder Providence is not more sage.
> Adversity is the first path to truth.
>   GEORGE GORDON BYRON

Adversity has the effect of eliciting talents which, in prosperous circumstances, would have lain dormant.   HORACE

The good things which belong to prosperity are to be wished, but the good things that belong to adversity are to be admired.   SENECA

If the way which, as I have shown, leads hither seems very difficult, it can nevertheless be found. It must indeed be difficult since it is so seldom discovered; for if salvation lay ready to hand and could be discovered without great labor, how could it be possible that it should be neglected almost by everybody? But all noble things are as difficult as they are rare.

BARUCH SPINOZA

> Then welcome each rebuff
> That turns earth's smoothness rough
> Each sting that bids nor sit nor stand, but go!
> Strive, and hold cheap the strain;
> Learn, nor account the pang; dare, never grudge the throe!

ROBERT BROWNING

Ask the man of adversity, how other men act towards him: ask those others, how he acts towards them. Adversity is the true touchstone of merit in both; happy if it does not produce the dishonesty of meanness in one, and that of insolence and pride in the other.   FULKE GREVILLE, LORD BROOKE

One thorn of experience is worth a whole wilderness of warning.

JAMES RUSSELL LOWELL

> He is the most wretched of men who has never felt
>   adversity
> Sweet are the uses of adversity,
> Which, like the toad, ugly and venomous,
> Wears yet a precious jewel in his head;
> And this our life, exempt from public haunt,
> Finds tongues in trees, books in the running brooks,
> Sermons in stones, and good in every thing.

WILLIAM SHAKESPEARE

Quiet minds cannot be perplexed or frightened, but go on in fortune or misfortune at their own private pace, like the ticking of a clock during a thunderstorm.   ROBERT LOUIS STEVENSON

If there were no clouds we should not enjoy the sun.   ANCIENT PROVERB

He that is down needs fear no fall.   JOHN BUNYAN

See also: AFFLICTION; COURAGE; FAILURE; FAITH; GRACE; GREATNESS; HEROISM; MATURITY; PEACE OF MIND; PERSEVERANCE; PERSPECTIVE; SUFFERING.

Affliction

In afflictions men generally draw their consolations out of books of morality, which indeed are of great use to fortify and strengthen the mind against the impressions of sorrow. Monsieur St. Evremont, who does not approve of this method, recommends authors who are apt to stir up mirth in the minds of the readers, and fancies Don Quixote can give more relief to a heavy heart than Plutarch or Seneca, as it is much easier to divert grief than to conquer it. This doubtless may have its effects on some tempers. I should rather have recourse to authors of a quite contrary kind, that give us instances of calamities and misfortunes and show human nature in its greatest distress.

                                                      JOSEPH ADDISON

> God ne'er afflicts us more than our desert,
> Though He may seem to over-act His part:
> Sometimes He strikes us more than flesh can
>   bear;
> But yet still less than grace can suffer here.
>   ROBERT HERRICK

It is not miserable to be blind; it is miserable to be incapable of enduring blindness.   JOHN MILTON

Never did I complain of the chances of fortune nor did I ever make a wry face at the resolution of fate, except on one occasion when I was reduced to going barefooted and had nothing with which to buy shoes. At that time I happened to enter the mosque at Kusa and did so with a heavy heart. There I observed a person who had no feet at all. At this I offered up praise and thanks to Almighty God and gladly submitted to this circumstance of being shoeless.   SA'DI

It is a very melancholy reflection, that men are usually so weak that it is absolutely necessary for them to know sorrow and pain to be in their right senses. Prosperous people (for happy there are none) are hurried away with a fond sense of their present condition, and thoughtless of the mutability of fortune. Fortune is a term which we must use, in such discourses as these, for what is wrought by the unseen hand of the Disposer of all things. But methinks the disposition of a mind which is truly great is that which makes misfortunes and sorrows little when they befall ourselves, great and lamentable when they befall other men. The most unpardonable malefactor in the world going to his death and bearing it with composure would win the pity of those who should behold him; and this not because his calamity is deplorable, but because he seems himself not to deplore it. We suffer for him who is less sensible of his own misery, and are inclined to despise him who sinks under the weight of his distress.   RICHARD STEELE

God says to man: "With thy very wounds I will heal thee."   THE TALMUD

The gem cannot be polished without friction, nor man perfected without trials.   CHINESE PROVERB

Lord Byron and Sir Walter Scott were both lame. Byron was embittered by his lameness, brooded on it till he loathed it, never entered a public place but his mind reverted to it, so that much of the color and zest of existence were lost to him. Scott, on the other hand, never complained or spoke one bitter word about his disability, not even to his dearest friend. In the circumstances it is not so very surprising that Sir Walter should have received a letter from Byron with this sentence in it: "Ah, Scott, I would give my fame to have your happiness."   ROBERT J. MCCRACKEN

Taxes are indeed very heavy; but if those laid on by the government were the only ones we had to pay, we might more easily discharge them; but we have many others, and much more grievous ones to some of us. We are taxed quite as heavily by idleness, three times as much by our pride, and four times as much by our folly; and from these taxes the commissioners cannot easily deliver us by allowing an abatement.   BENJAMIN FRANKLIN

It has done me good to be somewhat parched by the heat and drenched by the rain of life.   HENRY WADSWORTH LONGFELLOW

The truly great and good, in affliction, bear a countenance more princely than they are wont; for it is the temper of the highest hearts, like the palm tree, to strive upwards when it is most burdened.   SIR PHILIP SIDNEY

I hope when you know the worst you will at once leap into the river and swim through handsomely, and not, weatherbeaten by the divers blasts of irresolution, stand shivering upon the brink.   SIR JOHN SUCKLING

Come then, affliction, if my Father wills, and be my frowning friend. A friend that frowns is better than a smiling enemy.   ANONYMOUS

To be blind is bad, but worse is it to have eyes and not to see.

HELEN KELLER

As I look over my life, I find no disappointment and no sorrow I could afford to lose; the cloudy morning turned out the fairer day; the wounds of my enemies have done me good. So wondrous is this human life, not ruled by Fate, but Providence, which is Wisdom married unto Love, each infinite! What has been, may be. If I recover wholly, or but in part, I see new sources of power beside these waters of affliction I have stooped at.

THEODORE PARKER

We are not born to go weeping and complaining through life, even though it is an ill business turning to the world a smiling face when we carry in our breast a broken heart.   ROBERT LOUIS STEVENSON

See also: ADVERSITY; COURAGE; FAITH; GRACE; HEROISM; MATURITY; PATIENCE; PEACE OF MIND; PERSEVERANCE; PERSPECTIVE; PRAYER; SUFFERING.

Age

Old age has a great sense of calm and freedom. When the passions have relaxed their hold you have escaped, not from one master, but from many.

PLATO

As I approve of a youth that has something of the old man in him, so I am no less pleased with an old man that has something of the youth. He that follows this rule may be old in body, but can never be so in mind.   CICERO

One's age should be tranquil, as childhood should be playful. Hard work at either extremity of life seems out of place. At mid-day the sun may burn, and men labor under it; but the morning and evening should be alike calm and cheerful.   MATTHEW ARNOLD

It is remarkable that some of the most lively productions of several great writers have been the works of their maturest age. Johnson surpassed all his preceding labors in his last work, the popular *Lives of the Poets. The Canterbury Tales* of Chaucer were the effusions of his advanced age; and the congenial versions of Dryden were thrown out in the luxuriance of his later days. Milton might have been classed among the minor poets, had he not lived to be old enough to become the most sublime. Let it be a source of consolation, if not of triumph, in a long, studious life of true genius, to know that the imagination may not decline with the vigour of the frame which holds it; there has been no old age for many men of genius.

ISAAC D'ISRAELI

A graceful and honorable old age is the childhood of immortality. PINDAR

Lord, thou knowest better than I know myself that I am growing older and will some day be old. Keep me from the fatal habit of thinking I must say something on every subject and on every occasion. Release me from craving to straighten out everybody's affairs. Make me thoughtful but not moody; helpful but not bossy. With my vast store of wisdom, it seems a pity not to use it all, but Thou knowest Lord that I want a few friends at the end.

Keep my mind free from the recital of endless details; give me wings to get to the point. Seal my lips on my aches and pains. They are increasing, and love of rehearsing them is becoming sweeter as the years go by. I dare not ask for grace enough to enjoy the tales of others' pains, but help me to endure them with patience.

I dare not ask for improved memory, but for a growing humility, and a lessening cocksureness when my memory seems to clash with the memories of others. Teach me the glorious lesson that occasionally I may be mistaken.

Keep me reasonably sweet; I do not want to be a Saint—some of them are so hard to live with—but a sour old person is one of the crowning works of the devil. Give me the ability to see good things in unexpected places, and talents in unexpected people. And, give me, O Lord, the grace to tell them so. Amen.   ANONYMOUS

[Prayer for the Middle-aged]

A light heart lives long.   WILLIAM SHAKESPEARE

It is not by the gray of the hair that one knows the age of the heart.

EDWARD BULWER LYTTON

Old men's eyes are like old men's memories; they are strongest for things a long way off.   GEORGE ELIOT

The evening of a well-spent life brings its lamps with it.   JOSEPH JOUBERT

Nothing is more disgraceful than that an old man should have nothing to show to prove that he has lived long, except his years.   SENECA

The greatest glory of a building is not in its stones, nor in its gold. Its glory is in its age, and in that deep sense of voicefulness, of stern watching, of mysterious sympathy—nay, even of approval or condemnation—which we feel in walls that have long been washed by the passing waves of humanity. It is in their lasting witness against men, in their quiet contrast with the transitional character of all things, in the strength which, through the lapse of seasons and times, and the decline and birth of dynasties, and the changing of the face of the earth, and of the limits of the sea, maintains its sculptured shapeliness for a time insuperable, connects forgotten and following ages with each other, and half constitutes the identity, as it concentrates the sympathy, of nations: it is in that golden stair of time, that we are to look for the real light and color, and preciousness of architecture; and it is not until a building has assumed this character, till it has been intrusted with the fame, and hallowed by the deeds of men, till its walls have been witnesses of suffering, and its pillars rise out of the shadows of death, that its existence, more lasting as it is than that of the natural objects of the world around it, can be gifted with even so much as these possess, of language and of life.   JOHN RUSKIN

The seas are quiet when the winds give o'er;
So calm are we when passions are no more.
For then we know how vain it was to boast
Of fleeting things, so certain to be lost.
Clouds of affection from our younger eyes
Conceal that emptiness which age descries.

The soul's dark cottage, batter'd and decay'd,
Lets in new light through chinks that Time hath made
Stronger by weakness, wiser men become
As they draw near to their eternal home.
Leaving the old, both worlds at once they view
That stand upon the threshold of the new.
                                       EDMUND WALLER

Probably the happiest period in life most frequently is in middle age, when the eager passions of youth are cooled, and the infirmities of age not yet begun; as we see that the shadows, which are at morning and evening so large, almost entirely disappear at mid-day. THOMAS ARNOLD

Alonso of Aragon was wont to say in commendation of age, that age appears to be best in four things—old wood best to burn, old wine to drink, old friends to trust, and old authors to read. SIR FRANCIS BACON

It is not strange that that early love of the heart should come back, as it so often does when the dim eye is brightening with its last light. It is not strange that the freshest fountains the heart has ever known in its wastes should bubble up anew when the life-blood is growing stagnant. It is not strange that a bright memory should come to a dying old man, as the sunshine breaks across the hills at the close of a stormy day; nor that in the light of that ray, the very clouds that made the day dark should grow gloriously beautiful. NATHANIEL HAWTHORNE

I venerate old age, and I love not the man who can look without emotion upon the sunset of life, when the dusk of evening begins to gather over the watery eye, and the shadows of twilight grow broader and deeper upon the understanding. HENRY WADSWORTH LONGFELLOW

When we are young, we are slavishly employed in procuring something whereby we may live comfortably when we grow old; and when we are old, we perceive it is too late to live as we proposed. ALEXANDER POPE

Old age, to the unlearned, is winter; to the learned, it is harvest time.
YIDDISH PROVERB

See also: BLESSING; CHARACTER; DEATH; FAITH; GRACE; HEROISM; HOPE; HUMANITY; MATURITY; PEACE OF MIND; PERSPECTIVE; WISDOM.

Ambition

Of ambitions, it is less harmful the ambition to prevail in great things, than that other to appear in everything; for that breeds confusion, and mars busi-

ness; but yet it is less danger to have an ambitious man stirring in business
than great in dependences. He that seeketh to be eminent amongst able men
hath a great task; but that is ever good for the public; but he that plots to be
the only figure amongst ciphers is the decay of a whole age.

SIR FRANCIS BACON

Though ambition in itself is a vice, yet it is often the parent of virtues.

QUINTILIAN

Ambition hath no mean. It is either upon all fours or upon tiptoes.

GEORGE SAVILE, MARQUIS OF HALIFAX

It is the constant fault and inseparable evil quality of ambition, that it never
looks behind it.   SENECA

High seats are never but uneasy, and crowns are always stuffed with thorns.

JAMES GORDON BROOKS

If one advances confidently in the direction of his dreams, and endeavors to
live the life which he has imagined, he will meet with a success unexpected
in common hours. . . . If you have built castles in the air, your work need not
be lost; that is where they should be. Now put the foundations under them.

HENRY DAVID THOREAU

The rung of a ladder was never meant to rest upon, but only to hold a man's
foot long enough to enable him to put the other somewhat higher.

THOMAS H. HUXLEY

It is the nature of ambition to make men liars and cheats who hide the truth
in their hearts, and like jugglers, show another thing in their mouths; to cut
all friendships and enmities to the measure of their interest, and put on a
good face where there is no corresponding good will.   SALLUST

To be ambitious of true honor and of the real glory and perfection of our
nature is the very principle and incentive of virtue; but to be ambitious of
titles, place, ceremonial respects, and civil pageantry, is as vain and little as
the things are which we court.   SIR PHILIP SIDNEY

A noble man compares and estimates himself by an idea which is higher than himself; and a mean man, by one lower than himself. The one produces aspiration; the other ambition, which is the way in which a vulgar man aspires. HENRY WARD BEECHER

Ambition, that high and glorious passion, which makes such havoc among the sons of men, arises from a proud desire of honor and distinction, and, when the splendid trappings in which it is usually caparisoned are removed, will be found to consist of the mean materials of envy, pride, and covetousness. It is described by different authors as a gallant madness, a pleasant poison, a hidden plague, a secret poison, a caustic of the soul, the moth of holiness, the mother of hypocrisy, and, by crucifying and disquieting all it takes hold of, the cause of melancholy and madness. ROBERT BURTON

You cannot be anything if you want to be everything.
SOLOMON SCHECHTER

> Ambition is an idol, on whose wings
> Great minds are carried only to extreme;
> To be sublimely great or to be nothing.
> ROBERT SOUTHEY

See also: ACHIEVEMENT; ASPIRATION; DEDICATION; EXAMPLE; INSPIRATION; SELF-KNOWLEDGE; VISION.

America

While I would wish you to love America because it is your home, I would have you love the whole world and think of all the people in it as your countrymen. You will hear people more foolish than wicked say, "Our country, right or wrong," but that is a false patriotism and bad Americanism. When our country is wrong, she is worse than other countries when they are wrong, for she has more light than other countries, and we ought somehow to make her feel that we are sorry and ashamed for her.
WILLIAM DEAN HOWELLS

If all Europe were to become a prison, America would still present a loophole of escape; and, God be praised! that loophole is larger than the dungeon itself. HEINRICH HEINE

Observe good faith and justice toward all nations. Cultivate peace and harmony with all. Religion and morality enjoin this conduct. And can it be that good policy does not equally enjoin it? It will be worthy of a free, enlightened and at no distant period a great nation to give to mankind the magnanimous and too novel example of a people always guided by an exalted justice and benevolence. Who can doubt that, in the course of time and things, the fruits of such a plan would richly repay any temporary advantages which might be lost by a steady adherence to it? Can it be that Providence has not connected the permanent felicity of a nation with its virtue?

GEORGE WASHINGTON

We here in America have the vitalizing idea and the promising hope for which men live. The idea is not fully planted in fertile ground. Our conception of democracy is a democracy that puts its trust in the people. It is based on the worth of the human personality against deadly invasions of power. It stresses human dignity and individual diversity. It holds that a free society must not tolerate differences, but blend them in an inner strength. It knows that national unity cannot come from an imposed conformity. Its faith has a universal appeal, deeply rooted in human necessities and in human aspiration. It is predicated on the age-old principle that no prison can confine the human spirit. A freedom-thirsty world cannot be kept permanently in chains. Ultimately for all tyranny comes the final death knock on the door. Sooner or later the resurgent forces of the human spirit break through the barriers.

RAYMOND B. FOSDICK

We shall nobly save or meanly lose the last, best hope of earth.

ABRAHAM LINCOLN

To us Americans much has been given; of us much is required. With all our faults and mistakes, it is our strength in support of the freedom our forefathers loved which has saved mankind from subjection to totalitarian power.

NORMAN THOMAS

We came to America either ourselves or in the persons of our ancestors, to better the ideals of men, to make them see finer things than they had seen before, to get rid of the things that divide and to make sure of the things that unite. It was but an historical accident no doubt that this great country was called the "United States"; yet, I am very thankful that it has that word "United" in its title, and the man who seeks to divide man from man, group from group, interest from interest in this great Union is striking at its very heart.

WOODROW WILSON

The whole story of America—a story worth the telling and worth the understanding—began with an idea. This idea is actually the political expression of a basic law of nature—that there is strength in diversity. According to this idea, America is a place where people can be themselves. It is a human experience rather than a purely national or cultural experience. It is built upon fabulous differences—religion, race, culture, customs, political thinking. These differences, or pluralism, as the sociologists call it, are actually the mortar that hold the nation together. NORMAN COUSINS

Give me your tired, your poor,
Your huddled masses yearning to breathe free,
The wretched refuse of your teeming shore,
Send these, the homeless, tempest-tossed, to me:
I lift my lamp beside the golden door.

Not like the brazen giant of Greek fame,
With conquering limbs astride from land to land;
Here at our sea-washed, sunset gates shall stand
A mighty woman with a torch, whose flame
Is the imprisoned lightning, and her name
  Mother of exiles.

EMMA LAZARUS
[Inscription on Statue of
Liberty, New York Harbor]

Every genuine American holds to the ideal of justice for all men, of independence, including free speech and free action within the limits of law, of obedience to law, of universal education, of material well-being for all the well-behaving and industrious, of peace and good-will among men. These, however far short the nation may fall in expressing them in its actual life, are—no one will deny it—the ideals of our American democracy.

CHARLES ELIOT NORTON

See also: BROTHERHOOD; DEMOCRACY; EQUALITY; FREEDOM; LIBERTY; PATRIOTISM.

Aspiration

Speak only the truth; do not yield to anger; when asked to do so, give of the little thou hast. With these three steps thou shalt approach the gods.

BUDDHA

God gives no linen, but flax to spin. GERMAN PROVERB

> Ah, but a man's reach should exceed his grasp,
> Or what's a heaven for?
> ROBERT BROWNING

My Lord, I am ready on the threshold of this new day to go forth armed with thy power, seeking adventure on the high road, to right wrong, to overcome evil, to suffer wounds and endure pain if need be, but in all things to serve thee bravely, faithfully, joyfully, that at the end of the day's labor, kneeling for thy blessing, thou mayst find no blot upon my shield.

KNIGHT'S PRAYER
[Inscribed in Chester Cathedral]

> Life is a sheet of paper white
> Whereon each one of us may write
> His word or two, and then comes night.
>
> Greatly begin! though thou have time
> But for a line, be that sublime—
> Not failure, but low aim, is crime.
> JAMES RUSSELL LOWELL

Give me beauty in the inward soul; and may the inner and the outer be at one. May I consider wisdom to be wealth, and let me have only as much gold as a temperate man and only he can bear and carry. This prayer, I think, is enough for me. SOCRATES

Far away there in the sunshine are my highest aspirations. I may not reach them, but I can look up and see their beauty, believe in them, and try to follow where they lead. LOUISA MAY ALCOTT

Men make a great ado about the folly of demanding too much of life and of endeavoring to live according to that demand. It is much ado about nothing. I am not afraid that I shall exaggerate the values and significance of life, but that I shall not be up to the occasion which it is. I shall be sorry to remember that I was there, but noticed nothing remarkable; that I lived in the Golden Age, a hired man; visited Olympus even, but fell asleep after dinner, and did not hear the conversations of the gods; that I lived in Judea 1800 years ago, but I never knew there was such a one as Christ among my contemporaries.

HENRY DAVID THOREAU

Bad will be the day for every man when he becomes absolutely contented with the life that he is living, when there is not forever beating at the doors of his soul some great desire to do something larger.   PHILLIPS BROOKS

To go too far is as bad as to fall short.   CONFUCIUS

In great attempts it is glorious even to fail.   CASSIUS LONGINUS

Who shoots at the mid-day sun, though he be sure he shall never hit the mark, yet as sure he is he shall shoot higher than he who aims but at a bush.
     SIR PHILIP SIDNEY

There is nothing noble in being superior to some other men; the true nobility is in being superior to your previous self.   HINDU PROVERB

I find that the great thing is not so much where we stand as in what direction we are moving. To reach the port of heaven we must sail, sometimes with the wind and sometimes against it, but we must sail and not drift, nor lie at anchor.   OLIVER WENDELL HOLMES, JR.

Men stumble over pebbles, never over mountains.   ANONYMOUS

Grant me, Lord, a little light, but no more than a glowworm giveth which goeth about by night, to guide me through this life, this dream which lasteth but a day, wherein are many things on which to stumble, and many things at which to laugh, and others like unto a stormy path along which one goeth leaping.   PRAYER OF ANCIENT AZTEC CHIEFTAIN

Dost thou wish to rise? Begin by descending. You plan a tower that shall pierce the clouds? Lay first the foundation on humility.   SAINT AUGUSTINE

See also: AMBITION; DEDICATION; GOD; GOODNESS; IDEALS; INSPI-RATION; SELF-KNOWLEDGE; VIRTUE; VISION; WISDOM; WONDER; WORSHIP.

Atheism

Atheism and fanaticism are two monsters, which may tear society to pieces;
but the atheist preserves his reason, which checks his propensity to mischief, while the fanatic is under the influence of a madness which is constantly urging him on.   VOLTAIRE

I had rather believe all the fables in the Legend, and the Talmud, and the
Alcoran, than that this universal frame is without a mind; and, therefore,
God never wrought miracles to convince atheism, because his ordinary
works convince it. It is true, that a little philosophy inclineth Man's mind to
atheism, but depth in philosophy bringeth men's minds about to religion; for
while the mind of Man looketh upon second causes scattered, it may sometimes rest in them, and go no farther; but when it beholdeth the chain of
them confederate, and linked together, it must needs fly to Providence and
Deity.   SIR FRANCIS BACON

No man can succeed in life alone, and he cannot get the help he needs from
men.   INDIAN HUNTER

The fool hath said in his heart, there is no God.   THE BIBLE

          The very name of God
     Sounds like a juggler's charm; and, bold with joy,
     (Portentous sight!) the owlet Atheism,
     Sailing on obscene wings athwart the noon,
     Drops his blue-fringed lids and holds them close.
     And hooting at the glorious sun in heaven,
     Cries out, "Where is it?"
                         SAMUEL TAYLOR COLERIDGE

If God is not, then the existence of all that is beautiful and in any sense good,
is but the accidental and ineffectual by-product of blindly swirling atoms, or
of the equally unpurposeful, though more conceptually complicated, mech-
anisms of present-day physics. A man may believe that this dreadful thing
is true. But only the fool will say in his heart that he is glad that it is true.

For to wish there should be no God is to wish that the things which we love and strive to realize and make permanent, should be only temporary and doomed to frustration and destruction. . . . Atheism leads not to badness but only to an incurable sadness and loneliness.

WILLIAM PEPPERELL MONTAGUE

The legitimate powers of government extend to such acts only as are injurious to others. But it does me no injury for my neighbor to say there are twenty Gods, or no God.   THOMAS JEFFERSON

There are pseudo-atheists who believe that they do not believe in God and who in reality unconsciously believe in Him, because the God whose existence they deny is not God but something else. There are practical atheists who believe that they believe in God (and who perhaps believe in Him in their brains) but who in reality deny his existence by each one of their deeds. There are absolute atheists. Absolute atheism is in no way a mere absence of belief in God. It is rather a refusal of God, a fight against God, a challenge to God.   JACQUES MARITAIN

My atheism, like that of Spinoza, is true piety towards the universe and denies only gods fashioned by men in their own image, to be servants of their human interests.   GEORGE SANTAYANA

To say that there is no basis for personal and social ethics apart from one or another of the organized religions is untrue to observed fact and immensely derogatory to a God worth respect.   NORMAN THOMAS

Sometimes a nation abolishes God, but fortunately God is more tolerant.

ANONYMOUS

The legs of those who require proofs of God's existence are made of wood.

PERSIAN PROVERB

Atheists put on a false courage in the midst of their darkness and misapprehensions, like children who, when they fear to go in the dark, will sing or whistle to keep up their courage.   ALEXANDER POPE

Atheism can benefit no class of people; neither the unfortunate, whom it bereaves of hope, nor the prosperous, whose joys it renders insipid, nor the soldier, of whom it makes a coward, nor the woman whose beauty and sensibility it mars, nor the mother, who has a son to lose, nor the rulers of men, who have no surer pledge of the fidelity of their subjects than religion.

FRANÇOIS RENÉ DE CHATEAUBRIAND

The atheist is a man who has no invisible means of support.

LORD TWEEDSMUIR

See also: BELIEF; DISSENT; DOUBT; FAITH; GOD; MYSTERY; RELIGION.

Beauty

Within man is the soul of the whole, the wise silence, the universal beauty, to which every part and particle is equally related, the eternal One. When it breathes through his intellect, it is genius; when it breathes through his will, it is virtue; when it flows through his affection, it is love.

RALPH WALDO EMERSON

A thing of beauty is a joy forever,
Its loveliness increases; it will never
Pass into nothingness.

JOHN KEATS

The fountain of beauty is the heart, and every generous thought illustrates the walls of your chamber. If virtue accompanies beauty it is the heart's paradise; if vice be associate with it, it is the soul's purgatory. It is the wise man's bonfire, and the fool's furnace.　　　　FRANCIS QUARLES

For every beauty there is an eye somewhere to see it.
For every truth there is an ear somewhere to hear it.
For every love there is a heart somewhere to receive it.
But though my beauty meet no eye it still doth glow.
Though my truth meet no ear it still doth shine.
But when my love meets no heart it can only break.

IVAN PANIN

> Loveliest of lovely things are they
>   On earth that soonest pass away.
> The rose that lives its little hour
>   Is prized beyond the sculptured flower.
>   WILLIAM CULLEN BRYANT

After all, it is the divinity within that makes the divinity without; and I have been more fascinated by a woman of talent and intelligence, though deficient in personal charms, than I have been by the most regular beauty.

WASHINGTON IRVING

There is music even in the beauty and the silent note which Cupid strikes, far sweeter than the sound of an instrument; for there is a music wherever there is harmony, order, or proportion; and thus far we may maintain the music of the spheres.   SIR THOMAS BROWNE

Beauty is an all-pervading presence. It unfolds to the numberless flowers of the spring; it waves in the branches of the trees and in the green blades of grass; it haunts the depths of the earth and the sea, and gleams out in the hues of the shell and the precious stone. And not only these minute objects, but the ocean, the mountains, the clouds, the heavens, the stars, the rising and the setting sun, all overflow with beauty. The universe is its temple; and those men who are alive to it cannot lift their eyes without feeling themselves encompassed with it on every side. Now, this beauty is so precious, the enjoyment it gives so refined and pure, so congenial and so akin to worship, that it is pain living in the midst of it, and living almost as blind to it, as if, instead of this fair earth and glorious sky, they were tenants of a dungeon. An infinite joy is lost to the world by the want of culture of this spiritual endowment. The greatest truths are wronged if not linked with beauty, and they win their way most surely and deeply into the soul when arrayed in this their natural and fit attire.   WILLIAM ELLERY CHANNING

The spirit and the sense so easily grow dead to the impressions of the beautiful and the perfect that one ought every day to hear a little song, read a good poem, see a good picture, and, if it were possible, speak a few reasonable words.   JOHANN WOLFGANG VON GOETHE

Socrates called beauty a short-lived tyranny; Plato, a privilege of nature; Theophrastus, a silent cheat; Theocritus, a delightful prejudice; Carneades, a solitary kingdom. Domitian said that nothing was more grateful. Aristotle affirmed that beauty was better than all the letters of recommendation in the world; Homer, that it was a glorious gift of nature; and Ovid, alluding to him, calls it a favor bestowed by the gods. SIR WALTER RALEIGH

Youth is life as yet untouched by tragedy. . . . When youth has once grasped where Beauty dwells—with a real knowledge and not as a mere matter of literary phraseology—its self-surrender is absolute.
ALFRED NORTH WHITEHEAD

See also: ASPIRATION; GOD; GRACE; IDEALS; INSPIRATION; NATURE; VISION; WONDER; WORSHIP.

Being

It is not what he has, nor even what he does, which directly expresses the worth of a man, but what he is. HENRI-FREDERIC AMIEL

In German the word *sein* signifies both things: to be, and to belong to Him.
FRANZ KAFKA

Man cometh forth like a flower from concealment, and of a sudden shows himself in open day, and in a moment is by death withdrawn from open view into concealment again. The greenness of the flesh exhibits us to view, but the dryness of dust withdraws us from men's eyes. For whereas infancy is going on to childhood, childhood to youth, youth to manhood, and manhood to old age, and old age to death, in the course of the present life he is forced by the very steps of his increase upon those of decrease, and is ever wasting from the very cause whence he thinks himself to be gaining ground in the space of his life. For we cannot have a fixed stay here, whither we are come only to pass on. SAINT GREGORY THE GREAT

Your worth consists in what you are and not in what you have; what you are will show in what you do. THOMAS DAVIDSON

We ask the leaf, "Are you complete in yourself?" And the leaf answers, "No, my life is in the branches." We ask the branch, and the branch answers, "No, my life is in the root." We ask the root, and it answers, "No, my life is in the trunk and the branches and the leaves. Keep the branches stripped of leaves, and I shall die." So it is with the great tree of being. Nothing is completely and merely individual. HARRY EMERSON FOSDICK

The courage to take the anxiety of meaninglessness upon oneself is the boundary line up to which the courage to be can go. Beyond it is mere non-being. Within it all forms of courage are re-established in the power of the God above the God of theism. The courage to be is rooted in the God who appears when God had disappeared in the anxiety of doubt.

PAUL TILLICH

To Be is to live with God.   RALPH WALDO EMERSON

Love slays what we have been that we may be what we were not.

SAINT AUGUSTINE

See also: GOD; LIFE; MYSTERY; NATURE; RELIGION; REVERENCE; SOUL.

Belief

When the furrows have been turned and the seed sown, it is the brave man who trusts in the harvest.   ANONYMOUS

Nothing is so easy as to deceive one's self; for what we wish, that we readily believe.   DEMOSTHENES

All I know, all I want to know, is that I have found in my relations with my fellow men and in my glad beholding of the universe a reality of truth, goodness and beauty, and that I am trying to make my life as best I can a dedication to this reality. When I am in the thinking mood, I try to be rigorously rational, and thus not to go one step farther in my thoughts and language than my reason can take me. I then become uncertain as to whether I or any man can assert much about God, and fall back content into the mood of Job. When, however, in preaching or in prayer, in some high moment of inner communion or of profound experience with life among my fellows, I feel the pulse of emotion suddenly beating in my heart, and I am lifted up as though upon some sweeping tide that is more than the sluggish current of my days, I find it easy to speak as the poets speak, and cry, as so many of them cry, to God.

But when I say "God," it is poetry and not theology. Nothing that any theologian ever wrote about God has helped me much, but everything that poets have written about flowers, and birds, and skies, and seas, and the saviors of the race, and God—whoever He may be—has at one time or another reached my soul! More and more, as I grow older, I live in the lovely thought of these seers and prophets. The theologians gather dust upon the shelves of my library, but the poets are stained with my fingers and blotted with my tears. I never seem so near truth as when I care not what I think or believe, but only with these masters of inner vision would live forever.

JOHN HAYNES HOLMES

We are slow to believe that which if believed would hurt our feelings.

OVID

Trust in God and *do* something.
MARY LYON

It is a singular fact that many men of action incline to the theory of fatalism, while the greater part of men of thought believe in a divine providence.

HONORÉ DE BALZAC

Belief in God means believing that the ideals we cherish are real, that justice, peace, brotherhood, compassion and honesty actually emerge out of the very structure of the universe.
IRA EISENSTEIN

A little science estranges men from God, but much science leads them back to Him.
LOUIS PASTEUR

If I err in my belief that the souls of men are immortal, I gladly err; nor do I wish this error, in which I find delight, to be wrested from me.
CICERO

Some beliefs are like walled gardens. They encourage
exclusiveness, and the feeling of being especially privileged.
Other beliefs are expansive and lead the way
into wider and deeper sympathies.
Some beliefs are like shadows, darkening children's days
with fear of unknown calamities.
Other beliefs are like sunshine, blessing children
with the warmth of happiness.
Some beliefs are divisive, separating the saved from the
unsaved, friends from enemies.
Other beliefs are bonds in a universal brotherhood
where sincere differences beautify the pattern.

Some beliefs are like blinders, shutting off the power to
choose one's own direction.
> Other beliefs are like gateways opening up wide
> vistas for exploration.
Some beliefs weaken a person's selfhood. They blight the
growth of resourcefulness.
> Other beliefs nurture self-confidence and enrich the
> feeling of personal worth.
Some beliefs are rigid, like the body of death, impotent
in a changing world.
> Other beliefs are pliable, like the young sapling,
> ever growing with the upward thrust of life.

SOPHIA FAHS

I am not afraid of those tender and scrupulous consciences who are ever
cautious of professing and believing too much; if they are sincerely wrong, I
forgive their errors and respect their integrity. The men I am afraid of are
those who believe everything, subscribe to everything, and vote for everything. WILLIAM DAVIES SHIPLEY

It has been well said . . . that a man's religion is the chief fact with regard
to him. . . . By religion I do not mean here the church creed which he pro-
fesses, the articles of faith which he will sign and, in words or otherwise,
assert; not this wholly, in many cases not this at all. We see men of all kinds
of professed creeds attain to almost all degrees of worth or worthlessness
under each or any of them. This is not what I call religion, this profession
and assertion; which is often only a profession and assertion from the outwards. . . . But the thing a man does practically believe (and this often
enough without asserting it even to himself, much less to others), the thing
a man does practically lay to heart, and know for certain, concerning his vital
relations to this mysterious Universe, and his duty and destiny there, that is
in all cases the primary thing for him, and creatively determines all the
rest; . . . and I say, if you tell me what that is, you tell me, to a very great
extent, what the man is, what the kind of things he will do is.

Show me the man you honor, and I will know what kind of a man you are,
for it shows me what your ideal of manhood is, and what kind of a man you
long to be. THOMAS CARLYLE

Belief consists in accepting the affirmations of the soul; unbelief in denying
them. RALPH WALDO EMERSON

No matter what the world thinks about religious experience, the one who has it possesses the great treasure of a thing that has provided him with a source of life, meaning and beauty and that has given a new splendor to the world and mankind. CARL JUNG

See also: ATHEISM; DIVINE, THE; DOUBT; FAITH; GOD; HOPE; IMMOR-TALITY; MYSTERY; PRAYER; RELIGION; REVERENCE; SOUL.

The Bible

The world of the Bible is a great world. I have wandered through it all, but I have never made it all my own. But some friendly hills and valleys in it are mine by right of experience. Some chapters have comforted me; some have made me homesick; some have braced me like a bugle call; and some always enlarge me within by a sense of unutterable fellowship with a great, quiet Power that pervades all things and fills me. Such passages make up for each of us his Bible within the Bible, and the extent and variety of these claims he has staked out in it measure how much of the great Book has really entered into the substance of his life. WALTER RAUSCHENBUSCH

What a book! Great and wide as the world, rooted in the abysmal depths of creation and rising aloft into the blue mysteries of heaven. Sunrise and sunset, promise and fulfillment, birth and death, the whole human drama: everything is in this book. It is the book of books, *Biblia.* HEINRICH HEINE

Throughout the history of the Western world the Scriptures have been the great instigators of revolt against the worst forms of clerical and political despotism. The Bible has been the Magna Charta of the poor and of the oppressed. THOMAS H. HUXLEY

[The Bible] is, as it were, a kind of river, if I may so liken it, which is both shallow and deep, wherein both the lamb may find a footing and the elephant float at large. SAINT GREGORY THE GREAT

From century to century, even to this day, throughout the fairest regions of civilization, the Bible dominates existence. Its vision of life moulds states and societies. Its Psalms are more popular in every country than the poems of the nation's own poets. Beside this one book with its infinite editions all other literature seems "trifles light as air."   ISRAEL ZANGWILL

Nothing can surpass the Bible as lighting up the manifold problems of our life. There can be no worthwhile political or military education about Israel without profound knowledge of the Bible.

The Book of Books, written by the hand of the people of Israel in this Land, is the most widely read in the world, and more than any other has influenced human thought. Most religions have their origin in this Land, and many a nation owns an attachment of spirit and soul to it and to the events that have occurred in it during the last three thousand years. Of everything that happens here the echo resounds throughout the wide world.

DAVID BEN-GURION

The Bible is like a telescope. If a man looks *through* his telescope, then he sees worlds beyond; but if he looks *at* his telescope, then he does not see anything but that. The Bible is a thing to be looked through, to see that which is beyond; but most people only look at it; and so they see only the dead letter.

PHILLIPS BROOKS

Far from being a mere relic of ancient literature, a book on the shelf gathering dust, the Bible in our lives is living power, radiating anticipations, throwing illuminations.

More than two thousand years of reading and research have not succeeded in exploring its full meaning. Today it is as if it had never been touched, never been seen, as if we had not even begun to read it. What would be missing in the world, what would be the condition and faith of man, had the Bible not been preserved?   ABRAHAM JOSHUA HESCHEL

Even those who do not believe that the Bible is the revelation of God, will admit that it is the supreme revelation of man.   WILLIAM LYON PHELPS

Most people are bothered by those passages in Scripture which they cannot understand; but as for me, I always noticed that the passages in Scripture which trouble me most are those which I do understand.   MARK TWAIN

[The Bible is] a collection of literature, containing in a pre-eminent measure the growth of the consciousness of God in the human soul, as interpreted by the pre-eminent religious leaders of a pre-eminently religious people.

LYMAN ABBOTT

Our Jewish Bible has implanted itself in the table-talk and household life of every man and woman in the European and American nations.

RALPH WALDO EMERSON

The Bible is alive, it speaks to me; it has feet, it runs after me; it has hands, it lays hold on me. MARTIN LUTHER

The most learned, acute, and diligent student cannot, in the longest life, obtain an entire knowledge of this one volume. The more deeply he works the mine, the richer and more abundant he finds the ore; new light continually beams from this source of heavenly knowledge, to direct the conduct, and illustrate the work of God and the ways of men; and he will at last leave the world confessing, that the more he studied the Scriptures, the fuller conviction he had of his own ignorance, and of their inestimable value.

SIR WALTER SCOTT

The Bible is for the government of the people, by the people, and for the people. JOHN WYCLIFF

See also: ASPIRATION; BROTHERHOOD; CONSCIENCE; DEATH; FORGIVENESS; GOD; HOPE; JUSTICE; LOVE; MYSTERY; SELFLESSNESS; SOUL.

Blessings

Enjoy the blessings of this day: for this day only is ours; we are dead to yesterday and we are not yet born to the morrow. But if we look abroad and bring into one day's thoughts the evil of many, certain and uncertain, what will be and what will never be, our load will be as intolerable as it is unreasonable.

JEREMY TAYLOR

We are all nobly born; fortunate those who know it; blessed those who remember it. ROBERT LOUIS STEVENSON

What diamonds are equal to my eyes?
What labyrinths to my ears?
What gates of ivory or ruby leaves to the double
portal of my lips and teeth?

Is not sight a jewel?
Is not hearing a treasure?
Is not speech a glory?

O my Lord, pardon my ingratitude, and pity my dullness
  who am not sensible of these gifts.
The freedom of Thy bounty hath deceived me;
These things were too near to be considered.
Thou presenteth me with Thy blessings, and I was
  not aware.
But now I give thanks and adore and praise Thee for
  Thine inestimable favors.

           THOMAS TRAHERNE

May the blessing of light be on you, light without and light within. May the blessed Sunlight shine on you and warm your heart until it glows like a great peat fire, so that a stranger may come and warm himself at it, and also a friend. And may the light shine out of the two eyes of you like a candle set in two windows of a house, bidding the wanderer to come in out of the storm.

And may the blessing of the Rain be on you—the soft, sweet rain. May it fall upon your spirit so that all the little flowers may spring up, and shed their sweetness on the air. And may the blessings of the Great Rains be on you, may they beat upon your spirit and wash it fair and clean, and leave there many a shining pool where the blue of heaven shines reflected, and sometimes a star.

And may the blessing of the Earth be on you—the great and round earth; may you ever have a kindly greeting for them you pass as you're going along the roads. May the earth be soft under you when you lie upon it, tired at the close of the day.   ANCIENT GAELIC BLESSING

Reflect upon your present blessings, of which every man has many: not on your past misfortunes, of which all men have some.   CHARLES DICKENS

Today, I make my Sacrament of Thanksgiving. I begin with the simple things of my days: fresh air to breathe, cool water to drink, the taste of food, the protection of houses and clothes, the comforts of home. For all these I make an Act of Thanksgiving this day!

I bring to mind all the warmth of humankind that I have known: my mother's arms, the strength of my father, the playmates of my childhood; the wonderful stories brought to me from the lives of many who talked of days gone by when fairies and giants and all kinds of magic held sway; the tears I have shed, the tears I have seen: the excitement of laughter and the twinkle in the eye with its reminder that life is good. For all these I make an Act of Thanksgiving this day.

I finger one by one the messages of hope that awaited me at the crossroads: the smile of approval from those who held in their hands the reins of my security; the tightening of the grip in a simple handshake when I feared the step before me in the darkness; the whisper in my heart when the temptation was fiercest and the claims of appetite were not be be denied; the crucial word said, the simple sentence from an open page when my decision hung in the balance. From all these I make an Act of Thanksgiving this day.

HOWARD THURMAN

Things worth remembering:
The value of time,
The success of perseverance,
The pleasure of working,
The dignity of simplicity,
The worth of character,
The improvement of talent,
The influence of example,
The obligation of duty,
The wisdom of economy,
The virtue of patience,
The joy of originating,
The power of kindness.

ANONYMOUS

Blessings we enjoy daily, and for the most of them, because they be so common, men forget to pay their praises. But let not us, because it is a sacrifice so pleasing to Him who still protects us, and gives us flowers, and showers, and meat, and content.

IZAAK WALTON

Nothing raises the price of a blessing like its removal; whereas, it was its continuance which should have taught us its value.

There are three requisites to the proper enjoyment of earthly blessings: a thankful reflection, on the goodness of the giver; a deep sense of our own unworthiness; and a recollection of the uncertainty of our long possessing them. The first will make us grateful; the second, humble; and the third, moderate.

HANNAH MORE

See also: ADVERSITY; AFFLICTION; BEAUTY; CHEERFULNESS; DIVINE, THE; GOD; GRACE; HAPPINESS; HEALTH; PERSPECTIVE; SELF-KNOWLEDGE; WORSHIP.

Books

Except a living man there is nothing more wonderful than a book! A message to us from the dead—from human souls we never saw, who lived perhaps thousands of miles away. And yet these, in those little sheets of paper, speak to us, arouse us, terrify us, teach us, comfort us, open their hearts to us as brothers.   CHARLES KINGSLEY

The library is not a shrine for the worship of books. It is not a temple where literary incense must be burned or where one's devotion to the bound book is expressed in ritual. A library, to modify the famous metaphor of Socrates, should be the delivery room for the birth of ideas—a place where history comes to life.   NORMAN COUSINS

We may live without poetry, music and art;
We may live without conscience and live
    without heart;
We may live without friends; we may live
    without cooks;
But civilized man cannot live without books.
    EDWARD BULWER LYTTON

Say not, when I have leisure I will study; you may not have leisure.
                                                    THE MISHNAH

The two most engaging powers of an author are to make new things familiar and familiar things new.   SAMUEL JOHNSON

A book may be as great a thing as a battle.   BENJAMIN DISRAELI

Your unused learning is an unused taper:
A book, tight shut, is but a block of paper.
    CHINESE PROVERB

Books are the food of youth, the delight of old age; the ornament of prosperity, the refuge and comfort of adversity; a delight at home, and no hindrance abroad; companions by night, in traveling, in the country.　CICERO

Authors are like bees who pillage here and there among the flowers, but who succeed in producing honey which is entirely their own.　MONTAIGNE

As good almost kill a man as kill a good book; who kills a man kills a reasonable creature, God's image; but he who destroys a good book, kills reason itself, kills the image of God, as it were, in the eye.　JOHN MILTON

Many times the reading of a book has made the fortune of the man—has decided his way of life. 'Tis a tie between men to have been delighted with the same book.　RALPH WALDO EMERSON

Writing a book was an adventure. To begin with, it was a toy, an amusement: then it became a mistress, and then a master, and then a tyrant.
　WINSTON S. CHURCHILL

> The place that does
> Contain my books, the best companions, is
> To me a glorious court, where hourly I
> Converse with the old sages and philosophers;
> And sometimes for variety, I confer
> With kings and emperors, and weigh their counsels;
> Calling their victories, if unjustly got,
> Unto a strict account; and in my fancy,
> Deface their ill-plac'd statutes.
> 　JOHN FLETCHER

See also: EDUCATION; INSPIRATION; WISDOM.

Brotherhood

A man who stands alone, having decided to obey the truth, may be weak and slip back into his old ways. Therefore, stand ye together, assist one another, and strengthen one another's efforts. Be like unto brothers; one in love, one in holiness, and one in your zeal for the truth. Spread the truth and preach the doctrine in all quarters of the world, so that in the end all living creatures will be citizens of the kingdom of righteousness. This is the holy brotherhood.   BUDDHA

Brotherhood . . . is, in essence, a hope on the road—the long road—to fulfillment. To claim it to be already a full-grown fact is to be guilty of hypocrisy. To admit it to be always a fiction is to be guilty of cynicism. Let us avoid both.   T. V. SMITH

Let us neither express nor cherish any harsh feeling towards any citizen who, by his vote, has differed with us. Let us at all times remember that all Americans are brothers of a common country and should dwell together in the bonds of fraternal feeling.   ABRAHAM LINCOLN

Men become what they are, sons of God, by becoming what they are, brothers of their brothers.   MARTIN BUBER

All believers are brothers.   THE KORAN

That a few simple men should in one generation have invented so powerful and appealing a personality, so lofty an ethic and so inspiring a vision of human brotherhood, would be a miracle far more incredible than any recorded in the Gospel.   WILL DURANT

> Turn back, O man, forswear thy foolish ways,
> Old now is earth, and one may count her days;
> Yet thou, her child, whose head is crowned with flame,
> Still wilt not hear thine inner God proclaim—
> "Turn back, O man, forswear thy foolish ways." . . .
>   .   .   .   .
> Earth shall be fair, and all her peoples one;
> Nor till that hour shall God's whole will be done.
> Now, even now, once more from earth to sky,
> Peals forth in joy man's old undaunted cry—
> "Earth shall be fair, and all her folk be one."
>   ROBERT BROWNING

> Slav, Teuton, Kelt, I count them all
> My friends and brother souls,
> With all the peoples, great and small,
> That wheel between the poles.
>
> ALFRED, LORD TENNYSON

Somewhere in this plot of ground [5th Marine Division Cemetery, Iwo Jima] there may lie the man who could have discovered the cure for cancer. Under one of these Christian crosses, or beneath a Jewish Star of David, there may rest now a man who was destined to be a great prophet. Here lie men who loved America. . . . Now they lie here silently in this sacred soil, and we gather to consecrate this earth to their memory. . . .

Here lie officers and men, Negroes and white, rich men and poor. . . . Here are Protestants, Catholics, and Jews. . . . Here no man prefers another because of his faith, or despises him because of his color. Here there are no quotas of how many from each group are admitted or allowed. . . . Theirs is the highest and purest democracy. Among our dead there is no discrimination, no prejudice, no hatred. . . .

Any man among us the living who . . . lifts his hand in hate against a brother or thinks himself superior to those who happen to be in the minority, makes of this ceremony, and of the bloody sacrifice it commemorates, an empty, hollow mockery!　　　　　　　　ROLAND B. GITTELSOHN

Men are mystically united; a bond of brotherhood makes all men one.

THOMAS CARLYLE

> . . . The natural bond
> Of brotherhood is severed as the flax
> That falls asunder at the touch of fire.
> Lands intersected by a narrow firth
> Abhor each other. Mountains interposed
> Make enemies of nations who had else
> Like kindred drops been mingled into one.
> Thus man devotes his brother, and destroys.
>
> WILLIAM COWPER

Years ago I recognized my kinship with all human beings, and I made up my mind I was not one whit better than the meanest on earth. I said then and I say now that while there is a lower class, I am of it; while there is a criminal class, I am of it; while there is a soul in prison, I am not free.

EUGENE V. DEBS

Have we not all one father? Hath not one God created us? Why do we deal treacherously every man against his brother? THE BIBLE

The race of mankind would perish did they cease to aid each other. We cannot exist without mutual help. All therefore that need aid have a right to ask it from their fellow-men; and no one who has the power of granting can refuse it without guilt. SIR WALTER SCOTT

I am the darker brother.
They send me to eat in the kitchen
When company comes,
But I laugh,
And eat well,
And grow strong.

Tomorrow,
I'll sit at the table
when company comes.
Nobody'll dare
Say to me,
"Eat in the kitchen,"
Then.

Besides,
They'll see how beautiful I am
And be ashamed—

I, too, am America.
LANGSTON HUGHES

See also: AMERICA; COMPASSION; CONSCIENCE; DEMOCRACY; EQUAL-ITY; FRIENDSHIP; HUMANITY; INTERNATIONALISM; LOVE; PREJUDICE; RACIAL JUSTICE; RELIGION.

Character

I would rather be adorned by beauty of character than by jewels. Jewels are the gift of fortune, while character comes from within. PLAUTUS

Character, like a kettle, once mended, always requires repairs.
ANCIENT PROVERB

Keep the faculty of effort alive in you by a little gratuitous exercise each day. That is, be systematically ascetic or heroic in little unnecessary points, do every day or two something for no other reason that that you would rather not do it, so that when the hour of dire need draws nigh, it may find you not unnerved and untrained to stand the test.   WILLIAM JAMES

Without my work in natural science I should never have known human beings as they really are. In no other activity can one come so close to direct perception and clear thought, or realize so fully the errors of the senses, the mistakes of the intellect, the weaknesses and greatnesses of human charac- ter.   JOHANN WOLFGANG VON GOETHE

Fame is a vapor, popularity an accident, riches take wings. Only one thing endures and that is character.   ABRAHAM LINCOLN

The willow which bends to the tempest, often escapes better than the oak which resists it; and so in great calamities, it sometimes happens that light and frivolous spirits recover their elasticity and presence of mind sooner than those of a loftier character.   SIR WALTER SCOTT

> Who loves another's name to stain,
> he shall not dine with me again.
>   SAINT AUGUSTINE

If we had no faults, we should not take so much pleasure in noting those of others.   FRANÇOIS LA ROCHEFOUCAULD

He who when called upon to speak a disagreeable truth, tells it boldly and has done, is both bolder and milder than he who nibbles in a low voice and never ceases nibbling.   JOHANN KASPAR LAVATER

When wealth is lost, nothing is lost; when health is lost, something is lost; when character is lost, all is lost.   GERMAN PROVERB

A man is poor when he has lost the confidence of his friends; when people who are nearest to him do not believe in him; when his character is handi- capped by deceit and punctured by his dishonesty. He is poor when he makes money at the expense of his character, when principle does not stand out supreme in his ideals. When ideals are clouded he is in danger of the worst kind of poverty. To be in the poorhouse is not necessarily to be poor if one has maintained his integrity of character and stands foursquare to the world. If one has not bent the knee of principle to avarice he is not poor, though he may be compelled to beg bread.   ANONYMOUS

Character is what you are in the dark.   DWIGHT L. MOODY

I have been thinking, love, that for days now I have been sailing the lakes and each of the lakes is fed by a hundred and more confluent rivers. We look upon Niagara and say, wonderful—thinking nothing of all that makes its glory and majesty possible. We look upon a man or woman of character; we are lost in admiration, but we omit to consider the thousand influences, conscious and unconscious, which have gone to make up the result.

                                                    STEPHEN S. WISE
                    [in a letter to his future wife from Lake Superior in 1900]

It is character that counts in a nation as in a man. It is a good thing to have a keen, fine intellectual development in a nation, to produce orators, artists, successful businessmen; but it is an infinitely greater thing to have those solid qualities which we group together under the name of character: sobriety, steadfastness, the sense of obligation toward one's neighbor and one's God, hard common sense, and, combined with it, the lift of generous enthusiasm toward whatever is right.

These are the qualities which go to make up true national greatness.

                                                THEODORE ROOSEVELT

The highest of characters is his who is ready to pardon the moral errors of mankind as though he were every day guilty of some himself, and at the time is cautious of committing a fault as though he never forgave one.

                                                PLINY THE YOUNGER

The measure of a man's real character is what he would do if he knew he would never be found out.   THOMAS BABINGTON MACAULAY

The reputation of a thousand years may be determined by the conduct of one hour.   JAPANESE PROVERB

Cheerfulness

Wondrous is the strength of cheerfulness, and its power of endurance. The cheerful man will do more in the same time, will do it better, will persevere in it longer, than the sad or sullen. THOMAS CARLYLE

Of all subjective blessings, that which most directly makes us happy is a cheerful disposition: for this excellent trait is its own immediate reward. Precisely he who is cheerful always has reason to be so; namely, just because he feels that way. In judging the happiness of someone who is young, beautiful, rich, and honored, one wishes to know if he is cheerful as well. But if, on the other hand, he is cheerful, it makes no difference whether he is young or old, straight or hunchbacked, poor or rich; he is happy. Cheerfulness alone is comparable to the actual coin of happiness, and not, like everything else, only to its bank checks. ARTHUR SCHOPENHAUER

I had rather have a fool make me merry, than experience make me sad. WILLIAM SHAKESPEARE

Gladness of the heart is the life of man, and the joyfulness of a man prolongeth his days. THE APOCRYPHA

Always laugh when you can; it is a cheap medicine. Merriment is a philosophy not well understood. It is the sunny side of existence. GEORGE GORDON BYRON

A happy and cheerful life is not from without, but it has its source in the disposition within. The idea, however, deceives the most of mankind, just as clothes seem to warm a man, not by throwing out heat themselves (for in itself every garment is cold), but the heat which a man throws out from his own body is retained and wrapped in by a dress fitting close to the body, which does not admit of the heat being dissipated. PLUTARCH

I have always preferred cheerfulness to mirth. The latter I consider as an act, the former as a habit of the mind. Mirth is short and transient; cheerfulness, fixed and permanent. Those are often raised into the greatest transports of mirth, who are subject to the greatest depressions of melancholy; on the contrary, cheerfulness, though it does not give the mind such an exquisite gladness, prevents us from falling into any depths of sorrow. Mirth is like a flash of lightning, that breaks through a gloom of clouds and glitters for a moment; cheerfulness keeps up a kind of daylight in the mind, and fills it with a steady and perpetual serenity. Cheerfulness bears the same friendly regard to the mind as to the body; it banishes all anxious care and discontent; soothes and composes the passions and keeps them in a perpetual calm.
JOSEPH ADDISON

Cheerfulness is as natural to the heart of a man in strong health, as color to his cheek; and wherever there is habitual gloom, there must be either bad air, unwholesome food, improperly severe labor, or erring habits of life.
JOHN RUSKIN

See also: ADVERSITY; AFFLICTION; EXAMPLE; MATURITY; PERSPECTIVE; SELF-CONTROL; SELF-KNOWLEDGE.

Christianity

Christianity is not the religion of sorrow and gloom; it is the religion of the morning, and it carries in its heart the happiness of heaven.

Chrisitanity is not a restraint but an inspiration—not a weight but wings; not subtraction but addition.

Christianity brings bloom for faded hearts, rejuvenation for the prematurely old, imagination for the dry, literal mind.

Christianity is not a kill-joy at the feast of life, nor a kind of incarnate "don't"; it bristles with great affirmatives, fires the soul with permanent enthusiasms and durable loyalties.

Christianity leaves a trail of light wherever it goes; it can keep you cool under any confusion, bring you up smiling from any deeps, and utterly banish your fret and worry.

Christianity brings zest and sparkle to life; it is sunshine on the flowers rather than moonshine on the snow; it is life more abundant; it is leaving the little narrow life behind and leaving it forever.   HUGH ELMER BROWN

On the ancient minster at Basle are two sculptured groups: St. Martin, cutting his cloak in two with his sword to clothe a begger, and St. George, spurring his horse against the dragon that devastated the country. Every Christian man should embody both kinds of sainthood in one life.

WALTER RAUSCHENBUSCH

I doubt the possibility, or the propriety, of settling the religion of Jesus Christ in the models of man-made creeds and dogmas. It was a *spirit in life* that he laid stress on and taught, if I read aright. I know it to be so with me.

I cannot without mental reservations assent to long and complicated creeds and catechisms. If I could find a church that would simply ask for assent to the Savior's statement of the substance of the Law—"Thou shalt love the Lord thy God with all thy heart and with all thy soul and with all thy mind, and thy neighbor as thyself"—that church would I gladly unite with.

ABRAHAM LINCOLN

This is a cheerful world as I see it from my garden under the shadows of my vines. But if I were to ascend some high mountain and look out over the wide lands, you know very well what I should see: brigands on the highways, pirates on the sea, armies fighting, cities burning; in the amphitheaters men murdered to please applauding crowds; selfishness and cruelty and misery and despair under all roofs. It is a bad world, Donatus, an incredibly bad world. But I have discovered in the midst of it a quiet and holy people who have learned a great secret. They have found a joy which is a thousand times better than any pleasure of our sinful life. They are despised and persecuted, but they care not. They are masters of their souls. They have overcome the world. These people, Donatus, are the Christians—and I am one of them.

SAINT CYPRIAN

The Christian view of man knows no graded scale of essential and fundamental worth; there is no divine right of whites which differs from the divine rights of Negroes.

KYLE HASELDEN

When Christianity came up from the catacombs to become the official religion of Rome, it left something precious down in the dark. It gained extension; it lost intensity. It gained in bulk; it lost in savor.

HALFORD E. LUCCOCK

In the Christian religion we discern a transition from the religion of the cult to the prophetic religion of pure morals, from the religion of law to the religion of love, from the religion of priests to the religion of individual prayer and inward life, from the national God to the universal God.

SRI SARVEPALLI RADHAKRISHNAN

Scratch the Christian and you find the pagan—spoiled.   ISRAEL ZANGWILL

The Christian needs a reminder every hour: some defeat, surprise, adversity, peril; to be agitated, mortified, beaten out of his course, so that all remains of self will be sifted out.   HORACE BUSHNELL

> *See also:* ASPIRATION; BELIEF; BIBLE, THE; BLESSINGS; BROTHER-
> HOOD; CHURCH, THE; DIVINE, THE; FAITH; FELLOWSHIP; GOD; GRACE;
> HOPE; HUMILITY; IDEALS; JESUS CHRIST; LOVE; PEACE OF MIND;
> PRAYER; RELIGION; RESPONSIBILITY; REVERENCE; SAINTLINESS;
> SELFLESSNESS; SOUL; VIRTUE; WONDER; WORSHIP.

The Church

I believe in the Church Universal, the deposit of all ancient wisdom and the receptacle of modern science, which recognizes in all prophets and saints a harmony, in all scriptures a unity, and through all dispensations a continuity, which abjures all that separates and divides and always magnifies unity and peace, which harmonizes reason and faith, yoga and bhakti, asceticism and social duty . . . and which shall make all nations and sects one kingdom and one family in the fullness of time.   KESHAB CHANDRA SEN

> Wherever God erects a house of prayer,
> The Devil always builds a chapel there;
> And 'twill be found upon examination,
> The latter has the largest congregation.
>   DANIEL DEFOE

I never weary of great churches. It is my favorite kind of mountain scenery. Mankind was never so happily inspired as when it made a cathedral.
                     ROBERT LOUIS STEVENSON

It is of no avail to talk of the church in general, the church in the abstract, unless the concrete particular local church which the people attend can become a center of light and leading, of inspiration and guidance, for its specific community.   RUFUS M. JONES

The church will have nothing to do with current sins. She has the sword of the Spirit, but glues it in the scabbard! She puts on the breastplate of righteousness, but never goes into battle! She has her feet shod with the Gospel of peace, but will not travel. WENDELL PHILLIPS

The true meaning of the church has given way to the manipulations of the organization. In place of the sacraments, we have the committee meeting; in place of confession, the bazaar; in place of pilgrimage, the dull drive to hear the deadly speaker; in place of community, a collection of functions. This trivialization of religious life has made the middle-class search for religious meaning even more desperate. One begins to wonder after a time whether the search itself isn't pointless, since every church activity seems to lead further into a maze of superficiality which is stultifying the middle-class community. GIBSON WINTER

In the midst of all wrongs and sins of our day, is the church to say nothing, do nothing? If I thought so, I never would enter the church but once again, and then to bow my shoulder to their manifest work—to heave down strong pillars, though like Samson I buried myself under its ruins. A church must be not merely a church of theology but of religion; not of faith only, but of work, a church militant against every form of evil. . . . Its one great aim should be the building of a state where there is honorable work for every hand, bread for all mouths, clothing for all backs, culture for all minds, and love and faith in every heart. THEODORE PARKER

God builds his temple in the heart on the ruins of churches and religions.
RALPH WALDO EMERSON

Man is not yet so transfigured that he has ceased to keep the window of his mind and heart open toward Jerusalem, Galilee, Mecca, Canterbury, or Plymouth. The abstract proposal that we worship at any place where God lets down the ladder is not yet an adequate substitute for the deep desire to go up to some central sanctuary where the religious artist vindicates a concrete universal in the realm of the spirit. WILLARD L. SPERRY

It were better to be of no church, than to be bitter for any.
WILLIAM PENN

The church, like the Ark of Noah, is worth saving—not for the sake of the unclean beasts and vermin that almost filled it, and probably made most noise and clamor in it, but for the little corner of rationality that was as much distressed by the stink within as by the tempest without.
WILLIAM WARBURTON

The church is man when his awed soul goes out,
In reverence to a mystery that swathes him all
      about.
When any living man in awe gropes Godward in his
      search;
Then in that hour, that living man becomes the
      living church,
Then, though in wilderness or in waste, his
      soul is swept along
Down naves of prayer, through aisles of praise,
      up altar-stairs of song.
And where man fronts the Mystery with spirit
      bowed in prayer,
There is the universal church—the church of
      God is there.

                                          SAM WALTER FOSS

The Lord showed me, so that I did see clearly, that He did not dwell in these temples which men had commanded and set up, but in people's hearts. . . . His people were His temple, and He dwelt in them.   GEORGE FOX

See also: ASPIRATION; BROTHERHOOD; COMPASSION; FELLOWSHIP; GRACE; MYSTERY; PRAYER; RACIAL JUSTICE; RELIGION; REVERENCE; WONDER; WORSHIP.

Compassion

Great Spirit, grant that I may not criticise my neighbor until I have walked a mile in his moccasins.   INDIAN PRAYER

The root of the matter, if we want a stable world, is a very simple and old-fashioned thing, a thing so simple that I am almost ashamed to mention it for fear of the derisive smile with which wise cynics will greet my words. The thing I mean is love, Christian love, or compassion. If you feel this, you have a motive for existence, a reason for courage, an imperative necessity for intellectual honesty.   BERTRAND RUSSELL

The little I have seen of the world teaches me to look upon the errors of others in sorrow, not in anger. When I take the history of one poor heart that has sinned and suffered, and think of the struggles and temptations it has passed through, the brief pulsations of joy, the feverish inquietude of hope and fear, the pressure of want, the desertion of friends, I would fain leave the erring soul of my fellow-man with Him from whose hands it came.

                                                HENRY WADSWORTH LONGFELLOW

When God measures a man, He puts the tape around the heart instead of the head.   ANONYMOUS

Of what avail is an open eye, if the heart is blind?   SOLOMON IBN-GABIROL

Both [the North and the South] read the same Bible and pray to the same God; and each invokes His aid against the other. . . . The prayers of both could not be answered; that of neither has been answered fully. . . . Fondly do we hope, fervently do we pray, that this mighty scourge of war may speedily pass away. Yet, if God wills that it continue until all the wealth piled by the bondsman's two hundred and fifty years of unrequited toil shall be sunk, and until every drop of blood drawn with the lash shall be paid by another drawn with the sword, as was said three thousand years ago, so still it must be said, "The judgments of the Lord are true and righteous alto-gether."

   With malice toward none, with charity for all, with firmness in the right as God gives us to see the right, let us strive on to finish the work we are in, to bind up the nation's wounds, to care for him who shall have borne the battle and for his widow and his orphan, to do all which may achieve and cherish a just and lasting peace among ourselves and with all nations.

                                                          ABRAHAM LINCOLN

One wears his mind out in study, and yet has more mind with which to study.
   One gives away his heart in love, and yet has more heart to give away.
   One perishes out of pity for a suffering world, and is the stronger thereby.

                                                          MILTON STEINBERG

That person is cultured who is able to put himself in the place of the greatest number of other persons.   JANE ADDAMS

        The quality of mercy is not strain'd:
        It droppeth as the gentle rain from heaven
        Upon the place beneath; it is twice bless'd:
        It blesseth him that gives and him that takes.

'Tis mightiest in the mightiest: it becomes
The throned monarch better than his crown;
His scepter shows the force of temporal power,
The attribute to awe and majesty,
Wherein doth sit the dread and fear of kings;
But mercy is above this scepter'd sway,
It is enthroned in the hearts of kings,
It is an attribute to God himself;
And earthly power doth than show likest God's,
When mercy seasons justice . . .
⠀⠀⠀⠀⠀⠀⠀⠀. . . consider this,
That in the course of justice, none of us
Should see salvation: we do pray for mercy;
And that same prayer doth teach us all to render
The deeds of mercy.

⠀⠀⠀⠀⠀⠀⠀⠀⠀⠀⠀⠀⠀WILLIAM SHAKESPEARE

What is the law of nature? Is it to know that my security and that of my family, all my amusements and pleasures, are purchased at the expense of misery, deprivation, and suffering to thousands of human beings—by the terror of the gallows; by the misfortune of thousands stifling within prison walls; by the fears inspired by millions of soldiers and guardians of civilization, torn from their homes and besotted by discipline, to protect our pleasures with loaded revolvers against the possible interference of the famishing! Is it to purchase every fragment of bread that I put in my mouth and the mouths of my children by the numberless privations that are necessary to procure my abundance? Or is it to be certain that my piece of bread only belongs to me when I know that everyone else has a share, and that no one starves while I eat?

⠀⠀⠀⠀⠀⠀⠀⠀⠀⠀⠀⠀⠀LEO TOLSTOY

Among the attributes of God, although they are all equal, mercy shines with even more brilliancy than justice.

⠀⠀⠀⠀⠀⠀⠀⠀⠀⠀⠀⠀⠀CERVANTES

There are ten strong things. Iron is strong, but fire melts it. Fire is strong, but water quenches it. Water is strong, but the clouds evaporate it. Clouds are strong, but wind drives them away. Man is strong, but fears cast him down. Fear is strong, but wine allays it. Wine is strong, but sleep overcomes it. Sleep is strong, yet death is stronger; but loving kindness survives death.

⠀⠀⠀⠀⠀⠀⠀⠀⠀⠀⠀⠀⠀THE TALMUD

Man is never nearer the Divine than in his compassionate moments.

⠀⠀⠀⠀⠀⠀⠀⠀⠀⠀⠀⠀⠀JOSEPH H. HERTZ

See also: ADVERSITY; AFFLICTION; FORGIVENESS; KINDNESS; LOVE; SUFFERING.

Conscience

There is no witness so terrible, no accuser so potent, as the conscience that dwells in every man's breast.　　　　　　　　　　　　POLYBIUS

There is no class of men so difficult to be managed in a state as those whose intentions are honest, but whose consciences are bewitched.

NAPOLEON BONAPARTE

Tenderness of conscience is always to be distinguished from scrupulousness. The conscience cannot be kept too sensitive and tender; but scrupulousness arises from bodily or mental infirmity, and discovers itself in a multitude of ridiculous, superstitious, and painful feelings.　　　RICHARD CECIL

A good conscience enlists a multitude of friends; a bad conscience is distressed and anxious, even when alone. A good conscience fears no witness, but a guilty conscience is solicitous even in solitude. If we do nothing but what is honest, let all the world know it. But if otherwise, what does it signify to have nobody else know it, so long as I know it myself? Miserable is he who slights that witness.　　　　　　　　　　　　SENECA

Conscience is a thousand witnesses.　　　　　　　ANCIENT PROVERB

The relation is very close between our capacity to act at all and our conviction that the action we are taking is right. . . . Without that belief, most men will not have the energy and will to persevere in the action.

WALTER LIPPMANN

Conscience is the voice of the soul, as the passions are the voice of the body. No wonder they often contradict each other.　　JEAN JACQUES ROUSSEAU

A person may sometimes have a clear conscience simply because his head is empty.　　　　　　　　　　　　　　　RALPH W. SOCKMAN

The voice of conscience is so delicate that it is easy to stifle it; but it is also so clear that it is impossible to mistake it.   MADAME GERMAINE DE STAËL

It takes more than a soft pillow to insure sound sleep.   ANONYMOUS

Love is too young to know what conscience is;
But who knows not conscience is born of love?
WILLIAM SHAKESPEARE

He will easily be content and at peace, whose conscience is pure.
THOMAS À KEMPIS

While a jammed horn is recognized as abnormal, a jammed conscience is often regarded as the voice of God.   HARRY EMERSON FOSDICK

Conscience is justice's best minister. It threatens, promises, rewards, and punishes, and keeps all under its control. The busy must attend to its remonstrances, the most powerful submit to its reproof, and the angry endure its upbraidings. While conscience is our friend, all is peace; but if once offended, farewell to the tranquil mind.   MARY WORTLEY MONTAGUE

Be fearful only of thyself, and stand in awe of none more than of thine own conscience. There is a Cato in every man—a severe censor of his manners. And he that reverences this judge will seldom do anything he need repent of.
ROBERT BURTON

This little flame [conscience] should be the star of our life; it alone can guide our trembling ark across the tumult of the great waters.
HENRI FREDERIC AMIEL

All too often a clear conscience is merely the result of a bad memory.
ANCIENT PROVERB

Conscience warns us as friend before it punishes us as a judge.
KING STANISLAUS I

Courage

The strangest, most generous, and proudest of all virtues is true courage.

MONTAIGNE

> . . . Come, my friends,
> 'Tis not too late to seek a newer world.
> Push off, and sitting well in order, smite
> The sounding furrows; for my purpose holds
> To sail beyond the sunset, and the baths
> Of all the western stars, until I die.
> It may be that the gulfs will wash us down.
> It may be we shall touch the Happy Isles,
> And see the great Achilles whom we knew,
> Tho' much is taken, much abides; and tho'
> We are not now that strength which in old days
> Moved earth and heaven, that which we are, we are,
> One equal temper of heroic hearts,
> Made weak by time and fate, but strong in will,
> To strive, to seek, to find, and not to yield.

ALFRED, LORD TENNYSON

When none has the courage to be a man, stand thou up and be one.

HILLEL

Courage without discipline is nearer beastliness than manhood.

SIR PHILIP SIDNEY

Fortitude implies a firmness and strength of mind that enables us to do and suffer as we ought. It rises upon an opposition and, like a river, swells the higher for having its course stopped.　JEREMY COLLIER

To see what is right and not to do it, is want of courage.　CONFUCIUS

Courage conquers all things; it even gives strength to the body.   OVID

Courage consists not so much in avoiding danger as in conquering it.
                                                        ANCIENT PROVERB

Perfect courage means doing unwitnessed what we would be capable of with the world looking on.   FRANÇOIS LA ROCHEFOUCAULD

A scar nobly got is a good livery of honor.   WILLIAM SHAKESPEARE

Whatever you do, you need courage. Whatever course you decide upon, there is always someone to tell you you are wrong. There are always difficulties arising which tempt you to believe that your critics are right. To map out a course of action and follow it to an end, requires some of the same courage which a soldier needs. Peace has its victories, but it takes brave men to win them.   RALPH WALDO EMERSON

The courage we desire and prize is not the courage to die decently, but to live manfully.   THOMAS CARLYLE

Physical bravery is an animal instinct; moral bravery is a much higher and truer courage.   WENDELL PHILLIPS

Courage is what it takes to stand up and speak; courage is also what it takes to sit down and listen.   ANONYMOUS

Wealth, lost, something lost; honor lost, much lost; courage lost, all lost.
                                                JOHANN WOLFGANG VON GOETHE

'Tis nothing for a man to hold up his head in a calm; but to maintain his post when all others have quitted their ground and there to stand upright when other men are beaten down, this is divine and praiseworthy.   SENECA

True courage has so little to do with anger that there lies always the strongest suspicion against it where this passion is highest. True courage is cool

and calm. The bravest of men have the least of a brutal bullying insolence; and in the very time of danger are found the most serene, pleasant and free.
LORD SHAFTESBURY

To die, and thus avoid poverty or love, or anything painful, is not the part of a brave man, but rather of a coward; for it is cowardice to avoid trouble, and the suicide does not undergo death because it is honorable, but in order to avoid evil.   ARISTOTLE

Courage consists not in blindly overlooking danger, but in seeing it, and conquering it.   JEAN PAUL RICHTER

See also: ADVERSITY; AFFLICTION; CONSCIENCE; DEATH; DISSENT; DOUBT; FEAR; GRIEF; INTEGRITY; NON-CONFORMITY; SUFFERING; TRUTH.

Death

When Death, the great Reconciler, has come, it is never our tenderness we repent of, but our severity.   GEORGE ELIOT

I am standing upon the seashore; a ship at my side spreads her white sails to the morning breeze and starts for the blue ocean. She is an object of beauty and strength, and I stand and watch her until at length she hangs like a speck of white cloud just where the sea and sky come down to mingle with each other. Then someone at my side says, "There! She's gone!" Gone where? Gone from my sight—that is all. She is just as large in mast and hull and spar as she was when she left my side and is just as able to bear her load of living freight to the place of destination. Her diminished size is in me, not in her; and just at the moment when someone at my side says, "There! She's gone!" there are other eyes watching her coming and other voices ready to take up the glad shout, "There she comes!" And that is dying.   THE MIDRASH

I see what was, and is, and will abide;
Still glides the stream, and shall forever glide;
The form remains, the function never dies;
While we, the brave, the mighty, and the wise,
We men, who in the morn of youth defied
The elements, must vanish; — be it so!

Enough, if something from our hands have power
To live, and act, and serve the future hour;
And if, as toward the silent tomb we go,
Through love, through hope, and faith's transcendent
 dower,
We feel that we are greater than we know.
                    WILLIAM WORDSWORTH

Death is the liberator of him whom freedom cannot release, the physician of
him whom medicine cannot cure, and the comforter of him whom time cannot console.   CALEB C. COLTON

How do I know that the love of life is not a delusion; and that the dislike of
death is not like a child that is lost and does not know the way home?
                    CHUANG-TZE

Death closes all: but something ere the end,
Some work of noble note, may yet be done.
Not unbecoming men that strove with gods.
       ALFRED, LORD TENNYSON

A man has learned much who has learned how to die.   GERMAN PROVERB

I depart from life as from an inn, and not as from my home.   CICERO

When a man dies they who survive him ask what property he has left behind.
The angel who bends over the dying man asks what good deeds he has sent
before him.   THE KORAN

Let us reflect in another way, and we shall see that there is great reason to
hope that death is good; for one of two things: either death is a state of nothingness and utter unconsciousness, or, as men say, there is a change and
migration of the soul from this world to another. Now if you suppose that
there is no consciousness, but a sleep like the sleep of him who is undisturbed even by the sight of dreams, death will be an unspeakable gain. For
if a person were to select the night in which his sleep was undisturbed even
by dreams, and were to compare it with the other days and nights of his life,
and then were to tell us how many days and nights he had passed in the

course of his life better and more pleasantly than this one, I think that any man, I will not say a private man, but even the great king, will not find many such days or nights, when compared with the others. Now if death is like this, I say that to die, is gain: for eternity is then only a single night. But if death is the journey to another place, and there, as men say, all the dead are, what good, O my friends and judges, can be greater than this?   SOCRATES

We sometimes congratulate ourselves at the moment of waking from a troubled dream; it may be so at the moment of death. NATHANIEL HAWTHORNE

Not in the sky, not in the midst of the sea, not even in the clefts of the mountains is there a spot in the whole world where, if a man abide there, death could not overtake him.   DHAMMAPADA

If we treat the dead as if they were wholly dead, it shows want of affection; if we treat them as wholly alive, it shows want of sense. Neither should be done.   CONFUCIUS

Death rides a fast camel.   ARAB PROVERB

The rugged old Norsemen spoke of death as *Heimgang*—"home-going." So the snow-flowers go home when they melt and flow to the sea, and the rock-ferns, after unrolling their fronds to the light and beautifying the rocks, roll them up close again in the autumn and blend with the soil. Myriads of rejoicing living creatures, daily, hourly, perhaps every moment sink into death's arms, dust to dust, spirit to spirit—waited on, watched over, noticed only by their Maker, each arriving at its own Heaven-dealt destiny. All the merry dwellers of the trees and streams, and the myriad swarms of the air, called into life by the sunbeam of a summer morning, go home through death, wings folded perhaps in the last red rays of sunset of the day they were first tried. Trees towering in the sky, braving storms of centuries, flowers turning faces to the light for a single day or hour, having enjoyed their share of life's feast—all alike pass on and away under the law of death and love. Yet all are our brothers and they enjoy life as we do, share Heaven's blessings with us, die and are buried in hallowed ground, come with us out of eternity and return into eternity. "Our lives are rounded with a sleep."
                                                    JOHN MUIR

I watched a sail until it dropped from sight
Over the rounding sea. A gleam of white,

A last far-flashed farewell, and, like a thought
Slipt out of mind, it vanished and was not.

Yet to the helmsman standing at the wheel
Broad seas still stretched beneath the gliding keel.
Disaster? Change? He felt no slightest sign,
Nor dreamed he of that far horizon line.

So may it be, perchance, when down the tide
Our dear ones vanish. Peacefully they glide
On level seas, nor mark the unknown bound.
We call it death—to them 'tis life beyond.

ANONYMOUS

Termination of activity, cessation from movement and opinion, and in a sense their death, is no evil. Turn thy thoughts now to the consideration of thy life, thy life as a child, as a youth, thy manhood, thy old age, for in these also every change was a death. Is this anything to fear? Turn thy thoughts now to thy life under thy grandfather, then to thy life under thy mother, then to thy life under thy father; and as thou findest many other differences and changes and terminations, ask thyself: Is this anything to fear? In like manner, then, neither are the termination and cessation and change of thy whole life a thing to be afraid of. MARCUS AURELIUS

In the democracy of the dead, all men are equal. The poor man is as rich as the richest, and the rich man as poor as the pauper. The creditor loses his usury, and the debtor is acquitted of his obligation. There the proud man surrenders his dignity; the politician his honors; the worldling his pleasures; the invalid needs no physician; the laborer rests from toil. The wrongs of time are redressed; injustice is expiated, and the irony of fate is refuted.

ANONYMOUS

How plain that death is only the phenomenon of the individual or class. Nature does not recognize it. She finds her own again under new forms without loss. Yet death is beautiful when seen to be a law, and not an accident. It is as common as life. Men die in Tartary, in Ethiopia—in England— in Wisconsin. And after all what portion of this so serene and living nature can be said to be alive? Do this year's grasses and foliage outnumber all the past?

Every blade in the field—every leaf in the forest—lays down its life in its season as beautifully as it was taken up. It is the pastime of a full quarter of the year. Dead trees, sere leaves, dried grass and herbs—are not these a good

part of our life? And what is that pride of our autumnal scenery but the
hectic flush—the sallow and cadaverous countenance of vegetation, its
painted throes—with the November air for canvas?

When we look over the fields, are we not saddened because the particular
flowers or grasses will wither, for the law of their death is the law of new
life? Will not the land be in good heart because the crops die down from
year to year? The herbage cheerfully consents to bloom, and wither, and
give place to a new.

So it is with the human plant. We are partial and selfish when we lament
the death of an individual, unless our plaint be a paean to the departed soul,
and a sigh as the wind sighs over the fields, which no shrub interprets into
its private grief.   HENRY DAVID THOREAU

The tyrant dies and his rule is over; the martyr dies and his rule begins.
                                             SÖREN KIERKEGAARD

Death cannot kill what never dies. Death is but crossing the world, as
friends do the seas; they live in another still.   THOMAS TRAHERNE

The adventure of death . . . differs not from any other adventure of life save
that we face the uncertainty of our adventure thereunto not being free to
choose the hour of the inevitable rendezvous. I never resort to the soothing
commonplace—what all men have endured, we, too, may safely adventure.
Rather do I ask—who amongst us would wish to escape the greatest of adventures? Life is no more truly my birthright than it is my right to know that
I am about to set forth when the hour strikes. As for another, let the adventure of death signify hope unaltering and love unafraid; as for self, mine
cannot be less than courage unequaling and trust unafraid.
                                             STEPHEN S. WISE

There is nothing that Nature has made necessary which is more easy than
death; we are longer coming into the world than going out of it; and there
is not a minute of our lives wherein we may not reasonably expect it. Nay, it
is but a moment's work, this parting of soul and body.

What a shame is it then, to stand so long in fear of anything which is over
so soon! If it shall please God to add another day to our lives, let us thank-
fully receive it; but let us so compose ourselves tonight that we may have
no anxious dependence upon tomorrow.

He that can say, I have lived this day, makes the next clear again.

As the mother's womb holds us for nine months, making us ready, not for
the womb itself, but for life, just so, through our lives we are making our-

selves ready for another birth. Look forward without fear to that appointed hour, the last hour of the body but not of the soul. That day, which you fear as being the end of all things, is the birthday of your eternity.   SENECA

I look forward to my dissolution as to a secure haven, where I shall at length find a happy repose from the fatigues of a long journey.   CICERO

See also: AGE; COURAGE; DIVINE, THE; FEAR; GOD; GRACE; GRIEF; IMMORTALITY; LIFE; MATURITY; MYSTERY; PRAYER.

Dedication

There is no other way of serving the gods than by spending oneself for man.
CHINESE PROVERB

It is a felicitous and true saying of one of the wise men of old, that men never act in a manner more resembling God than when they are bestowing benefits; and what can be a greater good than for mortal men to imitate the everlasting God?   PHILO

I had rather be defeated in a cause that will ultimately triumph than triumph in a cause that will ultimately be defeated.   WOODROW WILSON

There is something in each of us that resents restraints, repressions, and controls, but we forget that nothing left loose ever does anything creative. No horse gets anywhere until he is harnessed. No steam or gas ever drives anything until it is confined. No Niagara is ever turned into light and power until it is tunneled. No life ever grows great until it is dedicated, focused, disciplined.   HARRY EMERSON FOSDICK

Give yourself to something great, enroll under the banner of a high cause, choose as your own some standard of self-sacrifice, attach yourself to a movement that makes not for your own gain but for the welfare of men, and you will have come upon a richly satisfying as well as engrossing adventure.
STEPHEN S. WISE

A man who lives right, and is right, has more power in his silence than another has by his words. Character is like bells which ring out sweet music and which, when touched, accidentally even, resound with sweet music.

PHILLIPS BROOKS

A good intention clothes itself with power.   RALPH WALDO EMERSON

Probably every generation sees itself as charged with remaking the world. Mine, however, knows that it will not remake the world. But its task is perhaps even greater, for it consists in keeping the world from destroying itself. As the heir of a corrupt history that blends blighted revolutions, misguided techniques, dead gods and worn-out ideologies, in which second-rate powers can destroy everything today, but are unable to win anyone over and in which intelligence has stooped to becoming the servant of hatred and oppression, that generation, starting from nothing but its own negations, has had to re-establish both within and without itself a little of what constitutes the dignity of life and death. Faced with a world threatened with disintegration, in which our grand inquisitors may set up once and for all the kingdoms of death, that generation knows that, in a sort of mad race against time, it ought to re-establish among nations a peace not based on slavery, to reconcile labor and culture again, and to reconstruct with all men an Ark of the Covenant.   ALBERT CAMUS

See also: ACHIEVEMENT; AMBITION; ASPIRATION; BIBLE, THE; CHARACTER; FAITH; GRACE; IDEALS; RELIGION; TRUTH; VISION; WORSHIP.

Democracy

Democracy is not just a word to be shouted at political rallies and then put back into the dictionary after Election Day. The service of democracy must be something much more than mere lip service. It is a living thing—a human thing—compounded of brains and muscle and heart and soul. The service of democracy is the birthright of every citizen, the White and the Colored; the Protestant, the Catholic and the Jew; the sons and daughters of every country in the world, who make up the people of the land. Dictators have forgotten—or perhaps they never knew—that the opinion of all the people, freely formed and freely expressed, without fear or coercion, is wiser than the opinion of any one man or any small group of men. We have more faith in the collective opinion of all Americans than in the individual opinion of any one American.   FRANKLIN D. ROOSEVELT

Democracy cannot be saved by supermen, but only by the unswerving devotion and goodness of millions of little men.   ADLAI STEVENSON

A democratic nation means a symphonic nation, a nation of many voices and many themes, each keeping individuality and freedom, and yet all harmonized together.   WALDO FRANK

> I swear to the Lord
> I still can't see
> Why Democracy means
> Everybody but me.
>   LANGSTON HUGHES

No attack on democracy can hide the fact that it can be replaced only by a system that substitutes coercion for persuasion—one that replaces the individual's choice with the choice of some ruler.   WILLIAM O. DOUGLAS

A democracy—that is a government of all the people, by all the people, for all the people; of course, a government of the principles of eternal justice, the unchanging law of God; for shortness' sake, I will call it the idea of Freedom.
                                             THEODORE PARKER

Political democracy, as it exists and practically works in America, with all its threatening evils, supplies a training school for making first-class men. It is life's gymnasium, not of good only, but of all.   WALT WHITMAN

Democracy is the worst type of government, *except* for all the other types that have been tried before.   WINSTON S. CHURCHILL

I believe in democracy because it releases the energies of every human being.

The great glory of our land is that nobody can predict from what family, from what region, from what race, even, the leaders of the country are going to come. The only way that government is kept pure is by keeping those channels open by which humble people rise to power, so that there will constantly be coming new blood into the veins of the body politic. We must keep open the channels by which obscure men may break the crust of any class to which they happen to belong, may spring up to higher levels and be counted among the leaders of the state.   WOODROW WILSON

Democracy is the only form of government that is founded on the dignity of man—not the dignity of some men, of rich men, of educated men or of white men, but of all men. Its sanction is not the sanction of force, but the sanction of human nature. Equality and justice, the two great distinguishing characteristics of democracy follow inevitably from the conception of men, as rational and spiritual beings.

In this light freedom takes on meaning. It is not freedom to do as we please but freedom to achieve that autonomy which we approach in proportion as we develop our rational and spiritual nature. It is not mere freedom to live that concerns us most, but freedom to live human lives. Men must be free to exercise those powers which make them men.

ROBERT MAYNARD HUTCHINS

Democracy is a cause that is never won, but I believe it will never be lost.

CHARLES A. BEARD

As I would not be a slave, so I would not be a master. This expresses my idea of democracy. Whatever differs from this, to the extent of the difference, is no democracy.

ABRAHAM LINCOLN

See also: AMERICA; BROTHERHOOD; DEDICATION; DISSENT; EQUALITY; FREEDOM; IDEALS; JUSTICE; LIBERTY; RACIAL JUSTICE; RELIGION; VISION.

Destiny

There is a tide in the affairs of men,
Which, taken at the flood, leads on to fortune;
Omitted, all the voyage of their life
Is bound in shallows and in miseries:
On such a full sea are we now afloat,
And we must take the current when it serves,
Or lose our ventures.

WILLIAM SHAKESPEARE

Even God cannot change the past.

AGATHON

All go unto one place; all are of the dust, and all turn to dust again.

Who knoweth the spirit of man that goeth upward, and the spirit of the beast that goeth downward to the earth?

Wherefore I perceive that there is nothing better, than that a man should rejoice in his own works; for that is his portion: for who shall bring him to see what shall be after him?   THE BIBLE

One cannot change one's fate; the road is predestined for each of us. But the way we walk it, the attitude with which we bear our fate, can be of great influence over events.   RICHARD BEER-HOFMANN

To live well, men need joy and hope concerning their destiny, and courage in facing it.   MILTON STEINBERG

> These struggling tides of life that seem
> In aimless wayward course to tend,
> Are eddies of the mighty stream
> That rolls to its appointed end.
>   WILLIAM CULLEN BRYANT

I cannot believe that God plays dice with the Cosmos.   ALBERT EINSTEIN

> We would pray for more than understanding.
> We would pray for a sense of common destiny
> In a world in time, made small by man's
> Achievement, weighted by selfishness, marred
> By power, but inescapably harnessed to
> Eternity by small glimpses and mighty
> Surges of man's aspiration to move
> From all levels of being to that high freedom
> Where the soul is won to his own keeping.
> So we would pray for a sense of common destiny
> Which arises in our will to be sharers
> Of the burden of all mankind, and
> Sharers of its total victories and defeats.
>   ARTHUR GRAHAM

See also: DIVINE, THE; FAITH; GOD; HEROISM; INSPIRATION; PURPOSE.

Dissent

Dissent

We settle things by a majority vote, and the psychological effect of doing that is to create the impression that the majority is probably right. Of course, on any fine issue the majority is sure to be wrong. Think of taking a majority vote on the best music. Jazz would win over Chopin. Or on the best novel. Many cheap scribblers would win over Tolstoy. And any day a prizefight will get a bigger crowd, larger gate receipts and wider newspaper publicity than any new revelation of goodness, truth or beauty could hope to achieve in a century.   HARRY EMERSON FOSDICK

A man may be a heretic in the truth; and if he believes things only because his pastor says so, or the assembly so determines, without knowing other reason, though his belief be true, yet the very truth he holds becomes his heresy.   JOHN MILTON

While I am not in favor of maladjustment, I view this cultivation of neutrality, this breeding of mental neuters, this hostility to eccentricity and controversy, with grave misgiving. One looks back with dismay at the possibility of a Shakespeare perfectly adjusted to bourgeois life in Stratford, a Wesley contentedly administering a country parish, George Washington going to London to receive a barony from George III, or Abraham Lincoln prospering in Springfield with nary a concern for the preservation of the crumbling Union.   ADLAI STEVENSON

It is perfectly possible for you and me to purchase intellectual peace at the price of intellectual death. The world is not without refuges of this description; nor is it wanting in persons who seek their shelter, and try to persuade others to do the same. The unstable and the weak have yielded and will yield to this persuasion, and they to whom repose is sweeter than the truth. But I would exhort you to refuse the offered shelter, and to scorn the base repose; to accept, if the choice be forced upon you, commotion before stagnation, the leap of the torrent before the stillness of the swamp.
                                                              JOHN TYNDALL

Democracy cannot survive without the guidance of a creative minority.
                                                            HARLAN F. STONE

A wise skepticism is the first attribute of a good critic.

JAMES RUSSELL LOWELL

I have never surrendered my mind to any church, or party, or individual yet, and I do not propose to begin now. I have ever counted it my highest duty, as well as my most precious privilege, to do my own thinking, reach my own opinions, stand by my own convictions—and I shall try to remain faithful to that duty to the end. For I was raised in a tradition which seems to be unfamiliar to this age. I was taught early in my life that one must be true to oneself—that independence of ideas and ideals was essential to dignity and self-respect—that Emerson was right when he said that "who would be a man must be a nonconformist." Nothing to me is quite so intolerable as running with the crowd, lining up with the church or the party, licking up the dust before the feet of the great leader.   JOHN HAYNES HOLMES

Speak, history! Who are life's victors? Unroll thy long
     annals and say:
Are they those whom the world called the victors, who won
     the success of a day?
The martyrs, or Nero? The Spartans who fell at Thermopylae's
     trust?
Or the Persians and Xerxes? His judges or Socrates? Pilate
     or Christ?

WILLIAM WETMORE STORY

There is beauty in music when voices, which are true, clear, distinct, blend to produce perfect consonance, perfect harmony, to achieve unity in diversity or diversity in unity—a good description might be discordant concord; better still, concordant discord.   SAINT FRANCIS DE SALES

I will obey God rather than you, and as long as I have breath I will not cease from exhorting you. God has sent me to attack this city, as if it were a great horse sluggish from its size, which needs to be roused by a gadfly. I think I am that gadfly. Are you not ashamed of caring so much for money and for reputation and for honor? Will you not think about wisdom and truth and how to make your soul better? I shall reproach you for indifference to what is most valuable and prizing what is unimportant. I shall do this to everyone I meet, young or old, for this is God's command to me.   SOCRATES

See also: CHARACTER; CONSCIENCE; DEMOCRACY; DOUBT; IDEALS; INTEGRITY; LIBERTY; MATURITY; NONCONFORMITY; RELIGION; WISDOM.

The Divine

Invisibly, very near us, touching us all, is a real world of divine order and beauty, whose mission it is to bring order and beauty where they can, to mortal souls who are struggling for such things.   JOHN MASEFIELD

It is well to think well; it is Divine to act well.   HORACE MANN

> A sense sublime
> Of something far more deeply interfused,
> Whose dwelling is the light of setting sun
> And the round ocean and the living air
> And the blue sky—and in the mind of man;
> A motion and a spirit that impels
> All thinking things, all objects of all thought
> And rolls through all things.
>   WILLIAM WORDSWORTH

The divine shall mean for us only such a primal reality as the individual feels impelled to respond to solemnly and gravely, and neither by a curse nor a jest.   WILLIAM JAMES

Whoever imagines that the wonderful order and incredible constancy of the heavenly bodies and their motions, whereon the preservation and welfare of all things depend, is not governed by an intelligent Being, is destitute of understanding. For shall we, when we see an artificial engine, a sphere or dial for instance, acknowledge at first sight that it is the work of art and understanding; and yet, when we behold the Heavens moved and whirled about with incredible velocity, constantly finishing their annual vicissitude, make any doubt that these are the performances, not only of reason, but of a certain excellent and Divine reason?   CICERO

Let men know what is divine. Let them know; that is all. If a Greek is stirred to the remembrance of God by the art of Phidias, an Egyptian by paying worship to animals, another man by a river, another by fire, have no anger in their divergences. Only let them know. Let them love. Let them remember.
                   MAXIMUS OF TYRE

What is there of the divine in a load of bricks? What is there of the divine in a barber's shop? Much. All.   RALPH WALDO EMERSON

> By a divine instinct, men's minds distrust
> Ensuing danger; as by proof we see
> The waters swell before a boisterous storm.
>   WILLIAM SHAKESPEARE

A man who is born with tendencies toward the Divine is fearless and pure in heart. He perseveres in that path to union with Brahman which the scriptures and his teacher have taught him. He is charitable. He can control his passions. He studies the scriptures regularly, and obeys their directions. He practices spiritual discipline. He is straightforward, truthful, and of an even temper. He harms no one. He renounces the things of this world. He has a tranquil mind and an unmalicious tongue. He is compassionate toward all. He is not greedy. He is gentle and modest. He abstains from useless activity. He has faith in the strength of his higher nature. He can forgive and endure. He is clean in thought and act. He is free from hatred and from pride. Such qualities are his birthright.   BHAGAVAD-GITA

Man's spiritual nature is no dream of theologians to vanish before the light of natural science. It is the greatest reality on earth. Everything here but the *B. J.* soul of man is a passing shadow. The only enduring substance is within. . . . In what a vain show we walk, while we toil without ceasing for the perishable, and remain blind and dead to the everlasting, the perfect, and the divine!   WILLIAM ELLERY CHANNING

See also: BELIEF; CHRISTIANITY; FAITH; GOD; GRACE; HOPE; INSPIRATION; JUDAISM; LOVE; MYSTERY; REVERENCE; WORSHIP.

Doubt

If you would be a real seeker after truth, it is necessary that at least once in your life you doubt, as far as possible, all things.   RENÉ DESCARTES

Serious doubt is confirmation of faith. It indicates the seriousness of the concern, its unconditional character.   PAUL TILLICH

Doubters invert the metaphor and insist that they need faith as big as a mountain in order to move a mustard seed.   ANONYMOUS

To question all things; never to turn away from any difficulty; to accept no doctrine either from ourselves or from other people without a rigid scrutiny by negative criticism, letting no fallacy, or incoherence, or confusion or thought, step by unperceived; above all, to insist upon having the meaning of the word clearly understood before using it, and the meaning of the proposition before assenting to it—these are the lessons we learn from ancient dialecticisms.   JOHN STUART MILL

God said to Moses: "You doubted me, but I forgive you that doubt. You doubted your own self and failed to believe in your own powers as a leader, and I forgive you that also. But you lost faith in this people and doubted the divine possibilities of human nature. That I cannot forgive. That loss of faith makes it impossible for you to enter the Promised Land."   THE MIDRASH

Knowledge of divine things is lost to us by incredulity.   HERACLITUS

> You call for faith:
> I show you doubt, to prove that faith exists.
> The more of doubt, the stronger faith, I say,
> If faith o'ercomes doubt.
>
> ROBERT BROWNING

There lives more faith in honest doubt, believe me, than in half the creeds.
                               ALFRED, LORD TENNYSON

To have doubted one's own first principles is the mark of a civilized man.
                               OLIVER WENDELL HOLMES, JR.

See also: DISSENT; FAITH; HERESY; INTEGRITY; KNOWLEDGE; MIND; NONCONFORMITY; TRUTH; WISDOM.

Education

Whom, then, do I call educated? First, those who control circumstances instead of being mastered by them; those who meet all occasions manfully and act in accordance with intelligent thinking; those who are honorable in all dealings, who treat good-naturedly persons and things that are disagreeable; and furthermore, those who hold their pleasure under control and are not overcome by misfortune; finally those who are not spoiled by success.

SOCRATES

The roots of education are bitter, but the fruit is sweet.　　ARISTOTLE

The entire object of true education is to make people not merely to do the right things, but enjoy them; not merely industrious, but to love industry; not merely learned, but to love knowledge; not merely pure, but to love purity; not merely just, but to hunger and thirst after justice.　JOHN RUSKIN

Every piece of marble has a statue in it waiting to be released by a man of sufficient skill to chip away the unnecessary parts. Just as the sculptor is to the marble, so is education to the soul. It releases it. For only educated men are free men. You cannot create a statue by smashing the marble with a hammer, and you cannot by force of arms release the spirit or the soul of man.　　CONFUCIUS

Education commences at the mother's knee, and every word spoken within the hearing of little children tends towards the formation of character.

HOSEA BALLOU

In the past the timespan of important change was considerably longer than that of a single human life. . . . Today this timespan is considerably shorter than that of human life, and accordingly our training must prepare individuals to face a novelty of conditions.　ALFRED NORTH WHITEHEAD

Fortunately or otherwise, we live at a time when the average individual has to know several times as much in order to keep informed as he did only thirty or forty years ago. Being "educated" today, requires not only more than a superficial knowledge of the arts and sciences, but a sense of interrelationship such as is taught in few schools. Finally, being "educated" today, in terms of the larger needs, means preparation for world citizenship; in short, education for survival.　NORMAN COUSINS

When we teach a child to read, our primary aim is not to enable it to decipher a waybill or receipt, but to kindle its imagination, enlarge its vision, and open for it the avenues of knowledge.　　CHARLES W. ELIOT

Experience is a good school, but the fees are high. HEINRICH HEINE

A statue lies hid in a block of marble, and the art of the statuary only clears away the superfluous matter and removes the rubbish. The figure is in the stone; the sculpture only finds it. What sculpture is to a block of marble, education is to a human soul. The philosopher, the saint, or the hero, the wise, the good or the great man, very often lies hid and concealed in a plebeian, which a proper education might have disinterred, and have brought to light. JOSEPH ADDISON

Change does not necessarily assure progress, but progress implacably requires change. . . . Education is essential to change, for education creates both new wants and the ability to satisfy them. HENRY STEELE COMMAGER

Education is not to teach men facts, theories or laws, not to reform or amuse them or make them expert technicians. It is to unsettle their minds, widen their horizons, inflame their intellect, teach them to think straight, if possible, but to think nevertheless. ROBERT MAYNARD HUTCHINS

It is much more difficult to overcome a bad habit, than it is to form a new one; for this reason, the Grecian flute-players were accustomed to charge double fees to those pupils who had been taught by inferior masters. MARY WRIGHT WEAVER

A visitor to Samuel Taylor Coleridge argued against religious instruction of the young, declaring that he was determined not to "prejudice" his children in favor of any form of religion and would allow them to choose for themselves at maturity. Coleridge retorted: "Why not let the clods choose for themselves between cockleberries and strawberries?" ANONYMOUS

Education, whether of black man or white man, that gives one physical courage to stand up in front of a cannon and fails to give one moral courage to stand up in defense of right and justice, is a failure. BOOKER T. WASHINGTON

Train up a child in the way he should go; and when he is old he will not depart from it. THE BIBLE

See also: ACHIEVEMENT; ASPIRATION; BOOKS; IDEALS; INSPIRATION; KNOWLEDGE; MATURITY; PERSERVERANCE; SELF-CONTROL; SELF-KNOWLEDGE; TRUTH; WISDOM.

Equality

A man is not an equalitarian in principle until he seeks and enjoys a reciprocal relation of equality; and the test of this is to be found not in a man's dislike of others' superiority, but in his dislike of their inferiority, and in his relish for a social relationship in which each looks upon the other with a level eye.   RALPH BARTON PERRY

Wealth in itself is a good, not an evil, but wealth in the hands of a few corrupts on one side and degrades on the other. No chain is stronger than its weakest link and the ultimate condition of any people is the condition of its lowest class. If the low are not brought up, the high must be brought down. In the long run, no nation can be freer than its most oppressed, richer than its poorest, wiser than its most ignorant. This is the fiat of the eternal justice that rules the world.   HENRY GEORGE

All men are by nature equal, made, all, of the same earth by the same Creator, and however we deceive ourselves, as dear to God is the poor peasant as the mighty prince.   PLATO

It is not the transient breath of poetic incense that women want; each can receive that from a lover. It is not life-long sway; she needs but to become a coquette, a shrew, or a good cook to be sure of that. It is not money, nor notoriety, nor the badges of authority, that men have appropriated to themselves. If demands made in their behalf lay stress on any of these particulars, those who make them have not searched deeply into the need. It is for that which at once includes all these and precludes them; which would not be forbidden power, lest there be temptation to steal and misuse it; which would not have the mind perverted by flattery from a worthiness of esteem. It is for that which is the birthright of every being capable to receive it, the freedom, the religious, the intelligent freedom of the universe, to use its means, to learn its secret as far as nature has enabled them, with God alone for their guide and their judge.   MARGARET FULLER

By the law of God, given by him to humanity, all men are free, are brothers, and are equals.   GUISEPPE MAZZINI

> Then the World-honored [Buddha] spake: "Pity and need
> Make all flesh kin. There is no caste in blood,
> Which runneth of one hue, nor caste in tears.
> Which trickle salt with all; neither comes man
> To birth with tilka-mark stamped on the brow,
>   nor sacred thread on neck.
> Who doth right deed is twice-born, and who doeth ill deeds vile."
>   SIR EDWIN ARNOLD

From any point of view, I had rather be what I am, a member of the Negro race, than be able to claim membership with the most favored of any other race. I have always been made sad when I have heard members of any race claiming rights and privileges, or certain badges of distinction, on the ground simply that they were members of this or that race, regardless of their own individual worth or attainments. I have been made to feel sad for such persons because I am conscious of the fact that mere connection with what is known as a superior race will not permanently carry an individual forward, and mere connection with what is regarded as an inferior race will not finally hold an individual back if he possesses intrinsic individual merit. Every persecuted individual and race should get much consolation out of the great human law, which is universal and eternal, that merit, no matter under what skin found, is in the long run recognized and rewarded. This I have said here, not to call attention to myself as an individual [born a slave], but to the race to which I am proud to belong.   BOOKER T. WASHINGTON

Society is a more level surface than we imagine. Wise men or absolute fools are hard to be met with; and there are few giants or dwarfs.
                                                    WILLIAM HAZLITT

When, in the course of human events, it becomes necessary for one people to dissolve the political bonds which have connected them with another, and to assume among the powers of the earth the separate and equal station to which the laws of nature and of nature's God entitle them, a decent respect to the opinions of mankind requires that they should declare the causes which impel them to separation. . . . We hold these truths to be self-evident: that all men are created equal; that they are endowed by their Creator with certain inalienable rights; that among these are life, liberty, and the pursuit of happiness. . . .   THOMAS JEFFERSON
[from opening paragraphs of the
Declaration of Independence]

They who say all men are equal speak an undoubted truth, if they mean that all have an equal right to liberty, to their property, and to their protection of the laws. But they are mistaken if they think men are equal in their station and employments, since they are not so by their talents.   VOLTAIRE

Every woman must have a new sense of dignity and self-respect, feeling that our mothers, during some periods in the long past, have been the ruling power, and that they used that power for the best interests of humanity. As history is said to repeat itself, we have every reason to believe that our turn will come again, it may not be for woman's supremacy, but for the as yet untried experiment of complete equality, when the united thought of man and woman will inaugurate a just government, a pure religion, and happy home, a civilization at last in which ignorance, poverty, and crime will exist no more.   ELIZABETH CADY STANTON

There is no king who has not had a slave among his ancestors, and no slave who has not had a king among his.   HELEN KELLER

It is not true that some human beings are by nature superior and others inferior. All men are equal in their natural dignity. Consequently there are no political communities which are superior by nature and none which are inferior by nature.   POPE JOHN XXIII

The origin of all mankind was the same: it is only a clear and a good conscience that makes a man noble, for that is derived from heaven itself. It was the saying of a great man that, if we could trace our descents, we should find all slaves to come from princes, and all princes from slaves; and fortune has turned all things topsy-turvy in a long series of revolutions: beside, for a man to spend his life in pursuit of a trifle that serves only when he dies to furnish out an epitaph, is below a wise man's business.   SENECA

> One place there is—beneath the burial sod—
> Where all mankind are equalized by death.
> Another place there is—the Fane of God,
> Where all are equal who draw living breath.
>   THOMAS HOOD

It is true that around every man a fatal circle is traced beyond which he cannot pass; but within the wide verge of that circle he is powerful and free. As it is with man, so with communities. The nations of our time cannot prevent the conditions of men from becoming equal, but it depends upon themselves whether the principle of equality is to lead them to servitude or freedom, to knowledge or barbarism, to prosperity or wretchedness.

ALEXIS DE TOCQUEVILLE

I have said so often that I regret that the slogan "Black Power" came into being because it has been so confusing. It gives the wrong connotation. It often connotes the quest for Black domination rather than Black equality. . . . But it is a slogan that we have to deal with now. . . .

    In the positive sense Black Power is a psychological call to manhood. This is desperately needed in the Black community because for all too many years people have been ashamed of themselves. All too many Black people have been ashamed of their heritage, and all too many have had a deep sense of inferiority. . . . Black Power is also economic pressure. . . . The Black man has enough buying power in many areas to make a difference in the profit and loss statements of many firms.   MARTIN LUTHER KING, JR.

See also: AMERICA; BROTHERHOOD; CHRISTIANITY; DEMOCRACY; FELLOWSHIP; HUMANITY; JUDAISM; PREJUDICE; RACIAL JUSTICE; RELIGION; VISION.

Evil

Even if the water falls drop by drop, it will fill the pot; and the fool will become full of evil, even though he gather it little by little.   DHAMMAPADA

A man can do only so much about the evil in the world, but this he can do with all the strength that is in him; he can withhold his consent to it.

HOWARD THURMAN

The evil that men do lives after them;
The good is oft interred with their bones.
WILLIAM SHAKESPEARE

Men never do evil so completely and cheerfully as when they do it from religious conviction.   BLAISE PASCAL

Yet there is one more cursed than them all,
That canker-worm, that monster, jealousy,
Which eats the heart and feeds upon the gall,
Turning all love's delight to misery,
Through fear of losing his felicity.
Ah, gods! that ever ye that monster placed
In gentle love, that all his joys defaced!

EDMUND SPENSER

The only intrinsic evil is the lack of love.   JOHN ROBINSON

Calumny is a vice of curious constitution. Trying to kill it keeps it alive.
Leave it to itself and it will die a natural death.   THOMAS PAINE

For as a picture is often more beautiful and worthy of commendation if some
colors in themselves are included in it, than it would be if it were uniform
and of a single color, so from an admixture of evil the universe is rendered
more beautiful and worthy of commendation.   PETER ABELARD

The devil's boots don't creak.   SCOTTISH PROVERB

[Envy is] the beginning of hell in this life, and a passion not to be excused.
ROBERT BURTON

There are a thousand hacking at the branches of evil to one who is striking at
the root.   HENRY DAVID THOREAU

As it is said of the greatest liar that he tells more truth than falsehoods, so
it may be said of the worst man that he does more good than evil.
SAMUEL JOHNSON

There is an evil which most of us condone and are even guilty of: indifference
to evil. We remain neutral, impartial, and not easily moved by the wrongs
done unto other people. Indifference to evil is more insidious than evil itself;
it is more universal, more contagious, more dangerous.
ABRAHAM JOSHUA HESCHEL

Heaven has a road, but no one travels it;
Hell has no gate but men will bore through to get there.
CHINESE PROVERB

See also: ADVERSITY; GOODNESS; IDEALS; PRIDE; RELIGION; SAINTLI-
NESS; SELFISHNESS; VALUE; VIRTUE; WISDOM.

Example

If a man has good corn, or wood, or boards, or pigs, to sell, or can make
better chairs or knives, crucibles, or church organs, than anybody else, you
will find a broad, hard-beaten road to his house, though it be in the woods.
RALPH WALDO EMERSON

It is not poverty that we praise, it is the man whom poverty cannot humble
or bend.   SENECA

We are lonelier; someone has gone from one's own life who was like the
certainty of refuge; and someone has gone from the world who was like a
certainty of honor.   ADLAI STEVENSON
[From eulogy for Eleanor Roosevelt before General Assembly
of the United Nations in 1962]

There is no power on earth that can neutralize the influence of a high, pure,
simple, and useful life.   BOOKER T. WASHINGTON

Every age has been illustrated by men who bore themselves like men, and
vindicated the cause of human nature—men who, in circumstances of great
trial, have adhered to moral and religious principle, to the cause of persecuted truth, to the interests of humanity, to the hope of immortality—who
have trodden underfoot the fairest gifts of fortune and the world in the pursuit of duty. . . . This is the greatest value of history, that it introduces us to
persons of this illustrious order; and its noblest use is by their examples to
nourish in us a conviction that elevated purity of motive and conduct is not
a dream of fancy, but that it is placed within our reach, and is the very end
of being.   WILLIAM ELLERY CHANNING

Our acts our angels are, for good or ill,
Our fatal shadows that walk by us still.
JOHN FLETCHER

The most complete revenge is not to imitate the aggressor.

MARCUS AURELIUS

Thou didst as one who passing through the night bears a light behind, that profits not himself but makes those who follow wise.   DANTE ALIGHIERI

Be noble! and the nobleness that lies
In other men, sleeping, but never dead,
Will rise in majesty to meet thine own.
JAMES RUSSELL LOWELL

A man that is fit to make a friend of, must have conduct to manage the engagement and resolution to maintain it. He must use freedom without roughness and oblige without design. Cowardice will betray friendship and covetousness will starve it. Folly will be nauseous, passion is apt to ruffle, and pride will fly out into contumely and neglect.   JEREMY COLLIER

To keep the body in good health is a duty, for otherwise we shall not be able to trim the lamp of wisdom, and keep our mind strong and clear. Water surrounds the lotus flower, but does not wet its petals.   BUDDHA

See also: ASPIRATION; CHARACTER; GOODNESS; GREATNESS; HEROISM; INSPIRATION; INTEGRITY; NONCONFORMITY; RELIGION; SAINTLINESS; SELFLESSNESS; TRUTH.

Faith

If you have not clung to a broken piece of your old ship in the dark night of the soul, your faith may not have the sustaining power to carry you through to the end of the journey.   RUFUS M. JONES

It is the heart that senses God, and not the reason. That is what faith is, God perceptible to the heart and not to reason.   BLAISE PASCAL

If faith be provisionally defined as conviction apart from or in excess of proof, then it is upon faith that the maxims of daily life, not less than the loftiest creeds and the most far-reaching discoveries, must ultimately lean.

ARTHUR JAMES BALFOUR

No ray of sunlight is ever lost, but the green which it wakes into existence needs time to sprout, and it is not always granted to the sower to live to see the harvest. All work that is worth anything is done in faith.

ALBERT SCHWEITZER

The only faith that wears well and holds its color in all weathers is that which is woven of conviction and set with the sharp mordant of experience.

JAMES RUSSELL LOWELL

Without faith man becomes sterile, hopeless, and afraid to the very core of his being.   ERICH FROMM

A visitor to our shores would probably come to the same conclusion at which St. Paul arrived in regard to the Athenians; namely, that we are "very religious." But the judgment might not imply a compliment any more than Paul wanted to so imply when he called attention to the worship of many gods in Athens, including the "unknown god." . . .

The "unknown god" in America seems to be faith itself. Our politicians are always adminishing the people to have "faith." Sometimes they seem to imply that faith is in itself redemptive. Sometimes this faith implies faith in something. That something is usually an idol. . . . Sometimes we are asked to have faith in ourselves, sometimes to have faith in humanity, sometimes to have faith in America. Sometimes it is hope, rather than faith, which is really intended. . . . The most disquieting aspect of such religiosity is that it is frequently advanced by popular leaders of the Christian church and is not regarded as a substitute, but as an interpretation of that faith. The Gospel admonition, "Repent ye, for the kingdom of heaven is at hand," is a challenge to submit all our achievements and ambitions and hopes to a much higher judge than those judges who support our self-esteem. This admonition would seem to have little affinity with the "power of positive thinking."

REINHOLD NIEBUHR

If God continually revealed Himself to men, faith could have no value, as we could not help believing; and if He never revealed himself, there could hardly be such a thing as faith.   BLAISE PASCAL

Faith is the bird that sings when the dawn is still dark.

SIR RABINDRANATH TAGORE

Nothing in life is more wonderful than faith—the one great moving force which we can neither weigh in the balance nor test in the crucible.

SIR WILLIAM OSLER

Without faith, we are as stained glass windows in the dark.   ANONYMOUS

Kierkegaard said that in the matter of faith every generation has to begin again. The people awakening to the significance of religion in the university would be inclined to agree with this statement. None of them works under the illusion that faith can be handed on from one generation to the next, or is concerned therefore for the transmission of dogma. What they are saying is that we must get over an entirely unacceptable notion that faith is a matter of indifference.   NATHAN M. PUSEY

Let us have faith that right makes might; and in that faith let us, to the end, dare to do our duty as we understand it.   ABRAHAM LINCOLN

Faith is the ear of the soul.   CLEMENT OF ALEXANDRIA

Faith means being grasped by a power that is greater than we are, a power that shakes us and turns us, and transforms and heals us. Surrender to this power is faith.   PAUL TILLICH

A man's religious faith (whatever more special items of doctrine it may involve) means for me essentially his faith in the existence of an unseen order of some kind in which the riddles of the natural order may be found explained.   WILLIAM JAMES

Faith is not an easy virtue; but, in the broad world of man's total voyage through time to eternity, faith is not only a gracious companion, but an essential guide.   THEODORE M. HESBURGH

Now faith is the substance of things hoped for, the evidence of things not seen.   THE BIBLE

As I survey the world at the age of one hundred [1956], I am distressed by its sin and sorrow, its needs and tragedies, its wars and rumors of wars. The power of evil is great, but the power of righteousness is greater. In the glory of this faith, though the clock of my life points to the evening hour, morning is in my heart. ARTHUR JUDSON BROWN

See also: BELIEF; CHRISTIANITY; DIVINE, THE; DOUBT; GOD; IMMORTALITY; JEWS; JUDAISM; MYSTERY; PRAYER; RELIGION; WORSHIP.

Fame

What's fame, after all, me la-ad? 'Tis apt to be what some wan writes on ye'er tombstone. FINLEY PETER DUNNE

No true and permanent Fame can be founded except in labors which promote the happiness of mankind. CHARLES SUMNER

Being famous is like having a string of pearls given you. It's nice, but after a while, if you think of it at all, it's only to wonder if they're real or cultured. W. SOMERSET MAUGHAM

Fame is a food that dead men eat. HENRY AUSTIN DOBSON

Sometimes the pinnacle of fame and the height of folly are twin peaks. ANONYMOUS

The temple of fame stands upon the grave; the flame upon its altars is kindled from the ashes of the dead. WILLIAM HAZLITT

Fame is no sure test of merit, but only a probability of such; it is an accident, not a property of man. THOMAS CARLYLE

What a heavy burden is a name that has too soon become famous. VOLTAIRE

Let us now praise famous men, and our fathers that begat us. The Lord hath wrought great glory by them through His great power from the beginning. Such as did bear rule in their kingdoms, men renowned for their power, giving counsel by their understanding, and declaring prophecies: leaders of the people by their counsels, and by their knowledge of learning meet for the people, wise and eloquent in their instructions: such as found out musical tunes, and recited verses in writing: rich men furnished with ability, living peaceably in their habitations: all these were honoured in their generations, and were the glory of their times. THE APOCRYPHA

He that pursues fame with just claims, trusts his happiness to the winds; but he that endeavors after it by false merit, has to fear, not only the violence of the storm, but the leaks of his vessel. SAMUEL JOHNSON

Fame is like a river, that beareth up things light and swollen, and drowns things weighty and solid. SIR FRANCIS BACON

See also: ACHIEVEMENT; AMBITION; ASPIRATION; CHARACTER; DEDI-CATION; GENIUS; GREATNESS; HUMILITY; MATURITY; PERSPECTIVE; SELF-KNOWLEDGE; WISDOM.

The Family

Whatever is great and good in the institutions and usages of mankind is an application of sentiments that have drawn their first nourishment from the soil of the family. FELIX ADLER

What a father says to his children is not heard by the world, but it will be heard by posterity. JEAN PAUL RICHTER

When a child goes away from home, he carries his mother's hand with him. CHINESE PROVERB

The ties of family and of country were never intended to circumscribe the soul. If allowed to become exclusive, engrossing, clannish, so as to shut out the general claims of the human race, the highest end of Providence is frustrated, and home, instead of being the nursery, becomes the grave of the heart. WILLIAM ELLERY CHANNING

I think it must somewhere be written that the virtues of mothers shall be visited on their children, as well as the sins of their fathers.

CHARLES DICKENS

An ounce of mother is worth a pound of clergy.   SPANISH PROVERB

Some parents bring up their children on thunder and lightning, but thunder and lightning never yet made anything grow. Rain or sunshine cause growth —quiet penetrating forces that develop life.   ANONYMOUS

One good mother is worth a thousand schoolmasters.   GEORGE HERBERT

The joys of parents are secret; and so are their griefs and fears. They cannot utter the one; nor will they utter the other. Children sweeten labors; but they make misfortunes more bitter. They increase the cares of life; but they mitigate the remembrance of death. The perpetuity by generation is common to beasts; but memory, merit, and noble works are proper to men.

SIR FRANCIS BACON

Who is best taught? He who has first learned from his mother.

THE TALMUD

Youth fades; love drops, the leaves of friendship fall;
A mother's secret hope outlives them all.
OLIVER WENDELL HOLMES, SR.

There is an enduring tenderness in the love of a mother to a son that transcends all other affections of the heart! It is neither to be chilled by selfishness, nor daunted by danger, nor weakened by worthlessness, nor stifled by ingratitude. She will sacrifice every comfort to his convenience; she will surrender every pleasure to his enjoyment; she will glory in his fame and exult in his prosperity. And if misfortune overtake him, he will be the dearer to her because of the misfortune; and if disgrace settle upon his name, she will still love and cherish him in spite of his disgrace; and if all the world beside cast him off, she will be all the world to him.   WASHINGTON IRVING

Only so far as a man is happily married to himself, is he fit for married life to another, and for family life generally.   NOVALIS

With partridges, it often occurs that some steal the eggs of others, in order to brood, and it is a strange but nevertheless well-attested fact that when the chick, hatched and nourished under the wing of the thievish partridge, first hears the cry of its true mother, it forthwith quits its thievish partridge, and hurries to meet and follow its own parent, drawn by its correspondence with her, which had remained hidden and as though sleeping in the depth of its nature, until the encounter of each with each.   SAINT FRANCIS DE SALES

God could not be everywhere, so He made mothers.   JEWISH PROVERB

In a child's lunch basket, a mother's thoughts.   JAPANESE PROVERB

I was present when an old mother, who had brought up a large family of children with eminent success, was asked by a young one what she would recommend in the case of some children who were too anxiously educated, and her reply was—"I think, my dear, a little wholesome neglect."
SIR HENRY TAYLOR

A mother is not a person to lean on, but a person to make leaning unnecessary.   DOROTHY CANFIELD FISHER

See also: FELLOWSHIP; GIVING; LOVE; MAN; MARRIAGE; MATURITY; SELFLESSNESS; VALUES.

Fear

Fear is one of the passions of human nature of which it is impossible to divest it. You remember the Emperor Charles V, when he read upon the tombstone of a Spanish nobleman, "Here lies one who never knew fear," wittily said, "Then he never snuffed a candle with his fingers."
SAMUEL JOHNSON

Our instinctive emotions are those that we have inherited from a much more dangerous world, and contain, therefore, a larger portion of fear than they should.   BERTRAND RUSSELL

Fear is more painful to cowardice than death to true courage.

SIR PHILIP SIDNEY

He who fears he will suffer, already suffers because of his fear.

MONTAIGNE

Fear is two-fold; a fear of solicitous anxiety, such as makes us let go our confidence in God's providence, and a fear of prudential caution, whereby, from a due estimate of approaching evil, we endeavor our own security. The former is wrong and forbidden; the latter not only lawful, but laudable.

ROBERT SOUTH

Let me assert my firm belief that the only thing we have to fear is fear itself— nameless, unreasoning, unjustified terror which paralyzes needed efforts to convert retreat into advance.   FRANKLIN D. ROOSEVELT

There is a virtuous fear which is the effect of faith, and a vicious fear which is the product of doubt and distrust. The former leads to hope as relying on God, in whom we believe; the latter inclines to despair, as not relying upon God, in whom we do not believe. Persons of the one character fear to lose God; those of the other character fear to find him.   BLAISE PASCAL

I fear God, yet am not afraid of Him.   SIR THOMAS BROWNE

The only failure a man ought to fear is failure in cleaving to the purpose he sees best.   GEORGE ELIOT

Those who love to be feared, fear to be loved; they themselves are of all people the most abject; some fear them, but they fear everyone.

SAINT FRANCIS DE SALES

As long as a man does not sin, he is feared; as soon as he sins, he himself is in fear.   THE MIDRASH

He that lives to live forever, never fears dying.   WILLIAM PENN

See also: COURAGE; DOUBT; PEACE OF MIND; SELF-CONTROL; SELF-KNOWLEDGE; WORRY.

Fellowship

Fellowship is life, and lack of fellowship is death; fellowship is heaven, and lack of fellowship is hell; and the things which ye do upon the earth, it is for fellowship's sake that ye do them.   WILLIAM MORRIS

We may not be able to meet in the same pew—would to God we did—but we can meet on our knees.   FULTON J. SHEEN

The true spirit of conversation consists in building on another man's observation, not overturning it.   EDWARD BULWER-LYTTON

People are often lonely because they build walls instead of bridges.

ANONYMOUS

Taught by no priest, but by our beating hearts:
Faith to each other, the fidelity
Of men whose pulse leaps with kindred fire
Who in the flash of eyes, the clasp of hands,
Nay, in the silent bodily presence, feel
The mystic stirrings of a common life
That makes the many one.

GEORGE ELIOT

The man who goes alone can start today; but he who travels with another must wait till that other is ready.   HENRY DAVID THOREAU

While there is infection in disease and sorrow, there is nothing in the world quite so irresistibly contagious as laughter and good humor.

CHARLES DICKENS

Pity and need
Make all flesh kin. There is no caste in blood

Which runneth of one hue; nor caste in tears
Which trickle salt with all.

SIR EDWIN ARNOLD

Julia Ward Howe was talking to Charles Sumner, the distinguished Senator from Massachusetts. She asked him to interest himself in the case of a person who needed help.

The Senator answered, "Julia, I've become so busy I can no longer concern myself with individuals."

"Charles," she replied, "that's remarkable. Even God hasn't reached that stage yet."

RALPH W. SOCKMAN

The problem of good fellowship between members of the various religious families seems to me to be a cardinal one for the new age of civilization.

JACQUES MARITAIN

See also: BROTHERHOOD; CHRISTIANITY; CHURCH, THE; FRIENDSHIP; HUMANITY; MANKIND; RELIGION.

Forgiveness

He who has not forgiven an enemy has never yet tasted one of the most sublime enjoyments of life.

JOHANN KASPAR LAVATER

Only forgiveness with reason can match sin without excuse.

EDWIN ARLINGTON ROBINSON

When thou forgivest, the man who has pierced thy heart stands to thee in the relation of the sea-worm that perforates the shell of the mussel, which straightway closes the wound with a pearl.

JEAN PAUL RICHTER

If anger is not restrained, it is frequently more hurtful to us than the injury that provokes it.

SENECA

The beginning of anger is madness, the end penitence.

THE TALMUD

Praised be my Lord for all those who pardon one another for His love's sake, and who endure weakness and tribulation; blessed are they who peaceably shall endure, for Thou, O most Highest, shalt give them a crown.

SAINT FRANCIS OF ASSISI

If you are suffering from a bad man's injustice, forgive him lest there be two bad men.   SAINT AUGUSTINE

Everything has two handles; the one soft and manageable, the other such as will not endure to be touched. If then your brother do you an injury, do not take it by the hot hard handle, by representing to yourself all the aggravating circumstances of the fact; but look rather on the soft side, and extenuate it as much as is possible, by considering the nearness of the relation, and the long friendship and familiarity between you, obligations to kindness which a single provocation ought not to dissolve. And thus you will take the accident by its manageable handle.   EPICTETUS

He who forgives ends the quarrel.   AFRICAN PROVERB

Say not, if people are good to us, we will do good to them, and if people oppress us we will oppress them: but resolve that if people do good to you, you will do good to them, and if they oppress you, oppress them not again.

MOHAMMED

You who are letting miserable misunderstandings run on from year to year, meaning to clear them up some day; you who are keeping wretched quarrels alive because you cannot quite make up your minds that now is the day to sacrifice your pride and kill them; you who are letting your neighbor starve—until you hear that he is dying of starvation; or letting your friend's heart ache for a word of appreciation or sympathy, which you mean to give him some day; if you could only know and see and feel all of a sudden that time is short, how it would break the spell! How you would go instantly and do the thing which you might never have another chance to do!

PHILLIPS BROOKS

See also: BROTHERHOOD; CHRISTIANITY; COMPASSION; FELLOWSHIP; FRIENDSHIP; GRACE; KINDNESS; LOVE; SELFLESSNESS.

Free Will

Behind all faith . . . lies the plain fact that man, as a creature of free will, cannot shirk the ultimate responsibility for his own fate.

PAUL ELMER MORE

There is in human conduct an element of will and choice. Without it freedom and democracy are meaningless, scarcely the substance of a dream.

NORMAN THOMAS

We who lived in the concentration camps can remember the men who walked through the huts comforting others, giving away their last piece of bread. They may have been few in number, but they offer sufficient proof that everything can be taken from a man but one thing: the last of his freedoms—to choose one's attitude in any given set of circumstances, to choose one's own way.

VIKTOR E. FRANKL

The freedom of the human self is a curse inasmuch as it is the source of spiritual evil in Man, but at the same time is an inestimable treasure inasmuch as it is also the source, the only source in Man, of spiritual good.

ARNOLD J. TOYNBEE

I believe that I am a free agent, inasmuch as, and so far as, I have a will, which renders me justly responsible for my actions, omissive as well as commissive.

SAMUEL TAYLOR COLERIDGE

Free Will does not say that everything that is physically conceivable is also morally possible. It merely says that of alternatives that really *tempt* our will more than one is really possible.

WILLIAM JAMES

When the cards are dealt and you pick up your hand, that is determinism; there's nothing you can do except to play it out for whatever it may be worth. And the way you play your hand is free will.

JAWAHARLAL NEHRU

Free will is not the liberty to do whatever one likes, but the power of doing whatever one sees ought to be done, even in the very face of otherwise overwhelming impulse. There lies freedom, indeed. GEORGE MACDONALD

See also: ASPIRATION; DISSENT; DOUBT; FREEDOM; GOD; GRACE; NON-CONFORMITY; RELIGIOUS FREEDOM; RESPONSIBILITY; SELF-KNOWLEDGE; WISDOM.

Freedom

Freedom is the end of government. To exalt men to self-rule is the end of all other rules; and he who would fasten on them his arbitrary will is their worst foe. WILLIAM ELLERY CHANNING

There are two freedoms—the false, where a man is free to do what he likes; the true, where a man is free to do what he ought. CHARLES KINGSLEY

We in this country, in this generation, are . . . by destiny rather than choice . . . the watchmen on the walls of freedom. We ask, therefore, that we may be worthy of our power and responsibility, that we may achieve in our time and for all time the ancient vision of peace on earth, good will toward men. That must always be our goal—and the righteousness of our cause must always underlie our strength. For as was written long ago: "Except the Lord keep the city, the watchmen waketh but in vain." JOHN F. KENNEDY
[From undelivered address, Dallas, Texas, November 22, 1963]

If a nation values anything more than freedom, it will lose its freedom; and the irony of that is that if it is comfort or money, it will lose that, too.
W. SOMERSET MAUGHAM

No man in this world attains to freedom from any slavery except by entrance into some higher servitude. There is no such thing as an entirely free man conceivable. PHILLIPS BROOKS

Not a grave of the murder'd for freedom, but grows seed
for freedom, in its turn to bear seed,
Which the winds carry afar and re-sow, and the rains

and the snows nourish.
Not a disembodied spirit can the weapons of tyrants let
    loose,
But it stalks invisibly over the earth, whispering,
    counseling, cautioning.

Liberty! let other despair of you! I never despair of
    you.

Is the house shut? Is the master away?
Nevertheless, be ready—be not weary of watching;
He will return soon—his messengers come anon.

                                        WALT WHITMAN

Freedom and responsibility are like Siamese twins: they die if they are
parted.   LILLIAN SMITH

Those who won our independence believed that the final end of the State
was to make men free to develop their faculties; and that in its government
the deliberative forces should prevail over the arbitrary. They valued liberty
both as an end and as a means. They believed liberty to be the secret of
happiness and courage to be the secret of liberty. They believed that freedom
to think as you will and to speak as you think are means indispensable to the
discovery and spread of political truth; that without free speech and assembly discussion would be futile; that with them discussion affords ordi-
narily adequate protection against the dissemination of noxious doctrine; that
the greatest menace to freedom is an inert people; that public discussion is a
political duty; and that this should be a fundamental principle of the American government.   LOUIS D. BRANDEIS

A man may not always eat and drink what is good for him; but it is better for
him and less ignominious to die of the gout freely than to have a censor
officially appointed over his diet, who after all could not render him immortal.   GEORGE SANTAYANA

Freedom consists not in refusing to recognize anything above us, but in respecting something which is above us; for by respecting it, we raise ourselves to it, and by our very acknowledgement make manifest that we bear
within ourselves what is higher, and are worthy to be on a level with it.

                                        JOHANN WOLFGANG VON GOETHE

It is better for a man to go wrong in freedom than to go right in chains.

THOMAS H. HUXLEY

We shall be outwardly free when we unbind ourselves from slavery within.

NICHOLAS BERDYAEV

No man is free who is not master of himself. EPICTETUS

Freedom is not worth having if it does not connote freedom to err.

MOHANDAS GANDHI

Men are free when they are in a living homeland . . . not when they are escaping to some wild west. The most unfree souls go west, and shout of freedom. Men are freest when they are most unconscious of freedom. The shout is the rattling of chains, always was. D. H. LAWRENCE

Till men have been some time free, they know not how to use their freedom. . . . The final and permanent fruits of liberty are wisdom, moderation, and mercy. Its immediate effects are often atrocious crimes, conflicting errors, scepticism on points the most clear, dogmatism on points the most mysterious. It is just at this crisis that its enemies love to exhibit it. They pull down the scaffolding from the half-finished edifice; they point to the flying dust, the falling bricks, the comfortless rooms, the frightful irregularity of the whole appearance, and then ask in scorn where the promised splendour and comfort are to be found? If such miserable sophisms were to prevail, there would never be a good house, or a good government in the world. . . .

There is only one cure for the evils which newly-acquired freedom produces, and that cure is freedom! THOMAS BABINGTON MACAULAY

See also: DEMOCRACY; EQUALITY; JUSTICE; LIBERTY; PATRIOTISM; RACIAL JUSTICE; RELIGIOUS FREEDOM; RESPONSIBILITY.

Friendship

The glory of friendship is not the outstretched hand, nor the kindly smile, nor the joy of companionship; it is the spiritual inspiration that comes to one when he discovers that someone else believes in him and is willing to trust him with his friendship.

The essence of friendship is a total magnanimity and trust. Friendship is for aid and comfort through all the relations and packages of life and death. It is fit for serene days, and graceful gifts, and country rambles; but also for rough roads and hard fare, shipwreck, poverty, and persecution. We are to dignify to each other the daily needs and offices of man's life, and embellish it by courage, wisdom, and unity. So that a friend may well be reckoned the masterpiece of nature.

The laws of friendship are great, austere and eternal, of one web with the laws of nature and of morals. Love, which is the essence of God, is not for levity, but for the total worth of man.

There are two elements that go to the composition of friendship, each so sovereign that I can detect no superiority in either. One is Truth. A friend is a person with whom I may be sincere. The other element in friendship is Tenderness. When a man becomes dear to me I have touched the goal of fortune.   RALPH WALDO EMERSON

By friendship you mean the greatest love, the greatest usefulness, the most open communication, the noblest sufferings, the severest truth, the heartiest counsel, and the greatest union of minds of which brave men and women are capable.   JEREMY TAYLOR

Be friends, in the truest sense, each to the other. There is nothing in all the world like friendship, when it is deep and real.   THOMAS DAVIDSON

Oh, the confort, the inexpressible comfort of feeling safe with a person; having neither to weigh thoughts nor measure words, but to pour them all out, just as they are, chaff and grain together, knowing that a faithful hand will take and sift them, keep what is worth keeping, and then, with the breath of kindness, blow the rest away.   GEORGE ELIOT

Just as the devout when they pray enter into the presence of God, so does the spirit, in beginning a letter, place itself in the presence of the absent friend. Every letter is an invocation, and the truest memory of a friend lies in what we have written to him.   ELLEN GLASGOW

A principal fruit of friendship is the ease and discharge of the fullness and swellings of the heart, which passions of all kinds do cause and induce. We know diseases of stoppings and suffocations are the most dangerous in the body, and it is not much otherwise in the mind. You may take sarza to open the liver, steel to open the spleen, flower of sulphur for the lungs, castoreum for the brain; but no receipt openeth the heart but a true friend, to whom you may impart griefs, joys, fears, hopes, suspicions, counsels, and whatsoever lieth upon the heart to oppress it, in a kind of civil shrift or confession.   SIR FRANCIS BACON

Faithful are the wounds of a friend.   THE BIBLE

> Great souls by instinct to each other turn,
> Demand alliance, and in friendship burn.
>   JOSEPH ADDISON

Even the utmost goodwill and harmony and practical kindness are not sufficient for friendship, for friends do not live in harmony merely, as some say, but in melody. We do not wish for friends to feed and clothe our bodies— neighbors are kind enough for that—but to do the like office to our spirits.
                                                  HENRY DAVID THOREAU

A true friend unbosoms freely, advises justly, asserts readily, adventures boldly, takes all patiently, defends courageously, and continues a friend unchangeably.   WILLIAM PENN

Next to the encounter of death in our own bodies, the most sensible calamity to an honest man is the death of a friend. The comfort of having a friend may be taken away, but not that of having had one. It is an ill construction of providence to reflect only upon my friend's being taken away, without any regard to the benefit of his once being given me. He who has lost a friend has more cause of joy that once he had him, than of grief that he is taken way. Shall a man bury his friendship with his friend?   SENECA

There is a truth and simplicity in genuine friendship, an unconstrained and spontaneous emotion, altogether incompatible with every kind and degree of artifice and simulation. I am persuaded, therefore, that it derives its origin not from the indigence of human nature, but from a distinct principle implanted in the breast of man; from a certain instinctive tendency which draws congenial minds into union, and not from a cool calculation of the advantages with which it is pregnant. . . . Experience shows that the more a man looks for his happiness within himself, and the more firmly he stands supported by the consciousness of his intrinsic merit, the more desirous he is to cultivate friendship, and the better friend he certainly proves.   CICERO

Blessed is the man who has the gift of making friends; for it is one of God's best gifts. It involves many things, but above all, the power of going out of one's self, and seeing and appreciating whatever is noble and loving in another man.

THOMAS CARLYLE

A friendship that makes the least noise is very often the most useful; for which reason I should prefer a prudent friend to a zealous one.

JOSEPH ADDISON

What a great blessing is a friend with a heart so trusty you may safely bury all your secrets in it, whose conscience you may fear less than your own, who can relieve your cares by his conversation, your doubts by his counsels, your sadness by his good humor, and whose very looks give you comfort.

SENECA

He that has a thousand friends has not one friend to spare,
And he who has one enemy shall meet him everywhere.

ARAB PROVERB

Friendship is one mind in two bodies.

MENCIUS

Three men are my friends:
He that loves me, he that hates me, he that is indifferent to me. Who loves me, teaches me tenderness. Who hates me, teaches me caution. Who is indifferent to me, teaches me self-reliance.

IVAN PANIN

We never know the true value of friends. While they live we are too sensible of their faults; when we have lost them we see only their virtues.

ANONYMOUS

A faithful friend is a strong defense, and he that hath found such a one hath found a treasure. Nothing doth countervail a faithful friend, and his excellency is invaluable. A faithful friend is the medicine of life.

THE APOCRYPHA

Friendship is composed of a single soul, inhabiting two bodies. ARISTOTLE

See also: BROTHERHOOD; FELLOWSHIP; GRACE; LOVE; MAN.

Genius

To carry the feelings of childhood into the powers of manhood, to combine the child's sense of wonder and novelty with the appearances which every day for years has rendered familiar, this is the character and privilege of genius, and one of the marks which distinguish it from talent.

SAMUEL TAYLOR COLERIDGE

The three indispensables of genius are understanding, feeling, and perseverance. The three things that enrich genius are contentment of mind, the cherishing of good thoughts, and exercising the memory.   ROBERT SOUTHEY

Genius is one per cent inspiration and ninety-nine per cent perspiration.

THOMAS ALVA EDISON

Genius is an infinite capacity for taking pains.   THOMAS CARLYLE

When a true genius appears in the world, you may know him by this sign, that the dunces are all in confederacy against him.   JONATHAN SWIFT

Of seven peasants I can make seven lords, but I cannot make one Hans Holbein, even of seven lords.   KING HENRY VIII

Genius is the father of a heavenly line, but the mortal mother is industry.

THEODORE PARKER

Common sense is instinct, and enough of it is genius.   JOSH BILLINGS

If we are to have genius we must put up with the inconvenience of genius, a thing the world will never do; it wants geniuses, but would like them just like other people.   GEORGE MOORE

All the means of action, the shapeless masses, the materials, lie everywhere about us. What we need is the celestial fire to change the flint into the transparent crystal, bright and clear. That fire is genius.

HENRY WADSWORTH LONGFELLOW

George Washington Carver [1864?-1943] put over the door of his laboratory at Tuskegee a sign suitable for every factory, office, or toolshed:

GOD'S LITTLE WORKSHOP

Everybody prizes the story of the day this superb Negro genius held a peanut in the palm of his hand and asked God to tell him its secret. God seemed to suggest that he should go back into his workshop and simply use the three laws God had already given him—temperature, pressure, and compatibility—and put together the different parts hidden in the peanut.

Dr. Carver, taking God at His word, found a wealth of revelation no other scientist had ever discovered: proteins, carbohydrates, oils, pigments, and cellulose. From these he made more than three hundred products from the peanut alone: rubber, shoe polishes, mock soups, dyes, stains, synthetic leathers, soaps, explosives, beverages, and milk.

This former slave boy, who had once been exchanged for a race horse, became one of the world's greatest scientists. And Dothan, Alabama, inaugurated a national festival honoring Dr. Carver's peanut which had brought prosperity to the farmers at a time when bankruptcy faced them as a result of the boll weevil. And Enterprise, Alabama, erected a statue to the boll weevil whose havoc had ruined their fields, but turned them, with gratitude, to the raising of peanuts and a multi-million-dollar business!

Their real debt, however, was to "God's Little Workshop" and to God's little black saint who handled water and light and earth as sacred discoveries for the help of all mankind.

MARGARET T. APPLEGARTH

See also: ACHIEVEMENT; AMBITION; ASPIRATION; GOD; GREATNESS; IMAGINATION; KNOWLEDGE; MYSTERY; SELF-KNOWLEDGE; VISION; WISDOM.

Giving

The golden ladder of giving is to give reluctantly, the gift of the hand, but not of the heart; to give cheerfully, but not in proportion to need: to give cheerfully and proportionately, but not until solicited; to give cheerfully, proportionately, and unsolicited, but to put the gift into the poor man's hand, thus creating shame; to give in such a way that the distressed may know their benefactor, without being known to him; to know the objects of our bounty, but remain unknown to them; to give so that the benefactor may not know those whom he has relieved, and they shall not know him; and to prevent poverty by teaching a trade, setting a man up in business, or in some other way preventing the need of charity. Giving is most blessed and most acceptable when the donor remains completely anonymous.   MAIMONIDES

True charity is the desire to be useful to others without thought of recompense.   EMANUEL SWEDENBORG

To him who is of kin to thee give his due, and to the poor and to the wayfarer: this will be best for those who seek the face of God; and with them it shall be well.

Whatever ye put out at usury to increase it with the substance of others shall have no increase from God: but whatever ye shall give in alms, as seeking the face of God, shall be doubled to you.   THE KORAN

He that gives should never remember, he that receives should never forget.   THE TALMUD

We should give as we would receive, cheerfully, quickly, and without hesitation, for there is no grace in a benefit that sticks to the fingers.   SENECA

The manner of giving shows the character of the giver more than the gift itself.   JOHANN KASPAR LAVATER

A kind man who makes good use of wealth is rightly said to possess a great treasure; but the miser who hoards up his riches will have no profit. Charity is rich in returns; charity is the greatest wealth, for though it scatters, it brings no repentance.

The charitable man is loved by all; his friendship is prized highly; in death his heart is at rest and full of joy, for he suffers not from repentance; he receives the opening flower of his reward and the fruit that ripens from it. Hard it is to understand: By giving away food, we get more strength; by bestowing clothing on others, we gain more beauty; by donating abodes of purity and truth, we acquire great treasures.

There is a proper time and a proper mode in charity; just as the vigorous warrior goes to battle, so is the man who is able to give. He is like a warrior, a champion strong and wise in action. Loving and compassionate, he gives with reverence, and banishes all hatred, envy and anger.

The charitable man has found the path of salvation. He is like the man who plants a sapling, securing thereby the shade, the flowers, and the fruit in future years. BUDDHA

It is only giving that stimulates. Impart as much as you can of your own spiritual being to those who are on the road with you, and accept as something precious what comes back to you from them. ALBERT SCHWEITZER

It is one of the most beautiful compensations of this life that no man can sincerely try to help another without helping himself.

RALPH WALDO EMERSON

What is a true gift? One for which nothing is expected in return.

CONFUCIUS

He gives double who gives unasked. ARAB PROVERB

See also: BLESSINGS; CHRISTIANITY; COMPASSION; DEDICATION; GRACE; GRATITUDE; IDEALS; JUDAISM; LOVE; RELIGION; SELFLESS-NESS; VIRTUE.

God, Contemplation of

Fall at the feet of the great God; He is not a stone. He liveth in water, in the dry land, in all things, and in all monarchs. He is in the sun, in the moon, in the sky. He is in fire, in wind, and beneath the earth. In what place is He not?

GOBIND SINGH

Live with men as if God saw you; converse with God as if men heard you.

SENECA

O Lord, pardon my three sins:
I have in contemplation clothed in form
Thee who art formless!
I have in praise described Thee who art
ineffable!

And in visiting shrines I have ignored
Thine omnipresence.

SANKARA

'Tis hard to find God, but to comprehend Him, as He is, is labor without end.

ROBERT HERRICK

I shall always be more certain that God is, than what He is.

WILLIAM ERNEST HOCKING

Each conception of spiritual beauty is a glimpse of God.

MOSES MENDELSSOHN

When Hadrian [Emperor from 117 to 138] conquered the world and returned to Rome, he said to his courtiers, "As I have conquered the world, I desire you to treat me as God."

They answered, "But you have not yet prevailed against His city and temple."

So he went and succeeded in destroying the temple and driving Israel out. He then returned and announced his success and repeated his request.

Now he had three philosophers. The first said to him, "No man who is inside the palace can rebel; go outside the palace, and then you will be God. He made heaven and earth, you must first get beyond these, His palace."

The second said, "It cannot be done, for He has said, 'The gods have not made the heavens and the earth shall perish under the heavens' (Jeremiah, chapter 10, verse 11)."

The third said, "Be pleased to stand by me in this hour of need!"

Hadrian said, "How?"

He replied, "I have a ship three miles out at sea, and it contains all my fortune."

Hadrian said, "I will send my legions and ships there to rescue it."

The philosopher said, "Why trouble your legions and your ships? Send a puff of wind."

Hadrian said, "Whence can I get wind to send?"

The philosopher retorted, "How then can you be God who created the wind?"

Hadrian went home displeased. THE TANHUMA

God is more truly imagined than expressed, and he exists more truly than is imagined. SAINT AUGUSTINE

To stand on one leg and prove God's existence is a very different thing from going down on one's knees and thanking Him.   SÖREN KIERKEGAARD

There is something in the nature of things which the mind of man, which reason, which human power, cannot effect, and certainly that which produces this must be better than man. What can this be but God?   CICERO

In a small house God has His corner, in a big house He has to stand in the hall.   SWEDISH PROVERB

As a house implies a builder; a dress, a weaver; a door, a carpenter; so the world proclaims God, its Creator.   THE TALMUD

See also: ASPIRATION; BELIEF; DIVINE, THE; MYSTERY; REVERENCE; WONDER; WORSHIP.

God, Definitions of

God is that indefinable something which we all feel but which we do not know. To me God is truth and love, God is ethics and morality, God is fearlessness, God is the source of light and life, and yet He is above and beyond all these. God is conscience. He is even the atheism of the atheist.

MOHANDAS GANDHI

Think'st thou in temporal speech God's
Name may uttered be?
It is unspeakable to all eternity.
ANGELUS SILESIUS

The attribution of personality to God, though much truer, I think, than the denial of it, is manifestly inadequate to the full reality we are struggling to express.   ARTHUR JAMES BALFOUR

In many forms we try
To utter God's infinity,
But the boundless hath no form,

And the Universal Friend
Doth as far transcend
An angel as a worm.

The great Idea baffles wit,
Language falters under it,
It leaves the learned in the lurch;
No art, nor power, nor toil can find
The measure of the Eternal Mind,
Nor hymn, nor prayer, nor church.
RALPH WALDO EMERSON

The name of this infinite and inexhaustible depth and ground of all being is God. That depth is what the word God means. It speaks of the depths of your life, of the source of your being. If you know that God means depth, you know much about Him. PAUL TILLICH

God is the Life-Spirit of the world, working unconsciously in nature and consciously in man, His Purpose, Will and Love. . . . God is to me an experience, well nigh impossible to explain, but felt as surely as the air we breathe or the sunshine in the midst of which we live. There are moments in our lives, if we struggle ever to be faithful to the best within us, when God appears as a veritable presence—One Who speaks His words of comfort, touches our hands in strength and guidance, and gives us companionship in moments of loneliness and pain. To all of us there come times when we are lifted up, so to speak, to the doing of things which of ourselves we could never have done.

He only is the religious man who, whatever his creed or lack of creed, has touched these mystic shores of his own spiritual knowledge. By prayer, by devotion to truth, by love of our fellow-men, by rigorous discipline to simple and pure modes of life, above all by valiant consecration to every emancipating cause, we find our way to God and see Him at the last as a comrade and a friend. JOHN HAYNES HOLMES

God must not be thought of as a physical being, or as having any kind of body. He is pure mind. He moves and acts without needing any corporeal space, or size, or form, or color, or any other property of matter. ORIGEN

God is a tailor who makes for the deer a coat that will last for a thousand years.

He is a shoemaker who provides boots for the deer that the deer will not outlive.

God is the best cook, because the heat of the sun supplies all the heat there is for cooking.

God is a butler who sets forth a feast for the sparrows and spends on them annually more than the total revenue of the King of France.

MARTIN LUTHER

God is an utterable sigh, planted in the depths of the soul.

JEAN PAUL RICHTER

> Ecclesiastes names Thee the Almighty.
> Maccabees names Thee Creator.
> Baruch names Thee Immensity.
> The Psalms name Thee Wisdom and Truth.
> The Book of Kings names Thee Lord.
> Exodus names Thee Providence.
> Leviticus names Thee Holiness.
> Esdras names Thee Justice.
> Creation calls Thee God.
> Man names Thee Father.
> But Solomon names Thee Compassion, and that
> is the most beautiful of all Thy Names.

VICTOR HUGO

It is essential that God be conceived as the deepest power in the universe; and second, he must be conceived under the form of a mental personality. God's personality is to be regarded, like any other personality, as something lying outside my own and other than me, and whose existence I simply come upon and find.

WILLIAM JAMES

Whatever the queer little word ["God"] means, it means something we can none of us quite get away from, or at; something connected with our deepest explosions.

D. H. LAWRENCE

God is a spirit: and they that worship Him, must worship Him in spirit and in truth.

THE BIBLE

See also: BEING; BELIEF; BIBLE, THE; DIVINE, THE; MYSTERY; VISION; WONDER.

God, Love of

One of the most convenient hieroglyphics of God is a circle; and a circle is endless; whom God loves, He loves to the end; and not for their own end, to their death, but to His end; and His end is that He might love them still.

JOHN DONNE

God often visits us, but most of the time we are not at home.

POLISH PROVERB

But my one unchanged obsession, wheresoe'er my feet have trod,
Is a keen, enormous, haunting, never-sated thirst for God.

GAMALIEL BRADFORD

You cannot love God with your father's heart.   SOLOMON SCHECHTER

Love and fear God; tremble and rejoice when you perform the commandments; if you have done a little wrong to your neighbour, let it seem to you large; if you have done him a big kindness, let it seem to you small; if he has done you a big evil, let it seem to you small; if he has done to you a small kindness, let it seem to you large.   RABBI JUDAH BEN TEMA

Allah, Most High, says: He who approaches near to me one span, I will approach to him one cubit; and he who approaches near to me one cubit, I will approach near to him one fathom; and whoever approaches me walking, I will come to him running, and he who meets me with sins equivalent to the whole world, I will greet him with forgiveness equal to it.

MISHKAT-UL-MASABIH

The greatest question of our time is not communism versus individualism, not Europe versus America, not even the East versus the West: it is whether man can bear to live without God.   WILL DURANT

If thou neglectest thy love to thy neighbor, in vain thou professest thy love to God; for by thy love to God, the love to thy neighbor is begotten, and by the love to thy neighbor, thy love to God is nourished.   FRANCIS QUARLES

The knowledge of God is very far from the love of Him.   BLAISE PASCAL

> Before this world's great frame, in which all things
> Are now contained, found any being place,
> Ere flitting Time could wag his eyas wings
> About that mightie bound which doth embrace
> The rolling Spheres, and parts their houres by space,
> That high eternall powre, which now doth move
> In all these things, mov'd in it selfe by love.
>   EDMUND SPENSER

The knowledge of God may be likened to a man, while love of God is like a woman. Knowledge has entry only to the outer rooms of God, and no one can enter into the inner mysteries of God save a lover.   RAMAKRISHNA

Dare to look up to God and say, Deal with me for the future as Thou wilt, I am of the same mind as Thou art; I am Thine: I refuse nothing that pleases Thee. Lead me where Thou wilt; clothe me in any dress Thou choosest. Is it Thy will that I should hold the office of a magistrate, that I should be in the condition of a private man, stay here or be in exile, be poor, be rich? I will make Thy defense to men in behalf of all these conditions. . . . If thou wouldst make a man happy, add not unto his riches, but take away from his desires.   EPICTETUS

See also: ASPIRATION; BEAUTY; BELIEF; BIBLE, THE; BLESSINGS; DIVINE, THE; GRACE; LOVE; RELIGION; SAINTLINESS; WONDER; WORSHIP.

God, Nature of

> Hast thou not known? Hast thou not heard,
> That the everlasting God, the Lord,
> The Creator of the ends of the earth,
> Fainteth not, neither is weary?
> There is no searching of His understanding.

He giveth power to the faint;
And to them that have no might He increaseth strength.
Even the youths shall faint and be weary,
And the young men shall utterly fall:

But they that wait upon the Lord shall renew their
    strength;
They shall mount up with wings as eagles;
They shall run, and not be weary;
And they shall walk, and not faint.

THE BIBLE

God Himself does not speak prose, but communicates with us by hints, omens, inferences and dark resemblances in objects lying all around us.

RALPH WALDO EMERSON

Everything we say about God is symbolic. Such a statement is an assertion about God which itself is not symbolic.   PAUL TILLICH

God comes with leaden feet, but strikes with iron hands. ENGLISH PROVERB

Who sees with equal eye, as God of all,
A hero perish or a sparrow fall,
Atoms or systems into ruin hurled
And now a bubble burst, and now a world, . . .
To Him no high, no low, no great, no small;
He fills, He bounds, connects and equals all.

ALEXANDER POPE

God is subtle, but He is not malicious.   ALBERT EINSTEIN

The nature of God is a circle whose center is everywhere and whose circumference is nowhere.   SAINT AUGUSTINE

God strikes not with both hands, for to the sea He made havens, and to rivers fords.   GEORGE HERBERT

Such is the First Mover: a principle upon which depend the heavens and the world of nature. Its life is such as the best which we enjoy: waking, perceiving, and thinking; and its thought, which is thought in the fullest sense, deals with that which is best in the fullest sense. It is an active contemplation, in which it contemplates itself: thought and its object being here identical. God's essential actuality is thus life at its very best; and this state persists for ever. We say therefore that God is a living being, eternal, and most good.   ARISTOTLE

As the bird alights on the bough, then plunges into the air again, so the thoughts of God pause but for a moment in any form.
                                                     RALPH WALDO EMERSON

The recent [Second] Inaugural Address. . . . I expect . . . to wear as well as—perhaps better than—anything I have produced; but I believe it is not immediately popular. Men are not flattered by being shown that there has been a difference of purpose between the Almighty and them. To deny it, however, in this case is to deny that there is a God governing the world. It is a truth which I thought needed to be told; and as whatever of humiliation there is in it falls most directly on myself, I thought others might afford for me to tell it.   ABRAHAM LINCOLN
                                                   [Letter to Thurlow Weed,
                                                          March 15, 1865]

With God, go over the sea—without Him, not over the threshold.
                                                       RUSSIAN PROVERB

Though the mills of God grind slowly,
     yet they grind exceeding small;
Though with patience He stands waiting,
     with exactness grinds He all.
                             FRIEDRICH VON LOGAU
            [translated by Henry Wadsworth Longfellow]

When God shuts a door, He opens a window.   JOHN RUSKIN

All things can be said of God, yet is nothing worthily said of God.
                                                       SAINT AUGUSTINE

See also: ASPIRATION; BEAUTY; BELIEF; BLESSINGS; DIVINE, THE; GRACE; LOVE; MYSTERY; NATURE; RELIGION; WONDER; WORSHIP.

God, Search for

If we cannot find God in your house or in mine, upon the roadside or the margin of the sea; in the bursting seed of opening flower; in the day duty or the night musing; in the general laugh and the secret grief, . . . I do not think we should discern Him any more on the grass of Eden, or beneath the moonlight of Gethsemane. JAMES MARTINEAU

All religion is based on the recognition of a superhuman Reality of which man is somehow conscious and towards which he must in some way orientate his life. The existence of the tremendous transcendent reality that we name God is the foundation of all religion in all ages and among all peoples. CHRISTOPHER DAWSON

Different creeds are but different paths to reach the Almighty. As with one gold, various ornaments are made having different forms and names, so one God is worshipped in different countries and ages, as different forms and names.

As one and the same material, water, is called by different names by different peoples, one calling it *water,* another *eau,* a third *aqua,* and another *pani,* so the one Everlasting-Intelligent-Bliss is invoked by some as Allah, and by others as God, and by others as Brahman.

As one can ascend to the top of a house by means of a ladder or a bamboo or a staircase or a rope, so diverse are the ways and means to approach God, and every religion in the world shows one of these ways. RAMAKRISHNA

Whatever road I take joins the highway that leads to Thee. PERSIAN PRAYER

All the doors that lead inward, to the sacred place of the Most High, are doors outward—out of self, out of smallness, out of wrong. GEORGE MACDONALD

Whosoever walks towards God one cubit, God runs towards him twain. HEBREW PROVERB

Canst thou by searching find out God? Canst thou find out the Almighty unto perfection?

It is as high as heaven; what canst thou do? Deeper than hell; what canst thou know?

The measure thereof is longer than the earth, and broader than the sea.

THE BIBLE

A humble knowledge of oneself is a surer road to God than a deep searching of the sciences.   THOMAS À KEMPIS

O senseless man, who cannot possibly make a worm, and yet will make gods by dozens.   MONTAIGNE

God has many names though He is only one being.   ARISTOTLE

When we know God, some likeness of God comes to be in us.

SAINT THOMAS AQUINAS

To have found God is not an end but in itself a beginning.

FRANZ ROSENZWEIG

Whoso draws near to God one step through doubtings dim
God will advance a mile in blazing light to him.

ANONYMOUS

As different streams having different sources and with wanderings crooked or straight, all reach the sea, so, Lord, the different paths which men take, guided by their different tendencies, all lead to Thee.   HINDU PRAYER

God is not dumb, that He should speak no more.
If thou hast wanderings in the wilderness,
And find'st not Sinai, 'tis thy soul is poor;
There towers the mountain of the voice no less,
Which whoso seeks shall find; but he who bends,
Intent on manna still and mortal ends,
Sees it not, neither hears its thundered lore.

JAMES RUSSELL LOWELL

See also: ASPIRATION; BEAUTY; BEING; BELIEF; BIBLE, THE; COMPAS-
SION; DIVINE, THE; MYSTERY; NATURE; SUFFERING; WONDER; WOR-
SHIP.

Goodness

The growing good of the world is partly dependent on unhistoric acts; and that things are not so ill with you and me as they might have been, is half owing to the number who lived faithfully a hidden life, and rest in unvisited tombs.   GEORGE ELIOT

The idea of the good is the highest wisdom. All things are useful and helpful only when added to this. If we lack understanding of the beautiful and the good, though we learn all else to perfection, it profits us nothing.   PLATO

>   Oh, yet we trust that somehow good
>   Will be the final goal of ill,
>   To pangs of nature, sins of will,
>   Defects of doubt and taints of blood;
>
>   That nothing walks with aimless feet;
>   That not one life shall be destroyed,
>   Or cast as rubbish to the void,
>   When God hath made the pile complete;
>
>   Behold, we know not anything;
>   I can but trust that good shall fall
>   At last—far off—at last, to all,
>   And every winter change to spring.
>   ALFRED, LORD TENNYSON

The true past departs not; no truth or goodness realized by man ever dies, or can die; but all is still here, and, recognized or not, lives and works through endless change.   THOMAS CARLYLE

Regard as trifling the great good you did to others, and as enormous the little good others did to you.   THE TALMUD

The scent of flowers does not travel against the wind, nor that of sandal-wood, or of Tagara and Mallika flowers; but the odor of good people travels even against the wind; a good man pervades every place.

DHAMMAPADA

The chief rival of goodness is not badness in itself, but the attractive spectacle of lives powerfully organized on low levels.   HARRY EMERSON FOSDICK

There is no odor so bad as that which arises from goodness tainted.

HENRY DAVID THOREAU

He who would do good to another, must do it in minute particulars.

WILLIAM BLAKE

Health, beauty, vigor, riches, and all the other things called goods, operate equally as evils to the vicious and unjust, as they do as benefits to the just.

PLATO

The first condition of human goodness is something to love; the second something to reverence.   GEORGE ELIOT

Monuments need not be erected for the righteous; their deeds are their memorials.   THE TALMUD

To do an evil action is base; to do a good action, without incurring danger, is common enough; but it is the part of a good man to do great and noble deeds, though he risks everything.   PLUTARCH

He who does good to those who do him wrong alone deserves the epithet of good.   PANCHATANTRA

Ther is an old proverbe, quod she [Dame Prudence] seith: That the good-nesse that thou mayst do this day, do it; and abyde nat ne delaye it nat til to-morwe.   GEOFFREY CHAUCER

Goodness is much more dangerous than vice because it is not subject to the constraints of conscience. RALPH WALDO EMERSON

See also: ASPIRATION; BEAUTY; CHARACTER; DIVINE, THE; EVIL; GREATNESS; IDEALS; INSPIRATION; KINDNESS; LOVE; SELF-CONTROL; VIRTUE.

Grace

There is no such way to attain to greater measure of grace as for a man to live up to the little grace he has. PHILLIPS BROOKS

Into all our lives, in many simple, familiar, homely ways, God infuses this element of joy from the surprises of life, which unexpectedly brighten our days, and fill our eyes with light. He drops this added sweetness into his children's cup, and makes it to run over. The success we are not counting on, the blessing we were not trying after, the strain of music in the midst of drudgery, the beautiful morning picture or sunset glory thrown in as we pass to or from our daily business, the unsought word of encouragement or expression of sympathy, the sentence that meant for us more than a writer or speaker thought—these and a hundred others that everyone's experience can supply are instances of what I mean. SAMUEL LONGFELLOW

But how lovely and how fitting the sound of the lively and impressive *I* of Socrates! It is the *I* of endless dialogue, and the air of dialogue is wafted around it in all its journeys, before the judges and in the last hour in prison. This *I* lived continually in the relation with man which is bodied forth in dialogue. . . .

How lovely and how legitimate the sound of the full *I* of Goethe! It is the *I* of pure intercourse with nature; nature gives herself to it and speaks unceasingly with it, revealing her mysteries to it but not betraying her mystery. . . .

And to anticipate by taking an illustration from the realm of unconditional relation: how powerful, even to being overpowering, and how legitimate, even to being self-evident, is the saying of *I* by Jesus! For it is the *I* of unconditional relation in which the man calls his *Thou* Father in such a way that he himself is simply Son, and nothing else but Son. MARTIN BUBER

These things are beautiful beyond belief:
The pleasant weakness that comes after pain,

> The radiant greenness that comes after rain,
> The deepened faith that follows after grief,
> And the awakening to love again.
>
> ANONYMOUS

The breeze of divine grace is blowing upon us all. But one needs to set the sail to feel this breeze of grace.   RAMAKRISHNA

What is grace? I know until you ask me; when you ask me, I do not know.   SAINT AUGUSTINE

God enters by a private door into every individual.   RALPH WALDO EMERSON

See also: ASPIRATION; BIBLE, THE; BLESSINGS; DIVINE, THE; GOODNESS; LOVE; PRAYER; RELIGION; REVERENCE; SAINTLINESS; WORSHIP.

Gratitude

He that urges gratitude pleads the cause both of God and men, for without it we can be neither sociable nor religious.   SENECA

> I hate ingratitude more in a man,
> Than lying, vainness, babbling, drunkenness
> Or any taint of vice, whose strong corruption
> Inhabits our frail blood.
>
> WILLIAM SHAKESPEARE

Dear Young Ladies,

I am deeply touched by your remembrance [a gift of an azalea plant from his Radcliffe College students].

It is the first time anyone ever treated me so kindly; so you may well believe that the impression on the heart of the lonely sufferer will be even more durable than the impression on your mind of all the teachings of Philosophy 2A.

I now perceive one immense omission in my Psychology,—the deepest principle of human nature is the craving to be appreciated, and I left it out altogether from the book, because I had never had it gratified till now.

I fear you have let loose a demon in me, and that all my actions will now be for the sake of such rewards.

However, I will try to be faithful to this one unique and beautiful azalea tree, the pride of my life and delight of my existence.

Winter and summer will I tend and water it—even with my tears. Mrs. James shall never go near it or touch it.

If it dies, I will die too; and if I die, it shall be planted on my grave.

Don't take all this too jocosely, but believe in the extreme pleasure you have caused me, and in the affectionate feeling with which I am and shall always be faithfully your friend,   WILLIAM JAMES

> Thou that hast given so much to me,
> Give one thing more—a grateful heart;
> Not thankful when it pleaseth me,
> As if thy blessings had spare days;
> But such a heart, whose pulse may be
> Thy praise.
>
> GEORGE HERBERT

Parents who expect gratitude from their children (there are even some who insist on it) are like usurers who gladly risk their capital if only they receive interest.   FRANZ KAFKA

Gratitude is one of those things that cannot be bought. It must be born with men, or else all the obligations in the world will not create it. A real sense of a kind thing is a gift of nature, and never was, nor can be acquired.

GEORGE SAVILE, MARQUIS OF HALIFAX

Gratitude is the fairest blossom which springs from the soul; and the heart of man knoweth none more fragrant.   HOSEA BALLOU

See also: BEAUTY; BEING; BLESSINGS; DIVINE, THE; GRACE; HAPPINESS; INSPIRATION; LIFE; LOVE; REVERENCE; WONDER; WORSHIP.

Greatness

Be not afraid of greatness; some are born great, some achieve greatness, and some have greatness thrust upon them.　　　　　WILLIAM SHAKESPEARE

It is not what the speaker says but who he is that gives weight to eloquence.
　　　　　EURIPIDES

Little minds are too much hurt by little things. Great minds perceive them all, and are not touched by them.　　　　　FRANÇOIS LA ROCHEFOUCAULD

Great men are nearly always the kindest; out of some instinctive knowledge they encourage the very people who do not elbow themselves ahead.
　　　　　STEFAN ZWEIG

If any man seeks for greatness, let him forget greatness and ask for truth, and he will find both.　　　　　HORACE MANN

The great man is he who does not lose his child's heart.　　　　　MENCIUS

A contemplation of God's works, a generous concern for the good of man-kind, and the unfeigned exercise of humility—these only denominate men great and glorious.　　　　　JOSEPH ADDISON

Consider whether we ought not to be more in the habit of seeking honor from our descendants than from our ancestors; thinking it better to be nobly re-membered than nobly born; and striving so to live, that our sons and son's sons, for ages to come, might still lead their children reverently to the doors out of which we had been carried to the grave, saying: "Look, this was his house, this was his chamber."　　　　　JOHN RUSKIN

If we win men's hearts throughout the world, it will not be because we are a big country but because we are a great country. Bigness is imposing. But greatness is enduring.　　　　　ADLAI E. STEVENSON

No saint, no hero, no discoverer, no prophet, no leader ever did his work cheaply and easily, comfortably and painlessly, and no people was ever great which did not pass through the valley of the shadow of death on its way to greatness.   WALTER LIPPMANN

A great man is affable in his conversation, generous in his temper, and immovable in what he has maturely resolved upon. And as prosperity does not make him haughty and imperious, so neither does adversity sink him into meanness and dejection: for if ever he shows more spirit than ordinary, it is when he is ill-used, and the world is frowning upon him. In short, he is equally removed from the extremes of servility and pride, and scorns either to trample on a worm, or cringe to an Emperor.   JEREMY COLLIER

See also: ACHIEVEMENT; ASPIRATION; CHARACTER; COURAGE; DESTINY; FAME; GENIUS; GRACE; HEROISM; INTEGRITY; RELIGION; VIRTUE.

Grief

If we could read the secret history of our enemies, we should find in each man's life sorrow and suffering enough to disarm all hostility.
                                    HENRY WADSWORTH LONGFELLOW

We should learn not to grow impatient with the slow healing process of time. We should discipline ourselves to recognize that there are many steps to be taken along the highway leading from sorrow to renewed serenity and that it is folly to attempt prematurely to telescope and compress these successive stages of recuperation into a miraculous cure. We should not demand of ourselves more than nature herself will permit. We should anticipate these stages in our emotional convalescence: unbearable pain, poignant grief, empty days, resistance to consolation, disinterestedness in life, gradually giving way under the healing sunlight of love, friendship, social challenge, to the new weaving of a pattern of action and the acceptance of the irresistible challenge of life.   JOSHUA LOTH LIEBMAN

Grief is to a man as certain as the grave;
Tempests and storms in life's whole progress rise,
And hope shines dimly through o'er-clouded skies;
Some drops of comfort on the favour'd fall,
But showers of sorrow are the lot of all.
                                    GEORGE CRABBE

You cannot prevent the birds of sorrow from flying over your head, but you can prevent them from building nests in your hair.   CHINESE PROVERB

I would maintain the sanctity of human joy and human grief. I bow in reverence before the emotions of every melted heart. We have a human right to our sorrow. To blame the deep grief which bereavement awakens, is to censure all strong human attachments. The more intense the delight in their presence, the more poignant the impression of their absence; and you cannot destroy the anguish unless you forbid the joy. A morality which rebukes sorrow rebukes love. When the tears of bereavement have had their natural flow, they lead us again to life and love's generous joy.   JAMES MARTINEAU

Grief is the agony of an instant; the indulgence of grief, the blunder of a life.
BENJAMIN DISRAELI

For the first sharp pangs there is no comfort; whatever goodness may surround us, darkness and silence still hang about our pain. But slowly the clinging companionship with the dead is linked with our living affections and duties, and we begin to feel our sorrow as a solemn initiation, preparing us for that sense of loving, pitying fellowship with the fullest human lot, which, I think, no one who has tasted it will deny to be the chief blessedness of our life. And especially to know what the last parting is, seems needful to give the utmost sanctity of tenderness to our relations with each other.
GEORGE ELIOT

The sun went up the morning sky with all his light, but the landscape was dishonored by this loss. For this boy, in whose remembrance I have both slept and awakened so oft, decorated for me the morning star, the evening cloud.

A boy of early wisdom, of a grave and even majestic deportment, of a perfect gentleness.

Every tramper that ever tramped is abroad, but the little feet are still.

He gave us his little innocent breath like a bird.

Sorrow makes us all children again, destroys all differences of intellect. The wisest knows nothing.   RALPH WALDO EMERSON

[From an entry of January 30,
1842 in his *Journal*]

It is very sad to lose your child just when he was beginning to bind himself to you; and I don't know that it is much consolation to reflect that the longer he had wound himself up in your heartstrings, the worse the tear would have been, which seems to have been inevitable sooner or later. One does not weigh and measure these things while grief is fresh, and in my experience a deep plunge into the waters of sorrow is the hopefullest way of getting through them on one's daily road of life again. No one can help another very much in these crises of life; but love and sympathy count for something.   THOMAS H. HUXLEY

It is with sorrows, as with countries, each man has his own.
                                    FRANÇOIS RENÉ DE CHATEAUBRIAND

The sorrow for the dead is the only sorrow from which we refuse to be divorced. Every other wound we seek to heal—every other affliction to forget; but this wound we consider it a duty to keep open—this affliction we cherish and brood over in solitude. Where is the mother who would willingly forget the infant that perished like a blossom from her arms, though every recollection is a pang? Where is the child that would willingly forget the most tender of parents, though to remember be but to lament? Who, even in the hour of agony, would forget the friend over whom he mourns? Who, even when the tomb is closing upon the remains of her he most loved; when he feels his heart, as it were, crushed in the closing of its portal, would accept of consolation that must be bought by forgetfulness?

No, the love which survives the tomb is one of the noblest attributes of the soul. If it has its woes, it has likewise its delights; and when the overwhelming burst of grief is calmed into the gentle tear of recollection, when the sudden anguish and the convulsive agony over the present ruins of all that we most loved is softened away into pensive meditation on all that it was in the days of its loveliness—who would root out such a sorrow from the heart? Though it may sometimes throw a passing cloud over the bright hour of gaiety, or spread a deeper sadness over the hour of gloom, yet who would exchange it, even for the song of pleasure or the burst of revelry? No, there is a voice from the tomb sweeter than song. There is a remembrance of the dead to which we turn even from the charms of the living.
                                                    WASHINGTON IRVING

There are wounds of the spirit which never close, and are intended in God's mercy to bring us nearer to Him, and to prevent us leaving Him, by their very perpetuity. Such wounds, then, may almost be taken as a pledge, or at least as a ground for the humble trust, that God will give us the great gift of perseverance to the end. . . . This is how I comfort myself in my own great bereavements.   JOHN HENRY NEWMAN

It is dangerous to abandon one's self to the luxury of grief; it deprives one of courage, and even of the wish for recovery.   HENRY-FREDERIC AMIEL

In the presence of a sorrow so great as this, when a life so young and full of promise [a gifted musician, dead at eighteen years of age] has fallen on sleep, we need all the sources of comfort within range of our mind and faith. We need the large horizons of comfort that are found in the hope of immortality.

Yet not alone do we need this large horizon of hope, but the comfort of a more humble and familiar insight. We need to say to ourselves, for example, that things are not incomplete because they are short-lived. Some flowers last in their blooming for many weeks; some for a few hours or days only; and yet each in its own way is perfect. So a life need not last many years to become complete; lived perfectly it can be, within its scope, a lovely thing. . . .

In the end, however, one comes back most of all to that undiscourageable faith that God does not make instruments like this, on which such music can be played, only to break them up as if he did not care. Some of the possibilities within such souls were unfolded here on earth, but many more in them this world could not unfold. Somewhere, sometime, they must come to bloom and fruitage. I am full of uncertainty about details, but I am profound in conviction about the major fact: This is a universe of open doors and not of blind alleys; and a personality like this goes on, and out, and up.

HENRY EMERSON FOSDICK

See also: ADVERSITY; AFFLICTION; COURAGE; DEATH; IMMORTALITY; MATURITY; PEACE OF MIND; PRAYER; RELIGION; SELF-CONTROL; SOLITUDE; SUFFERING.

Happiness

Those only are happy who have their minds fixed on some object other than their own happiness; on the happiness of others, on the improvement of mankind, even on some art or pursuit, followed not as a means but as itself an ideal end. Aiming thus at something else, they find happiness by the way. . . . Ask yourself whether you are happy, and you cease to be so. The only chance is to treat, not happiness, but some end external to it, as the purpose of life.   JOHN STUART MILL

If a laborer were to dream for twelve hours every night that he was a king, I believe he would be almost as happy as a king who should dream for twelve hours every night that he was a laborer.   BLAISE PASCAL

Happiness is like a sunbeam, which the least shadow intercepts, while adversity is often as the rain of spring.   CHINESE PROVERB

Search for a single, inclusive good is doomed to failure. Such happiness as life is capable of comes from the full participation of all our powers in the endeavor to wrest from each changing situation of experience its own full and unique meaning.　　　　　　　　　　　　　　JOHN DEWEY

Peace is that state in which fear of any kind is unknown. But Joy is a positive thing; in Joy . . . something goes out from oneself to the universe, a warm, possessive effluence of love. There may be Peace without Joy, and Joy without Peace, but the two combined make happiness.
　　　　　　　　　　　　　　LORD TWEEDSMUIR

The habit of being happy enables one to be freed, or largely freed, from the domination of outward conditions.　　　ROBERT LOUIS STEVENSON

Anthony sought for happiness in love; Brutus in glory; Caesar in dominion; the first found disgrace, the second disgust, the last ingratitude, and each destruction.　　　　　　　　　　　　　CALEB C. COLTON

If there is a scarcity of happiness in this world, it is because more people try to share it than produce it.　　　　　　　ANONYMOUS

Fun I love; but too much fun is, of all things, the most loathsome. Mirth is better than fun, and happiness is better than mirth.　　WILLIAM BLAKE

The supreme happiness of life is the conviction of being loved for yourself, or, more correctly, being loved in spite of yourself.　　VICTOR HUGO

It is only a poor sort of happiness that could ever come by caring very much about our own narrow pleasures. We can only have the highest happiness, such as goes along with true greatness, by having wide thoughts and much feeling for the rest of the world as well as ourselves; and this sort of happiness often brings so much pain with it, that we can only tell it from pain by its being what we would choose before everything else, because our souls see it is good.　　　　　　　　　　　　GEORGE ELIOT

Bless me, O God, in this life with but peace of my conscience, command of my affections, the love of Thyself and my dearest friends; and I shall be happy enough to pity Caesar.　　　　　　SIR THOMAS BROWNE

The happiness of your life depends upon the character of your thoughts.

MARCUS AURELIUS

See also: AGE; ASPIRATION; BLESSING; CHARACTER; CHEERFULNESS; DIVINE, THE; FRIENDSHIP; GRACE; MATURITY; PEACE OF MIND; PERSPECTIVE; SUFFERING.

Heroism

No man has earned the right to intellectual ambition until he has learned to lay his course by a star which he has never seen—to dig by the divining rod for springs which he may never reach. In saying this, I point to that which will make your study heroic. For I say unto you in all sadness of conviction, that to think great thoughts you must be heroes as well as idealists.

OLIVER WENDELL HOLMES, JR.

The ultimate question which every man has to face and answer for himself is: Will you be a hero or a coward?　　WILLIAM ERNEST HOCKING

Cowards die many times before their deaths;
The valiant never taste of death but once.

WILLIAM SHAKESPEARE

It is more difficult, and calls for higher energies of soul, to live a martyr than to die one.　　HORACE MANN

To stand held only by the invisible chains of higher duty, and, so standing, to let the fire creep up to the heart—that is the truer heroism.

PHILLIPS BROOKS

He stood upon the world's broad threshold. Wide
　　The din of battle and of slaughter rose;
He saw God stand upon the weaker side,
　　That sank in seeming loss before its foes;
Many there were who made great haste and sold
　　Unto the coming enemy their swords.
He scorned their gifts of fame, and power, and gold,

And underneath their soft and flowery words,
Heard the cold serpent hiss; therefore he went
And humbly joined him to the weaker part,
Fanatic named, and fool, yet well content
So he could be the nearer to God's heart,
And feel its solemn pulses sending blood
Through all the widespread veins of endless good.

JAMES RUSSELL LOWELL
[*In memory of Wendell Phillips*]

The hero is he who lives in the inward sphere of things, in the True, Divine, Eternal, which exists always. . . . His life is a piece of the everlasting heart of nature itself.

THOMAS CARLYLE

The greatest hero is he who makes his enemy his friend.

THE TALMUD

Life, misfortunes, isolation, abandonment, poverty, are battlefields which have their heroes; obscure heroes, sometimes greater than the illustrious heroes.

VICTOR HUGO

See also: ADVERSITY; AFFLICTION; ASPIRATION; CHARACTER; COUR-
AGE; DEDICATION; GREATNESS; IDEALS; INTEGRITY; NONCONFORM-
ITY; SUFFERING; VIRTUE.

Hope

I avow my faith that we are marching toward better days. Humanity will not be cast down. We are going on—swinging bravely forward along the grand high road—and already behind the distant mountains is the promise of the sun.

WINSTON S. CHURCHILL

Ours is a sad, disillusioned world. Too many people on this blood-soaked, battered globe live in constant fear and dread; fear of hunger and want, dread of oppression and slavery. Poverty, starvation, disease and repression stalk the world, and over us all hangs the menace of war like a gloomy shroud. But everywhere people cling to their hope and their faith in freedom and justice and peace—though fear, anguish, even death are their daily lot.

ADLAI STEVENSON

Hope is the pillar that holds up the world.
Hope is the dream of a waking man.
                                    PLINY THE YOUNGER

Within us we have a hope which always walks in front of our present narrow experience; it is the undying faith in the infinite in us.
                                    SIR RABINDRANATH TAGORE

He who wants to enjoy the glory of the sunrise must live through the night.
                                    ANONYMOUS

The march of Providence is so slow and our desires so impatient; the work
of progress is so immense and our means of aiding it so feeble; the life of
humanity is so long, that of the individual so brief, that we often see only the
ebb of the advancing waves, and are thus discouraged. It is history that
teaches us to hope.   ROBERT E. LEE

The *Encyclopaedia Britannica* devotes many columns to the topic of love,
and many more to faith. But hope, poor little hope! She is not even listed!
                                    KARL MENNINGER

He who has health has hope, and he who has hope has everything.
                                    ARAB PROVERB

　　　See also: ADVERSITY; AFFLICTION; BELIEF; COURAGE; DIVINE, THE;
FAITH; INSPIRATION; MATURITY; RELIGION; VIRTUE; VISION.

Humanity

In the midst of all triumphs of Christianity, it is well that the stately syn-
agogue should lift its walls by the side of the aspiring cathedral, a perpetual
reminder that there are many mansions in the Father's earthly house as well
as in the heavenly one; that civilized humanity, longer in time and broader in
space than any historical form of belief, is mightier than any one institution
or organization it includes.   OLIVER WENDELL HOLMES, SR.

We have rudiments of reverence for the human body, but we consider as nothing the rape of the human mind.   ERIC HOFFER

If you really want to help your fellow-man, you must not merely have in you what would do them good if they should take it from you, but you must be such a man that they can take it from you. The snow must melt upon the mountain and come down in a spring torrent, before its richness can make the valley rich.   PHILLIPS BROOKS

Humanism can only be properly expressed through tolerance and consideration toward other human beings; freedom of expression; respect for the essential dignity and worth of the human individual, with equal opportunity for each to develop freely to his fullest capacity in a cooperative community.
                                                                      KENNETH KAUNDA

It may well be that the lively sense of universal brotherhood and of the bright hopes of the future may stir in humanity those qualities which will enable it to survive the dread agencies which have fallen into its as yet untutored hands.   WINSTON S. CHURCHILL

I can see [September, 1918] the dawn of a better day of humanity. The people are awakening. In due course of time they will come to their own.

When the mariner, sailing over tropic seas, looks for release from his weary watch, he turns his eyes toward the Southern Cross, burning luridly above the tempest-tossed ocean. As the midnight approaches, the Southern Cross begins to bend, and the whirling worlds change their places, and with starry finger-points the Almighty marks the passage of time upon the dial of the universe, and though no bell may beat the glad tidings, the lookout knows that the midnight is passing—that relief and rest are close at hand.

Let the people take heart and hope everywhere, for the cross is bending, the midnight is passing, and joy cometh with the morning.
                                                                      EUGENE V. DEBS

I do and I must reverence human nature . . . I know how it is despised, how it has been oppressed, how civil and religious establishments have for ages conspired to crush it. I know its history. I shut my eyes on none of its weaknesses and crimes. . . . But injured, trampled on, and scorned as our nature is, I still turn to it with intense sympathy and strong hope. I bless it for its kind affections, for its strong and tender love. I honor it for its struggles against oppression, for its growth and progress under the weight of so many chains and prejudices, for its achievements in science and art, and still more for its examples of heroic and saintly virtue. These are marks of a divine origin and the pledges of a celestial inheritance; and I thank God that my own lot is bound up with that of the human race.

WILLIAM ELLERY CHANNING

The human tragedy reaches its climax in the fact that after all the exertions and sacrifices of hundreds of millions of people and of the victories of the Righteous Cause, we have still not found Peace or Security, and that we lie in the grip of even worse perils than those we have surmounted.

WINSTON S. CHURCHILL

My dedication, therefore, is to the cause of man in the attainment of that which is within the reach of man.

I will work for human unity under a purposeful peace. I will work for the growth of a moral order that is in keeping with the universal order.

In this way do I affirm faith in life and life in faith.   NORMAN COUSINS

Thinking of the earth without mankind is almost impossible. But the awful silence of Auschwitz was foreboding and remains an obsessive memory—so much so that the incredible is more real now than before I went there. Is it really too much, I ask myself, to hope that the politics of humanity will triumph over the politics of power before the whole world is turned into an Auschwitz? Perhaps. But if there is no such hope, what is there to pray for?

JOHN COGLEY

See also: BROTHERHOOD; INTERNATIONALISM; MANKIND; RELIGION.

Humility

Should you ask me: what is the first thing in religion? I should reply: the first, second, and third thing therein is humility.   SAINT AUGUSTINE

Humility like darkness reveals the heavenly lights.   HENRY DAVID THOREAU

Humility is the first of the virtues—for other people.

OLIVER WENDELL HOLMES, SR.

Let every day be a day of humility; condescend to all the weaknesses and infirmities of your fellow-creatures, cover their frailties, love their excellencies, encourage their virtues, relieve their wants, rejoice in their prosperities, compassionate in their distress, receive their friendship, overlook their unkindness, forgive their malice, be a servant of servants, and condescend to do the lowest offices to the lowest of mankind. WILLIAM LAW

Be humble and you will remain entire.
The sage does not display himself, therefore he shines.
He does not approve himself, therefore he is noted.
He does not praise himself, therefore he has merit.
He does not glory in himself, therefore he excels.

TAO TÊ CHING

Nothing is more scandalous than a man who is proud of his humility.

MARCUS AURELIUS

If thou wilt know anything profitably, love to be unknown, and of no account. How many perish in this world because they rather choose to be great than humble, becoming vain in their imaginations. He is truly great that is great in love.

Presume not upon thyself, but place thy hope in God. Do what lieth in thy power, and God will assist thy good-will. Trust not in thy knowledge, nor in any living creature, but in the grace of God, who helpeth the humble, and humbleth the proud.

It hurts thee not if thou thinkest thyself worse than all men, but it hurts thee much to prefer thyself before any one man. The humble enjoy continual peace, but in the heart of the proud is envy and frequent indignation.

THOMAS À KEMPIS

Professions of humility are the very cream, the very essence of pride; the really humble man wishes to be, and not to appear so.

SAINT FRANCIS DE SALES

Humility is the Hall-mark of Wisdom. Socrates, whom the Oracle (that is, the united opinion of the world in which he moved) pronounced to be the wisest man, was content with the title of a lover, rather than a professor, of wisdom. JEREMY COLLIER

Many would be scantily clad if clothed in their humility. ANONYMOUS

Think of your own sins the first part of the night while you are awake, and of the sins of others the second part of the night while you are asleep.

CHINESE PROVERB

Humility is the most difficult of all virtues to achieve; nothing dies harder than the desire to think well of oneself.   T. S. ELIOT

In our respective parts yesterday, you could not have been excused to make a short address, nor I a long one. I am pleased to know that, in your judgment, the little I did say was not entirely a failure.   ABRAHAM LINCOLN

[Letter to Edward Everett,
November 20, 1863, the day
after Lincoln delivered his
address at the dedication
of the national cemetery at
Gettysburg, Pennsylvania]

Though humility be a virtue, an affected one is none.   WILLIAM PENN

A mountain shames a molehill until they are both humbled by the stars.

ANONYMOUS

It is no great thing to be humble when you are brought low; but to be humble when you are praised is a great and rare attainment.

SAINT BERNARD OF CLAIRVAUX

The great act of faith is when man decides that he is not God.

OLIVER WENDELL HOLMES, JR.

I believe that the first test of a truly great man is his humility. I do not mean by humility, doubt of his own powers. But really great men have a curious feeling that the greatness is not in them, but through them. And they see something divine in every other man.   JOHN RUSKIN

Let another man praise thee, and not thine own mouth; a stranger, and not thine own lips.   THE BIBLE

See also: AMBITION; ASPIRATION; EXAMPLE; GOODNESS; GRACE; LOVE; PERSPECTIVE; PRIDE; SAINTLINESS; SELFLESSNESS; VIRTUE.

Ideals

The highest flights of charity, devotion, trust, patience, bravery, to which the wings of human nature have spread themselves have been flown for religious ideals.   WILLIAM JAMES

If one advances confidently in the direction of his dreams, and endeavors to live the life which he imagined, he will meet with a success unexpected in common hours. In proportion as he simplifies his life, the laws of the universe will appear less complex, and solitude will not be solitude, nor poverty poverty, nor weakness weakness. If you have built castles in the air, your work need not be lost; that is where they should be. Now put foundations under them.   HENRY DAVID THOREAU

In heaven there is laid up a pattern of the Eternal City which he who desires may behold; and beholding, may set his own house in order. But whether such a one exists, or ever will exist in fact, is no matter, for he (the wise man) will live after the manner of that city, having nothing to do with any other.   PLATO

Ideals are like stars: you will not succeed in touching them with your hands, but, like the seafaring man on the desert of waters, you choose them as your guides, and, following them, you reach your destiny.   CARL SCHURZ

Deviate an inch, lose a thousand miles.   CHINESE PROVERB

Every man has at times in his mind the ideal of what he should be, but is not. This ideal may be high and complete, or it may be quite low and insufficient; yet in all men that really seek to improve, it is better than the actual character—man never falls so low that he can see nothing higher than himself.
                                                          THEODORE PARKER

All the great things are simple, and many can be expressed in a single word: freedom; justice; honor; duty; mercy; hope.   WINSTON S. CHURCHILL

We wish to preserve the fire of the past, not the ashes.   WILLIAM JAMES

If we work upon marble it will perish; if we work upon brass, time will efface it; if we rear temples, they will crumble into dust; but if we work upon immortal minds, if we imbue them with principles, with just the fear of God and love of our fellow-men, we engrave on those tablets something which will brighten all eternity.   DANIEL WEBSTER

Let then our first act every morning be to make the following resolve for the day:
I shall not fear anyone on earth.
I shall fear only God.
I shall not bear ill will toward anyone.
I shall not submit to injustice from anyone.
I shall conquer untruth by truth.
And in resisting untruth I shall put up with all suffering.
MOHANDAS GANDHI

God hides some ideal in every human life. At some time we feel a trembling fearful longing to do some good thing. Life finds its noblest spring of excellence in the hidden impulse to do our best.   ROBERT COLLYER

So many people go through life filling the storeroom of their minds with odds and ends of a grudge here, a jealousy there, a pettiness, a selfishness—all ignoble. The true task of a man is to create a noble memory, a mind filled with grandeur, forgiveness, restless ideals, and the dynamic ethical ferment, preached by all religions at their best.   LEO BAECK

See also: ASPIRATION; BELIEF; CHARACTER; DEDICATION; DIVINE, THE; EDUCATION; EXAMPLE; GOODNESS; HEROISM; INTEGRITY; VIRTUE; WISDOM.

Immortality

I am a better believer, and all serious souls are better believers, in immortality than we can give grounds for. The real evidence is too subtle or is higher than we can write down in propositions. I have always thought that faith in immortality is proof of the sanity of a man's nature.

RALPH WALDO EMERSON

Divine Wisdom, intending to detain us some time on earth, has done well to cover with a veil the prospect of the life to come; for if our sight could clearly distinguish the opposite bank, who would remain on this tempestuous coast of time? MADAME GERMAINE DE STAËL

> Whence this pleasing hope, this fond desire,
> This longing for immortality?
> 'Tis the divinity that stirs within us:
> 'Tis heaven itself that points out an hereafter,
> And intimates eternity to man.
>
> JOSEPH ADDISON

There is, I know not how, in the minds of men, a certain presage, as it were, of a future existence; and this takes the deepest root, and is most discoverable, in the greatest geniuses and most exalted souls. CICERO

I have never seen what to me seemed an atom of proof that there is a future life. And yet—I am strongly inclined to expect one. MARK TWAIN

Vast possibilities suggest themselves to us of an order of existence wholly different from all that we have ever known; what may be the nature of that other life it is impossible to know and it is useless to speculate. . . . Only this I feel warranted in holding fast to—that the root of my selfhood, the best that is in me, my true and only being, cannot perish. In regard to that the notion of death seems to me to be irrelevant. . . . I let go my hold on the empirical, transient self, I see it perish with the same indifference which the materialist asserts, for whom man is but a compound of physical matter and physical force. It is the real self, the eternal self, upon which I tighten my hold. I affirm the real, the irreducible existence of the essential self, though I know not the *how* or *where* of its survival. I affirm that there verily is an eternal divine life, a best beyond the best I can think or imagine. What I retain is the conviction that the spiritual self is an eternal self, and cannot perish. FELIX ADLER

Without a belief in personal immortality, religion is surely like an arch resting on one pillar, like a bridge ending in an abyss. MAX MÜLLER

Here in this world He bids us come, there in the next He shall bid us welcome. JOHN DONNE

I believe in my survival after death. Like many others before me, I have experienced "intimations of immortality." I can no more explain these than the brown seed can explain the flowering tree. Deep in the soil in time's mid-winter, my very stirring and unease seem a kind of growing pain toward June.   ROBERT HILLYER

I trouble not myself about the manner of future existence. I content myself with believing, even to positive conviction, that the power that gave me existence is able to continue it, in any form and manner He pleases, either with or without this body; and it appears more probable to me that I shall continue to exist hereafter than that I should have had existence, as I now have, before that existence began.   THOMAS PAINE

The grave itself is but a covered bridge leading from light to light through a brief darkness.   HENRY WADSWORTH LONGFELLOW

The dust goes to its place, and man to his own. It is then I feel my immortality. I look through the grave into heaven. I ask no miracle, no proof, no reasoning, for me. I ask no risen dust to teach me immortality. I am conscious of eternal life.   THEODORE PARKER

> Is this the end? I know it cannot be,
> Our ships shall sail upon another sea;
> New islands yet shall break upon our sight,
> New continents of love and truth and might.
>   JOHN WHITE CHADWICK

See also: BEING; BELIEF; BIBLE, THE; CHRISTIANITY; DIVINE, THE; FAITH; MYSTERY; RELIGION; SOUL; WONDER.

Inspiration

Perpetual inspiration is as necessary to the life of goodness, holiness and happiness as perpetual respiration is necessary to animal life.
                                                      WILLIAM LAW

High art, high morals, high faith, are impossible among those who do not believe their own inspirations, but only court them for pleasure or profit.
                                                      JAMES MARTINEAU

Men grind and grind in the mill of truism, and nothing comes out but what was put in. But the moment they desert the tradition for a spontaneous thought, then poetry, wit, hope, virtue, learning, anecdote, all flock to their aid.   RALPH WALDO EMERSON

Life seems to me like a Japanese picture which our imagination does not allow to end with the margin.   OLIVER WENDELL HOLMES, JR.

Aspiration shows us the goal and the distance to it; inspiration encourages with a view to how far we have come. Aspiration gives us the map of the journey; inspiration furnishes the music to keep us marching.
                                                                                                  RALPH W. SOCKMAN

A teacher who is attempting to teach without inspiring the pupil with a desire to learn is hammering on cold iron.   HORACE MANN

The notion that inspiration is something that happened thousands of years ago, and was then finished and done with, . . . the theory that God retired from business at that period and has not been heard from since, is as silly as it is blasphemous.   GEORGE BERNARD SHAW

There are one-story intellects, two-story intellects, and three-story intellects with skylights. All fact collectors, who have no aim beyond their facts, are one-story men. Two-story men compare, reason, generalize, using the labors of the fact-collectors as well as their own. Three-story men idealize, imagine, predict; their best illumination comes from above, through the skylight.   OLIVER WENDELL HOLMES, SR.

The past is our cradle, not our prison, and there is danger as well as appeal in its glamor. The past is for inspiration, not imitation, for continuation, not repetition.   ISRAEL ZANGWILL

Every great advance in science has issued from a new audacity of imagination.   JOHN DEWEY

See also: AMBITION; ASPIRATION; DIVINE, THE; IDEALS; PRAYER; RELIGION; VISION; WONDER.

Integrity

A good name is to be chosen rather than great riches and favor is better than silver or gold.   THE BIBLE

To confess a fault freely is the next thing to being innocent of it.
                                                            PUBLILIUS SYRUS

On honesty God's favor is bestowed,
I never saw one lost in a straight road.
                                                            SAADI

A man who cannot mind his own business, is not to be trusted with the king's.   GEORGE SAVILE, MARQUIS OF HALIFAX

The reputation of a man is like his shadow: It sometimes follows and sometimes precedes him; it is sometimes longer and sometimes shorter than his natural size.   FRENCH PROVERB

I would not deliver my conscience into the keeping of the angels. My conscience is my own.   STEPHEN S. WISE
[January 5, 1906, in letter
to the president and members
of Temple Emanu-El, New York]

Compromise makes a good umbrella, but a poor roof; it is a temporary expedient, often wise in party politics, almost sure to be unwise in statesmanship.   JAMES RUSSELL LOWELL

When a scholar speaks what he ought not to speak by guile of speech to gain some end, and when he does not speak, by guile of silence to gain some end—both these cases are of a piece with breaking through a neighbor's wall.
                                                            MENCIUS

Hateful to me even as the gates of Hades is he that hideth one thing in his heart and uttereth another. HOMER

> Who is the honest man?
> He that doth still and strongly good pursue,
> To God, his neighbor, and himself most true:
> Whom neither force nor fawning can
> Unpin, or wrench from giving all their due.
> GEORGE HERBERT

What a man is in himself, what accompanies him when he is alone, what no one can give or take away is obviously more essential to him than everything he has in the way of possessions, or even what he may be in the eyes of the world. ARTHUR SCHOPENHAUER

Fraud and deceit are ever in a hurry. Take time for all things. Great haste makes great waste. BENJAMIN FRANKLIN

An honest man's the noblest work of God. ALEXANDER POPE

See also: ASPIRATION; CHARACTER; CONSCIENCE; COURAGE; GOD; GOODNESS; GREATNESS; IDEALS; RELIGION; RESPONSIBILITY; TRUTH; VIRTUE.

Internationalism

The narrow-minded ask, "Is this man a stranger, or is he of our tribe?" But to those in whom love dwells, the whole world is but one family. HINDU PROVERB

It was in West Africa in 1927 that a blood specimen was taken from a black native named Asibi who was sick with yellow fever. This specimen was inoculated into a rhesus monkey which had just been received from India. Asibi recovered, but the monkey died of the disease. All the vaccine manufactured since 1927, both by the Rockefeller Foundation and other agencies as well, derives from the original strain of virus obtained from this humble native. Carried down from the present day from one laboratory and by enormous multiplication, it has offered immunity to yellow fever to millions of people in many countries. Through the creative imagination of science, the blood of one man in West Africa has been made to serve the whole human race.   ROCKEFELLER FOUNDATION REPORT

We the peoples of the United Nations

Determined

> To save succeeding generations from the scourge of war, which twice in our lifetime has brought untold sorrow to mankind, and

> To reaffirm faith in fundamental human rights, in the dignity and worth of the human person, in the equal right of men and women and of nations large and small, and

> To establish conditions under which justice and respect for the obligations arising from treaties and other sources of international law can be maintained, and

> To promote social progress and better standards of life in larger freedom, and for these ends

> To practice tolerance and live together in peace with one another as good neighbors, and

> To unite our strength to maintain international peace and security and

> To insure, by the acceptance of principles and the institution of methods, that armed force shall not be used, save in the common interest, and

> To employ international machinery for the promotion of the economic and social advancement of all peoples

have resolved to combine our efforts to accomplish these aims.

PREAMBLE TO THE CHARTER
OF THE UNITED NATIONS

The man of science . . . suffers a truly tragic fate. Striving in great sincerity for clarity and inner independence, he himself, through his sheer superhuman efforts, has fashioned the tools which are being used to make him a slave and to destroy him also from within. He cannot escape being muzzled by those who have the political power in their hands. As a soldier he is forced to sacrifice his own life and to destroy the lives of others even when he is convinced of the absurdity of such sacrifices. He is fully aware of the fact that universal destruction is unavoidable since the historical developmen has led to the concentration of all economic, political, and military power in the hands of national states. He also realizes that mankind can be saved only if a supranational system, based on law, would be created to eliminate for good the methods of brute force. ALBERT EINSTEIN

To the main road there is only one hope: we must return to the main road from which we have wandered. We must substitute for propaganda the power of understanding the truth that is really true; for the patriotism current today, the noble kind of patriotism which aims at ends that are worthy of the whole of mankind; for idolized nationalisms, a humanity with a common civilization; for the condition into which we have plunged, a restored faith in the civilized man; for the preoccupation with the problems of living, a concern with the processes and ideals of true civilizations; for a mentality stripped of all true spirituality, a faith in the possibility of progress.

ALBERT SCHWEITZER

We [the United States of America and the Union of Soviet Socialist Republics] are tied together as no two peoples have been tied together before. We have it within our joint power to pulverize the species of which we are a part, including untold numbers of people with whom neither of us has any quarrel. We are in a race, both of us, to the ultimates—in folly or splendor.

Something else we have in common—a shared helplessness as the mutual terror deepens. All of us understand the consequences of the folly; neither one craves the distinction of belonging to the last generation of civilized men on earth. Yet the certainty of disaster represented by the present drift is exceeded only by the uncertainty of how to avert it. . . .

Mutual enlightenment can keep the monument of modern man from becoming a ruin; but enlightenment depends not just on good will but on the existence and exchange of knowledge. . . .

In whatever we say to the Russians, we should never forget the magic of freedom; but we can always remember that an awareness of a common destiny unlocks the mind, stimulates insight, and releases energy for mutual adventure. The end is not uniformity. It is not even combined operations. The end is a world whose inhabitants, whatever their political and economic values, place proper value on human life. NORMAN COUSINS

I have said on many occasions that a dead soldier, whether American or Vietnamese, is my brother—a dead child in the arms of his father or his mother, is my child. To me there is no distinction between an American or Vietnamese, a Jew or an Arab. I look at the human community from the global point of view. I have tried to develop this global concept, this planetary concept.

Long before I came to the United States, I was brought up in a Buddhist family as some of you must have been aware. I was trained to cherish these moral and spiritual values above all other values.

In my view, there is today no such thing as national peace—or national security, or national progress—confined within the boundaries of a particular nation or a particular state. The world is so interdependent, much more interdependent than ever before. National peace, national security and national progress depend primarily on international peace, international security, and the development of international resources.   U THANT

I like the words of Sir Rabindranath Tagore's poem, "Listen to the rumbling of the clouds, O heart of mine. Be brave, break through and leave for the unknown. . . ."

I think that these lines express in a very noble way the attitude we must take to this venture called the United Nations. We may listen to the rumbling of the clouds, but we can never afford to lose that kind of confidence in ourselves and in the wisdom of man which makes us brave enough to break through and leave, always for the unknown.

DAG HAMMARSKJÖLD

I am not born for one corner; the whole world is my native land.   SENECA

An American soldier wounded on a battlefield in the Far East owes his life to the Japanese scientist Kitasato, who isolated the bacillus of tetanus. A Russian soldier saved by a blood transfusion is indebted to Landsteiner, an Austrian. A German is shielded from typhoid fever with the help of a Russian, Metchnikoff. A Dutch marine in the East Indies is protected from malaria because of the experiments of an Italian, Grassi; while a British aviator in North Africa escapes death from surgical infection because a Frenchman, Pasteur, and a German, Koch, elaborated a new technique.

In peace, as in war, we are beneficiaries of knowledge contributed by every nation in the world. Our children are guarded from diphtheria by what a Japanese and a German did; they are protected from smallpox by the work of an Englishman; they are saved from rabies because of a Frenchman; they are cured of pellagra through the researches of an Austrian. From birth to death they are surrounded by an invisible host—the spirits of men who never thought in terms of flags or boundary lines and who never served a lesser loyalty than the welfare of mankind.   RAYMOND B. FOSDICK

See also: BROTHERHOOD; CHRISTIANITY; FELLOWSHIP; HUMANITY; MANKIND; PEACE.

Israel

The State of Israel is a surprise, yet the modern mind hates to be surprised. Never before has a nation been restored to its ancient hearth after a lapse of 1,897 years. This extraordinary aspect is bound to carry some shock to the conventional mind, to be a scandal to the mediocre mind and a foolishness to the positivists. It requires reordering of some notions.

Israel is a miracle in disguise. Things look natural and conceal what is a radical surprise. Zion rebuilt becomes a harbinger of a new understanding, of how history is intertwined with the mystery. ABRAHAM JOSHUA HESCHEL

In Israel, in order to be a realist you must believe in miracles.

DAVID BEN-GURION

If I were to sum up the [Zionist] Basel Congress [of 1897] in a single phrase—which I would not dare to make public—I would say: In Basel I created the Jewish State. Were I to say this aloud I would be greeted by universal laughter. But perhaps five years hence, in any case certainly fifty hence, everyone will perceive it [Palestine Partition Plan adopted by UN in 1947]. THEODOR HERZL

What we see [in Palestine in 1929] is a deep-founded, full-rounded civilization, reared in an inhospitable country, amid a primitive people, by the labor of men's hands and the sacrifice of their heroic hearts. I know of nothing in history to compare with it, unless it be the early settlement of New England.

Palestine [now Israel] may be made not merely a battleground but a laboratory. It needs but the presence of a determined mind, a courageous heart, an idealistic spirit, to make this country an experiment station for the healing of the ills of man. And it is just this which the Jew brings to Palestine in Zionism. Here in this adventure is the dream of a society of justice, righteousness and peace. Here on the scene of this adventure are all the diversive and divisive elements out of which this dream must fashion the substance of its reality. If the Jew succeeds in what he has so heroically undertaken, he will have discovered the solution of all social problems. It is in this sense that Zionism is far more than the hope of Israel. It is the hope, also, of the world. JOHN HAYNES HOLMES

Let no American imagine that Zionism is inconsistent with patriotism. Multiple loyalties are objectionable only if they are inconsistent. A man is a better citizen of the United States for being also a loyal citizen of his state, and of his city; for being loyal to his family, and to his profession or trade; for being loyal to his college or lodge. . . . Every American Jew who aids in advancing the Jewish settlement in Palestine [now Israel], through he feels that neither he nor his descendants will ever live there, will likewise be a better man, a better American, for doing so.   LOUIS D. BRANDEIS

There is no experiment in human uplift now [1939] to be seen on the face of the earth which can compare to the work of the Jews in Palestine [now Israel]. If I were a Jew, I would deem it the highest honor life can hold to take part in a work so noble.   NORMAN MacLEAN
[Chaplain to King George VI and moderator
of the Church of Scotland]

The Jew, even though he was driven from the land, never surrendered his love for it. The Jew literally transplanted Zion into his very consciousness. He imagined that he continued to live in the land of his dreams. He might be living in the cold north or to the sunny south, yet he prayed for rain or for dew when it was the season for these in Israel. . . .

"The land without a people," to use a phrase of Zangwill, "waited for the people without a land."   ISRAEL HERBERT LEVINTHAL

I think it is necessary to say that what is basic and what is needed in the Middle East is peace. Peace for Israel is one thing. Peace for the Arab side of that world is another thing.

Peace for Israel means security, and we must stand with all of our might to protect its right to exist, its territorial integrity, and the right to use whatever sea lanes it needs. I see Israel, and never mind saying it, as one of the great outposts of democracy in the world, and a marvelous example of what can be done, how desert land almost can be transformed into an oasis of brotherhood and democracy.

On the other hand, we must see what peace for the Arab means in a real sense of security on another level. Peace for the Arabs means a kind of economic security that they so desperately need. These nations, as you know, are a part of that third world of hunger, of disease, of illiteracy. I think that as long as these condidtions exist there will be tensions, there will be the endless quest to find scapegoats. So there is a need for a Marshall Plan for the Middle East, where we lift those who are at the bottom of the economic ladder and bring them into the mainstream of economic activity.

          MARTIN LUTHER KING, JR.

The idea of Zion is rooted in deeper regions of the earth and rises into loftier regions of the air; and neither its deep roots nor its lofty heights, neither its memory of the past nor its ideal for the future, both of the self-same texture, must be repudiated. If Israel renounces the mystery, it renounces the heart of reality itself. National forms without the eternal purpose from which they have arisen signify the end of Israel's specific fruitfulness. The free development of the latent power of the nation without a supreme value to give it purpose and direction does not mean regeneration but the mere sport of a common self-deception behind which spiritual death lurks in ambush. If Israel desires less then it is intended to fulfil then it will even fail to achieve the lesser goal.   MARTIN BUBER

When I think of the liberation of Palestine,
When my eye conceives the great black English line
Spanning the world news of two thousand years,
My heart leaps forward like a hungry dog,
My heart is thrown back on its tangled chain,
My soul is hangdog in a Western chair.

When I think of the battle for Zion I hear
The drop of chains, the starting forth of feet,
And I remain chained in a Western chair.
My blood beats like a bird against a wall,
I feel the weight of prisons in my skull
Falling away; my forebears stare through stone.

When I see the name of Israel high in print
The fences crumble in my flesh; I sink
Deep in a Western chair and rest my soul.
I look the stranger clear to the blue depths
Of his unclouded eye. I say my name
Aloud for the first time unconsciously.

Speak of the tillage of a million heads
No more. Speak of the evil myth no more
Of one who harried Jesus on his way
Saying, *Go faster*. Speak no more
Of the yellow badge, *secta nefaria*.
Speak the name only of the living land.
                               KARL SHAPIRO

A young American who had read the Israeli philosopher Martin Buber, and who had worked for six weeks in a Marxist collective in Galilee, had a chance to talk with Dr. Buber.

"Dare I ask you a personal question?" he said. "In your writings you are deeply religious, You also see hope of regeneration through the collective settlements. But many of the collective settlements are militantly atheistic. Isn't that a kind of paradox?"

"I can answer you," replied Dr. Buber, "only by a quotation from the Talmud. 'Would that they had forgotten My name and done that which I commanded of them!' "   STRINGFELLOW BARR

See also: ACHIEVEMENT; ADVERSITY; ASPIRATION; BIBLE, THE; DEDICATION; DIVINE, THE; FAITH; GOD; JEWS; JUDAISM; PATRIOTISM; RELIGION.

Jesus Christ

Jesus Christ belonged to the true race of prophets. He saw with open eyes the mystery of the soul. Drawn by its severe harmony, ravished with its beauty, he lived in it, and had his being there. Alone in all history he estimated the greatness of man. One man was true to what is in you and me. He saw that God incarnates himself in man, and evermore goes forth anew to take possession of his World.

RALPH WALDO EMERSON

        Lamb of God, Man of Sorrow,
        Son of David, Man or God,
        Man of Nazareth, Carpenter's Son—
        There are names you may call him,
        Recount them like a litany of beads
        Precious with memory and magic with hope.
        Hold them in your hand to delight the senses,
        Fingering the busy work of the spirit.
        Say them again—Christ, Savior,
        Great Friend of Man, Man of the Cross.
        From all languages the names come,
        Their images dancing to your placid joy.
        But they do not contain him, not gentle Jesus,
        Pharisee of the Pharisees, Lord of Gethsemane.
        Those who have known life contain him,
        Those who have gulped the common cup of
            struggle and tragedy.
        Say the names again. Say Gandhi,
        Saint Francis. Say Schweitzer. Say King.
        Yes, say King behind bars in Atlanta jail.

Recount the litany of those who knew
Destiny among "the least of these."
Then stop the moving finger, cast off
The aloof, vicarious observer role,
For the chant is short, the cycle incomplete.
A name is missing, and with it
Something of love is lost from history.

ARTHUR GRAHAM

I am no more of a Christian than Pilate was, or you are, gentle hearer; and yet, like Pilate, I greatly prefer Jesus of Nazareth to Amos or Caiaphas; and I am ready to admit that I see no way out of the world's misery but the way which would have been found by his will.   GEORGE BERNARD SHAW

Mankind in its totality offers an assemblage of low beings, selfish, and superior to the animal only in that its selfishness is more reflective. From the midst of this uniform mediocrity, there are pillars that rise toward the sky, and bear witness to a nobler destiny. Jesus is the highest of these pillars which show to man whence he comes, and whither he ought to tend. In him was condensed all that is good and elevated in our nature.

Whatever may be the unexpected phenomena of the future, Jesus will not be surpassed. His worship will constantly renew its youth, the tale of his life will cause ceaseless tears, his sufferings will soften the best hearts; all the ages will proclaim that, among the sons of men, there is none born who is greater than Jesus.   ERNEST RENAN

It was night-time, and He was alone.

And He saw afar off the walls of a round city, and went toward the city.

And when He came near He heard within the City the tread of the feet of joy, and the laughter of the mouth of gladness, and the loud noise of many lutes. And he knocked at the gate and certain of the gatekeepers opened to Him.

And He beheld a house that was of marble, and had fair pillars of marble before it. The pillars were hung with garlands, and within and without there were torches of cedar. And He entered the house.

And when He had passed through the hall of chalcedony and the hall of jasper, and reached the long hall of feasting, He saw lying on a couch of sea-purple one whose hair was crowned with red roses and whose lips were red with wine.

And He went behind him and touched him on the shoulder, and said to him: "Why do you live like this?"

And the young man turned round and recognized Him, and made answer, and said: "But I was a leper once, and you healed me. How else should I live?"

And He passed out of the house and went again into the street.

And after a little while He saw one whose face and raiment were painted and whose feet were shod with pearls. And behind her came slowly, as a hunter, a young man who wore a cloak of two colors. Now the face of the woman was as the fair face of an idol, and the eyes of the young man were bright with lust.

And He followed swiftly, and touched the hand of the young man, and said to him: "Why do you look at this woman in such wise?"

And the young man turned round and recognized Him, and said: "But I was blind once, and you gave me sight. At what else should I look?"

And He ran forward and touched the painted raiment of the woman, and said to her: "Is there no other way in which to walk save the way of sin?"

And the woman turned round and recognized Him, and laughed, and said: "But you forgave me my sins, and the way is a pleasant way."

And He passed out of the city.

And when He had passed out of the city, He saw, seated by the roadside, a young man who was weeping.

And He went toward him and touched the long locks of his hair, and said to him: "Why are you weeping?"

And the young man looked up and recognized Him, and made answer: "But I was dead, and you raised me from the dead. What else should I do but weep?"

OSCAR WILDE

I cannot understand why you feel that I must come back, as you put it, to the God of Israel through Jesus Christ, His son. We do not believe that Jesus is in any unique sense the Son of God. He was a son of Israel, which fact Christendom for the most part has forgotten, and his was the immediacy of access to God which is the portion and privilege of all His children.

STEPHEN S. WISE

[October 9, 1933, in letter to a Southern Baptist who had asked him to "become a 'Paul' . . . and be the anointed of God to lead this poor struggling world back to the God of Israel, thru Jesus Christ His son."]

If Shakespeare should come into the room, we would all rise; but if Jesus Christ should come in, we would all kneel.

CHARLES LAMB

In the best sense of the word, Jesus was a radical. . . . His religion has been so long identified with conservatism—often with conservatism of the obstinate and unyielding sort—that it is almost startling for us sometimes to remember that all of the conservatism of his own times was against him; that it was the young, free, restless, sanguine, progressive part of the people who flocked to him.   PHILLIPS BROOKS

For nearly fifty years the New Testament has been a main concern in my studies, and I think I am a good reader who listens impartially to what is said.

From my youth onwards I have found in Jesus my great brother. That Christianity has regarded him as God the Savior has always appeared to me a fact of highest importance which, for his sake and my own, I must endeavor to understand. My own fraternally open relationship to him has grown ever more stronger and clearer, and today I see him more strongly and clearly than ever before.

I am more certain than ever that a great place belongs to him in Israel's history of faith.   MARTIN BUBER

Two thousand years ago lived One who saw the absurdity of a man loving only his friend. He saw that this meant faction, lines of social cleavage, with untimate discord; and so He painted the truth large and declared we should love our enemies and do good to those who might despitefully use us. He was one of the erring, the weak, the insane, the poor; and so free was He from prejudice and fear that we have confounded Him with Deity, and confused Him with the maker of the worlds. He was one set apart, because He had no competition in the matter of love. It is not necessary for us to leave our task and pattern our lives after His; but if we can imitate His divine patience and keep thoughts of discord out of our lives, we, too, can work such wonders that men will indeed truthfully say that we are the Sons of God.   ELBERT HUBBARD

When I think of Mahatma Gandhi I think of Jesus Christ. The Nazarene, or divine personality, taught the law of love and laid down a program of soul force for its fulfillment; He sought to establish the Kingdom of Heaven on earth, so also with Gandhi. This Indian is a saint in personal life; he teaches the law of love and soul force as its practice; and he seeks the establishment of a new social order, which shall be a Kingdom of the Spirit. If I believed in the "Second Coming," as I do not, I should dare to assert that Gandhi was Jesus come back to earth. When I think of Romain Rolland, I think of Tolstoi. When I think of Lenin, I think of Napoleon. But when I think of Gandhi, I think of Jesus. He lives his life; he speaks his word; he suffers, strives, and will some day nobly die, for his kingdom upon earth.

                                                    JOHN HAYNES HOLMES
                                                    [Written in 1921]

If Jesus Christ were to come today people would not even crucify him. They would ask him to dinner, and hear what he has to say, and make fun of it.

THOMAS CARLYLE

See also: BELIEF; BIBLE, THE; CHRISTIANITY; COMPASSION; DIVINE, THE; GRACE; HUMILITY; LOVE; SAINTLINESS; SELFLESSNESS; SUFFERING.

Jews

The Jews gave to the world its three greatest religions, reverence for law, and the highest conceptions of morality. LOUIS D. BRANDEIS

Because I am a Jew, I was Abraham, shatterer of idols.
Because I am a Jew, I was Moses, challenger of justice, pursuing kings.
Because I am a Jew, I was Elijah, destroyer of the Baalim.
Because I am a Jew, I was Isaiah, dreamer of a warless world.
Because I am a Jew, I was Amos, enacter of justice from man to man.
Because I am a Jew, I was Ezra, bringer back from exile of God's people.
Because I am a Jew, I was the Maccabean warrior for Israel's unfettered life.
Because I am a Jew, I was Bar Kochba, terrible, though vain awakener of my people.
Because I am a Jew, through medieval centuries of darkness I held aloft the torch of light and reason, passing through the flaming terror of the Inquisition without fear.
Because I am a Jew, I was Spinoza, truth-revealer of the modern world.
Because I am a Jew, I was Mendelssohn, conciliator between the Ghetto and the world without.
Because I am a Jew, I was Theodor Herzl, insistent upon the Jew's right and duty of self-determination.
Because I am a Jew, I must suffer wrong without wrath; I must do justice, and be more than a man in forbearance to man, and all of man in greatness of act before God and man. STEPHEN S. WISE

We are conscious today that many centuries of blindness have clouded our eyes so that we can no longer either see the beauty of Thy Chosen People or recognize in their faces the features of our privileged brethren. We realize that the mark of Cain stands upon our foreheads. Across the centuries our brother Abel has lain in the blood which we drew or shed the tears we

caused by forgetting Thy love. Forgive us for the curse we falsely attached
to their name as Jews. Forgive us for crucifying Thee a second time in their
flesh. For we knew not what we did. . . .   POPE JOHN XXIII

> [Prayer composed by John XXIII in 1963, three months
> before his death, and intended by him to be read aloud
> in all Roman Catholic churches of the world on a
> designated date]

The Hebrews have done more to civilize men than any other nation. If I were
an atheist, and believed in blind eternal fate, I should still believe that fate
had ordained the Jews to be the most essential instrument for civilizing the
nations.   JOHN ADAMS

Not long ago I was reading the Sermon on the Mount with a rabbi. At nearly
each verse he showed me very similar passages in the Hebrew Bible and
Talmud. When we reached the words, "Resist not evil," he did not say,
"This too is in the Talmud," but asked, with a smile, "Do the Christians
obey this command?" I had nothing to say in reply, especially as at that
particular time, Christians, far from turning the other cheek, were smiting
the Jews on both cheeks.   LEO TOLSTOY

Jerusalem, we were forced to leave when driven out by conquerors, but we
never abandoned, never relinquished you. Our parting was a pain to which
we would never reconcile ourselves.
   "The site has been captured, occupied, and recaptured by various people
since the Old Stone Age and the Pleistocene period. During the past 3,500
years it has been held by Egyptians, Jebusites, Jews, Babylonians, Romans,
Arabs, Turks, Britons, and now Jews again," writes the *Christian Century*
without realizing that if Jerusalem had been only the city of Jebusites,
Turks, and Arabs, there would have been no Christian century.
          ABRAHAM JOSHUA HESCHEL

In the sight of an anti-Semite, Jews can do nothing right. If they are rich,
they are birds of prey. If they are poor, they are vermin. If they are in favor
of war, they are exploiters of bloody feuds for their own profit. If they are
anxious for peace, they are either instinctive cowards or traitors. If they give
generously, they are doing it for some selfish purpose of their own. If they
don't give, then what would one expect from a Jew?
          DAVID LLOYD GEORGE

The burden of our history is unmistakable: the enemy of the Jew is the enemy of freedom. Those who organize the pogrom of today will attack to-

morrow the general foundation of freedom. That is why the moral stature of the nation is set by its recognition that the claim of its Jew to freedom is the claim of its own people to strike off its chains. When it is silent before the agony of the Jew, it collaborates in the organization of its future servitude.

HAROLD LASKI

I wish your nation [the Jewish people] may be admitted to all privileges of citizens in every country of the world. This country has done much. I wish it may do more; and annul every narrow idea in religion, government and commerce. Let the wits joke; the philosophers sneer; what then? It has pleased the Providence of the "first cause," the universal cause, that Abraham should give religion, not only to Hebrews, but to Christians and Mahometans, the greatest part of the civilized world.

JOHN ADAMS

We are not one other example of the species "nation"; we are the only example of the species "Israel."

MARTIN BUBER

The same wonder-working Deity who long since delivering the Hebrews from their Egyptian oppressors planted them in the promised land. . . . For happily the government of the United States which gives to bigotry no sanction, to persecution no assistance, requires only that they who live under its protection, should demean themselves as good citizens in giving it on all occasions their effectual support.

GEORGE WASHINGTON

Were I of Jew blood, I do not think I could ever forgive the Christians; the ghettos would get in my nostrils like mustard or lit gunpowder.

ROBERT LOUIS STEVENSON

The pursuit of knowledge for its own sake, an almost fanatical love of justice, and a desire for personal independence—these are features of the Jewish tradition which make me thank my stars that I belong to it.

ALBERT EINSTEIN

See also: ADVERSITY; AFFLICTION; BIBLE, THE; CHRISTIANITY; DIVINE, THE; GOD; IDEALS; ISRAEL; JESUS CHRIST; JUDAISM; RELIGION; SUFFERING.

Judaism

Judaism is not only religion and it is not only ethics: it is the sum total of all the needs of a nation, placed on a religious basis. Judaism is a nation and a religion at one and the same time.   JOSEPH KLAUSNER

I, Maurice Samuel, an American citizen, and a lover of this country, feel that the best I can offer it springs from my identification with the development of Judaism. In the deep moral struggles of America (as of the rest of the Western world) the issue lies between the cooperative and the competitive interpretations of life, between essential Christianity and its matrix and ally, Judaism, on the one hand, and paganism, open or concealed, on the other. If I identify myself with a Judaism that is such in name only, hence with an Israel that is a purely nationalistic state, I serve neither Judaism nor America, whatever approvals I can obtain for the deception. If, under the slogan of an exclusive Americanism, I dissociate myself from creative Judaism and a creative Israel, I am practicing another deception: I am depriving America of my best potentialities and calling it good Americanism.

                                                    MAURICE SAMUEL

"How odd of God to choose the Jews," mused a cynic.
To which the reply is: "It's not so odd. The Jews chose God."
                                                    ANONYMOUS

The Jew has to help mold tomorrow by continued loyalty to his ideals inherited from a long yesterday.

Judaism is not a song that is sung; it is a continuing symphony which each Jew may either swell with harmony or mar with discord.

It is a symphony which echoes forth to the world Judaism's faith in man's possibilities of good and his power of regeneration to a nobler future.

The past is a foundation on which Jews have to continue building and developing in loyal keeping with what has been achieved by the master builders of the past.

It is that past which compellingly gives us the dedicated purpose to remain a people for the present and the future.

Noblesse oblige.

The past is my heritage, the present my responsibility, the future my challenge as a Jew.   DAVID DE SOLA POOL

Christianity needs confrontation with Judaism. By this I do not mean only the profound moral truth that the treatment of Jews is one of the tests of Christianity, and a test in which the Christian performance has been poor. I mean also the profound religious and theological truth that whenever Christian thought loses touch with Judaism, it loses touch with a part of itself. Whenever in Christian history Christians have neglected their ties with the ancient people of God, they have been impoverished in both faith and understanding.

JAROSLAV PELIKAN

FRIAR: Nathan, you are a Christian.
               Yes, I swear
               You are a Christian—better never lived.
NATHAN: Indeed, the very thing that
                 makes me seem
               Christian to you, makes you a
                     Jew to me.

GOTTHOLD EPHRAIM LESSING
[From Nathan the Wise]

In the economy of humanity, to Israel was assigned the function to be the "people of the Book." Duty was his dower. Righteousness through private sanctification and social cooperation in enjoining justice was his incessant obsession. His history was so guided that in every deeper measure the consciousness took possession of Israel that this priesthood was his task at the altar of humanity. No merit of his entitled him to this sacerdotal mitre. Modestly he ascribed his appointment to the "merit" of his fathers. Their "love" had won for him the call to his responsibilities. The grace of God had chosen him not to higher prerogatives but to sterner obligations.

EMIL G. HIRSCH

See also: ADVERSITY; ASPIRATION; BELIEF; BIBLE, THE; CHRISTIANITY; COURAGE; DIVINE, THE; GOD; ISRAEL; JESUS CHRIST; JEWS; SUFFERING.

Judgment

Foolish men imagine that because judgment for an evil thing is delayed, there is no justice, but only accident here below. Judgment for an evil thing is many times delayed some day or two, some century or two, but it is sure as life, it is sure as death!

THOMAS CARLYLE

Those who have nothing, but wish they had, are damned with the rich. For God does not consider what we possess but what we covet.

SAINT AUGUSTINE

The lessons taught by history are:

First, whom the gods would destroy they
   first make mad with power.

Second the mills of God grind slowly,
   yet they grind exceeding small.

Third, the bee fertilizes the flower it robs.

Fourth, when it is dark enough you can see the stars.

CHARLES A. BEARD

Those who cannot remember the past are condemned to repeat it.

GEORGE SANTAYANA

One tear met another tear floating down the river. Said the first tear, "I am the tear of the woman who lost her lover." The other tear replied, "And I am the tear of the woman who got him."   OLD CHINESE TALE

There is no man so good, who, were he to submit all his thoughts and actions to the law, would not deserve hanging ten times in his life.   MONTAIGNE

God strikes with his finger, and not with all his arm.   GEORGE HERBERT

It was not the guns that broke Napoleon on the Moscow road; it was the might of the snowflakes.   JAMES REID

Never point a finger of scorn at another, for in so doing you are pointing three fingers of scorn at your own self.   BURMESE PROVERB

See also: ADVERSITY; AFFLICTION; BELIEF; BIBLE, THE; CHARACTER; GOD; JUSTICE; RACIAL JUSTICE; RELIGION; RESPONSIBILITY; SUFFERING.

Justice

Shall justice fail and perish out of the world of men?
Shall wrong continually endure?
Injustice cannot stand. No armies, no alliance, can hold it up.
The arc of the moral universe is long, but it bends toward justice.

THEODORE PARKER

Justice and power must be brought together, so that whatever is just may be powerful, and whatever is powerful may be just.   BLAISE PASCAL

Justice has nothing to do with expediency. It has nothing to do with any temporary standard whatever. It is rooted and grounded in the fundamental instincts of humanity.   WOODROW WILSON

One hour of justice is worth a hundred of prayer.   ARAB PROVERB

All knowledge that is divorced from justice must be called cunning rather than wisdom.   PLATO

That amid our highest civilization men faint and die with want is not due to the niggardliness of nature, but to the justice of man.   HENRY GEORGE

See also: COMPASSION; CONSCIENCE; EQUALITY; IDEALS; LIBERTY; RACIAL JUSTICE; RELIGION.

Kindness

The ministry of kindness is a ministry which may be achieved by all men, rich and poor, learned and illiterate. Brilliance of mind and capacity for deep thinking have rendered great service to humanity, but by themselves they are impotent to dry a tear or mend a broken heart.   ANONYMOUS

A man takes contradiction and advice much more easily than people think, only he will not bear it when violently given, even though it is well founded. Hearts are flowers; they remain open to the softly falling dew, but shut up in the violent downpour of rain.   JEAN PAUL RICHTER

I expect to pass through this world but once. Any good thing, therefore, that I can do, or any kindness that I can show a fellow being, let me do it now. Let me not defer or neglect it, for I shall not pass this way again.
                    STEPHEN GRELLET

> The best portion of a good man's life,
> His little, nameless, unremembered acts of kindness
>   and of love.
>   WILLIAM WORDSWORTH

Not to aid one in distress is to kill him in your heart.   AFRICAN PROVERB

Jests that give pain are no jests.   CERVANTES

> Think that day lost to whose descending sun
> Views from thy hand no noble action done.
>   JACOB BOBART

Believe nothing against another, but on good· authority; nor report what may hurt another, unless it be a greater hurt to some other to conceal it.
                    WILLIAM PENN

To injure none by thought, word or deed, to give to others, and be kind to all —this is the constant duty of the good.   MAHABHARATA

He who sees a need and waits to be asked for help is as unkind as if he had refused it.   DANTE ALIGHIERI

When a Moslem visits a sick brother, he gathers the fruits of paradise from the time he leaves his home until he returns.   ISLAMIC SAYING

Life is short and we have not too much time for gladdening the hearts of those who are traveling the dark way with us. Oh, be swift to love! Make haste to be kind!   HENRI FREDERIC AMIEL

Whoever gives a small coin to a poor man has six blessings bestowed upon him, but he who speaks a kind word to him obtains eleven blessings.   THE TALMUD

An eye can threaten like a loaded and levelled gun, or can insult like hissing or kicking; or, in its altered mood, by beams of kindness, it can make the heart dance with joy.   RALPH WALDO EMERSON

See also: BLESSINGS; CHARACTER; CHRISTIANITY; COMPASSION; FRIENDSHIP; GIVING; GOODNESS; GRACE; JUDAISM; LOVE; SAINTLINESS; SELFLESSNESS.

Knowledge

My truth is as dark to thee as thy truth is dark to me until the Lord enlightens all our understanding.   JOHN SALTMARSH

A spirited mind never stops within itself; it is always aspiring and going beyond itself; it has impulses beyond its power of achievement. If it does not advance and press forward and stand at bay and clash, it is only half alive. Its pursuits are boundless; its food is wonder, the chase, and ambiguity.   MONTAIGNE

The preservation of the means of knowledge among the lowest ranks is of more importance to the public than all the property of all the rich men in the country.   JOHN ADAMS

All wish to know, but none want to pay the price.   JUVENAL

A mind enlightened is like heaven; a mind in darkness is like hell.

CHINESE PROVERB

Carelessness does more harm than a want of knowledge.

BENJAMIN FRANKLIN

The human mind is never stationary; when it is not progressive, it is necessarily retrograde. He who imagines at any period of his life, that he can advance no farther in moral or intellectual improvements, is as little acquainted with the extent of his own powers as the voyager was with that of the terrestrial globe, who supposed he had erected pillars at the end of the world, when he had only left a monument how much farther he might have proceeded.

CICERO

It seems to me, then, to rest with us, the college women of this generation, to see to it that the girls of the next generation are given favorable conditions for this higher kind of scholarly development. To advance the boundaries of human knowledge however little is to exercise our highest human faculty. There is no more altruistic satisfaction, no purer delight. I am convinced that we can do no more useful work than this—to make it possible for the few women of creative and constructive genius born in any generation to join the few men of genius of their generation in the service of their common cause.

M. CAREY THOMAS

It was remarked by the ancients that the Pentathlete, who divided his attention among several exercises, though he could not vie with a boxer in the use of a cestus, or with one who had confined his attention to running in the contest of the stadium, yet enjoyed far greater general vigor and health than either.

It is the same with the mind. The inferiority in technical skill is often more than compensated by the superiority in general intelligence.

This is peculiarly the case in politics. States have always been best governed by men who have taken a wide view of public affairs, and who have rather a general acquaintance with many sciences than a perfect mastery of one.

The union of the political and military departments in Greece contributed not a little to the splendor of its early history. After their separation more skillful generals appeared, but the breed of statesmen dwindled and they became almost extinct. Themistocles or Pericles would have been no match for Demosthenes in the assembly or Iphicrates in the field. But surely they were incomparably better fitted than either for the supreme direction of affairs.

THOMAS BABINGTON MACAULAY

It is in knowledge as in swimming; he who flounders and splashes on the surface, makes more noise, and attracts more attention than the pearl-diver who quietly dives in quest of treasures to the bottom.

WASHINGTON IRVING

If you have knowledge, let others light their candles at it.

MARGARET FULLER

See also: ACHIEVEMENT; ASPIRATION; BOOKS; EDUCATION; GENIUS; GOD; GRACE; MANKIND; MATURITY; SELF-KNOWLEDGE; TRUTH; WISDOM.

Liberty

Liberty is a word to conjure with, not to vex the ear in empty boastings; for liberty means justice, and justice is the natural law—the law of health and strength, of fraternity and cooperation. As the sun is the lord of life, as his beams support all growth, and call forth all the infinite diversities of being and beauty, so is liberty to mankind. It is not for an abstraction that in every age the witnesses of liberty have stood forth, and the martyrs of liberty suffered. We speak of liberty as one thing, and virtue, wealth, knowledge, national strength and national independence as other things. But of all these liberty is the source, the mother, the necessary condition. She is to virtue what light is to color; she is to wealth what sunshine is to grain; she is to knowledge what eyes are to sight; she is the genius of invention, the brawn of national strength, the spirit of national independence. . . . Where liberty sinks, there virtue fades, wealth diminishes, knowledge is forgotten, and empires once mighty in arms and art decline. Only in broken gleams and partial light has the sun of liberty yet beamed among men, but all progress hath she called forth. Shall we not trust her?　　　HENRY GEORGE

Many politicians of our time are in the habit of laying it down as a self-evident proposition, that no people ought to be free till they are fit to use their freedom. The maxim is worthy of the fool in the old story, who resolved not to go into the water till he had learned how to swim. If men are to wait

for liberty till they become wise and good in slavery, they may indeed wait
forever. THOMAS BABINGTON MACAULAY

Liberty is to democracy what air is to fire, an element without which it instantly expires. But it could not be less folly to abolish liberty, because it
nourishes factions than it would be to wish the annihilation of air . . . because it imparts to fire its destructive agency. JAMES MADISON

I doubt that I deserve the laurel wreath, for poetry has always been merely
an instrument with me, a sort of divine plaything. If you would honor me,
lay a sword rather than a wreath upon my coffin, for I was, above all else, a
soldier in the war for the liberation of mankind. HEINRICH HEINE

The only liberty that is valuable, is a liberty connected with order; that not
only exists with order and virtue, but which cannot exist at all without them.
It inheres in good and steady government, as in its substance and vital principle. EDMUND BURKE

In the past, personal and political liberty depended to a considerable extent
upon governmental inefficiency. The spirit of tyranny was always more
than willing; but its organization and material equipment were generally
weak. Progressive science and technology have changed all this completely.
ALDOUS HUXLEY

To live without let or hindrance would be life indeed, and so the spirit actually lives in its happier moments, in laughter or in quick thought. Yet there
is a snare in this vital anarchy. It is like the liberty to sign cheques without
possessing a bank account. You may write them for any amount; but it is
only when a precise deposit limits your liberty that you may write them to
any purpose. GEORGE SANTAYANA

The people are the only sure reliance for the preservation of our liberty. The
will of the people is the only legitimate foundation of any government, and
to protect its free expression should be our first object. THOMAS JEFFERSON

If liberty is to be saved, it will not be by the doubters, the men of science, or
the materialists; it will be by religious conviction, by the faith of individuals,
who believe that God wills man to be free but also pure.
SAMUEL TAYLOR COLERIDGE

Dictatorship involves costs which the American people will never pay: The cost of our spiritual values. The cost of the blessed right of being able to say what we please. The cost of freedom of religion. The cost of seeing our capital confiscated. The cost of being cast into a concentration camp. The cost of being afraid to walk down the street with the wrong neighbor. The cost of having our children brought up not as free and dignified human beings, but as pawns molded and enslaved by a machine.

If the avoidance of these costs means taxes on my income; if avoiding these costs means taxes on my estate at death, I would bear those taxes willingly as the price of my breathing and my children breathing the free air of a free country, as the price of a living and not a dead world.

FRANKLIN D. ROOSEVELT

Give me the liberty to know, to utter, and to argue freely according to conscience, above all liberties.   JOHN MILTON

To suppose that our civil and political liberties are secure because they are abstractly defined in written constitutions is to mistake the legal form for the living substance of freedom.   CARL BECKER

See also: BLESSINGS; BROTHERHOOD; DEMOCRACY; EQUALITY; FREE WILL; FREEDOM; IDEALS; JUSTICE; RACIAL JUSTICE; RELIGIOUS FREEDOM.

Life

There are nine requisites for contented living; health enough to make work a pleasure; wealth enough to support your needs; strength to battle with difficulties and overcome them; grace enough to confess your sins and forsake them; patience enough to toil until some good is accomplished; charity enough to see some good in your neighbor; love enough to move you to be useful and helpful to others; faith enough to make real the things of God; hope enough to remove all anxious fears concerning the future.

JOHANN WOLFGANG VON GOETHE

So live that you wouldn't be ashamed to sell the family parrot to the town gossip.   WILL ROGERS

Away with funeral music—set
The pipe to powerful lips—
The cup of life's for him that drinks
And not for him that sips.
ROBERT LOUIS STEVENSON

One cannot step twice in the same river, for fresh waters are forever flowing round us. HERACLITUS

The great victories of life are oftenest won in a quiet way, and not with alarms and trumpets. BENJAMIN N. CARDOZO

Go with mean people and you will think life is mean. Then read Plutarch, and the world is a proud place, with heroes and demigods standing around us, who will not let us sleep. RALPH WALDO EMERSON

Only a life lived for others is a life worth while. ALBERT EINSTEIN

That God can write straight with crooked lines does not entitle creatures to write crooked lines in the book of their lives. KARL RAHNER

Here in this poor, miserable, hampered, despicable Actual, wherein thou now standest, here or nowhere is thy Ideal; work it out therefrom, and working, believe, live, be free. O thou, that pinest in the imprisonment of the Actual, and criest bitterly to the gods for a kingdom wherein to rule and create, know this for a truth: the thing thou seekest is already here, "here or nowhere," couldst thou only see. THOMAS CARLYLE

We cannot control the evil tongues of others; but a good life enables us to disregard them. PUBLIUS VALERIUS CATO

I wish you the courage to be warm when the world would prefer that you be cool.
  I wish you success sufficient to your needs; I wish you failure to temper that success.
  I wish you joy in all your days; I wish you sadness so that you may better measure joy.
  I wish you gladness to overbalance grief.

I wish you humor and a twinkle in the eye.

I wish you glory and the strength to bear its burdens.

I wish you sunshine on your path and storms to season your journey.

I wish you peace—in the world in which you live and in the smallest corner of the heart where truth is kept.

I wish you faith—to help define your living and your life.

More I cannot wish you—except perhaps love—to make all the rest worthwhile.
ROBERT A. WARD

There are parts of a ship which taken by themselves would sink. The engine would sink. The propeller would sink. But when the parts of a ship are built together, they float. So with the events of my life. Some have been tragic. Some have been happy. But when they are built together, they form a craft that floats and is going someplace. And I am comforted.
RALPH W. SOCKMAN

To save one man's life is better than to build a seven-story pagoda.
CHINESE PROVERB

If you have known how to compose your life, you have accomplished a great deal more than the man who knows how to compose a book. Have you been able to take your stride? You have done more than the man who has taken cities and empires. The great and glorious masterpiece of man is to live to the point. All other things—to reign, to hoard, to build—are, at most, but inconsiderable props and appendages.
MONTAIGNE

Providence has given us hope and sleep, as a compensation for the many cares of life.
VOLTAIRE

Get your grammar right! Live in the active voice rather than in the passive, thinking more about what you do than about what happens to you. Live in the indicative mood rather than in the subjunctive, concerned with things as they are, rather than as they might be. Live in the present tense, facing the duty at hand without regret for the past or worry about the future.

Live in the first person, criticizing yourself, rather than finding fault with others. Live in the singular number, caring more for the approval of your own conscience than for the applause of the crowd. If you want a verb to conjugate you cannot do better than to take the verb to love.
WILLIAM DE WITT HYDE

The value of life is not the end of it, but the use we make of it.   MOLIÈRE

The art of living is more like that of wrestling than of dancing; the main thing is to stand firm and be ready for an unforeseen attack.

MARCUS AURELIUS

Life is action and passion. It is expected of a man that he share in the action and passion of his time under penalty of being judged not to have lived.

OLIVER WENDELL HOLMES, JR.

We come into this world crying while all around us are smiling. May we so live that we go out of this world while everybody around us is weeping.

PERSIAN PROVERB

Life, like a dome of many-coloured glass,
Stains the white radiance of eternity.
PERCY BYSSHE SHELLEY

But man is a frivolous and incongruous creature, and perhaps, like a chess player, loves the process of the game, not the end of it. And who knows (there is no saying with certainty), perhaps the only goal on earth to which mankind is striving lies in this incessant process of attaining, in other words, in life itself, and not in the thing to be attained, which must always be expressed as a formula, as positive as twice two makes four, and such positiveness is not life, gentlemen, but is the beginning of death.

FYODOR DOSTOYEVSKI

Instead of accepting the stale cult of death that the fascists have erected, as the proper crown for the servility and the brutality that are the pillars of their states, we must erect a cult of life; life in action, as the farmer and the mechanic know it; life in expression, as the artist knows it; life as the lover feels it and as the parent practices it; life as it is known to men of good will who meditate in the cloister, experiment in the laboratory, or plan intelligently in the factory or the government office.   LEWIS MUMFORD

According to an ancient Greek legend, a woman came down to the River Styx to be ferried across to the region of the departed spirits. Charon, the kindly ferryman, reminded her that it was her privilege to drink of the waters of Lethe, and thus forget the life she was leaving. Eagerly she said, "I will forget how I have suffered." "And," added Charon, "remember too that you will forget how you have rejoiced." The woman said, "I will forget my failures." The old ferryman added, "And also your victories." She continued, "I will forget how I have been hated." "And also how you have been loved," added Charon. Then she paused to consider the whole matter, and the end of the story is that she left the draught of Lethe untasted, preferring to retain the memory even of sorrow and failure rather than to give up the memory of life's loves and joys. RALPH W. SOCKMAN

Who can decide offhand which is absolutely better, to live or to understand life? We must do both alternately, and a man can no more limit himself to either than a pair of scissors can cut with a single one of its blades.

WILLIAM JAMES

See also: ASPIRATION; BEING; BIBLE, THE; DEATH; DESTINY; GOD; GRACE; HEROISM; MYSTERY; PERSPECTIVE; SELF-KNOWLEDGE; YOUTH.

Love

Love is the doorway through which the human soul passes from selfishness to service and from solitude to kinship with all mankind. ANONYMOUS

Love does not consist in gazing at each other but in looking together in the same direction. ANTOINE DE SAINT-EXUPÉRY

True humor springs not more from the head than from the heart; it is not contempt, its essence is love. THOMAS CARLYLE

> True love's the gift which God has given
> To man alone beneath the heaven:
> It is not fantasy's hot-fire,
> Whose wishes soon as granted fly.
>
> . . . .
>
> It is the secret sympathy,
> The silver link, the silken tie,
> Which heart to heart and mind to mind
> In body and in soul can bind.
>
> SIR WALTER SCOTT

Love is the crowning grace of humanity, the holiest right of the soul, the golden link which binds us to duty and truth, the redeeming principle that chiefly reconciles the heart of life, and is prophetic of eternal good.

PETRARCH

Ah, love, let us be true
To one another! for the world, which seems
To lie before us like a land of dreams,
So various, so beautiful, so new,
Hath really neither joy, nor love, nor light,
Nor certitude, nor peace, nor help for pain;
And we are here as on a darkling plain
Swept with confused alarms of struggle and flight,
Where ignorant armies clash by night.

MATTHEW ARNOLD

A palace without affection is a poor hovel, and the meanest hut with love in it is a palace for the soul. ROBERT G. INGERSOLL

A man who was entirely careless of spiritual things died and went to hell. He was much missed on earth by his old friends.

His business manager went down to the gates of hell to see if there were any chance of bringing him back. But, though he pleaded for the gates to be opened, the iron bars never yielded.

His cricket captain went also and besought Satan to let him out just for the remainder of the season. But there was no response.

His minister went also and argued, saying, "He was not altogether bad. Let him have another chance. Let him out just this once."

Many other friends of his went also and pleaded with Satan saying, "Let him out. Let him out. Let him out."

But when his mother came, she spake no word of his release. Quietly, and with a strange catch in her voice, she said to Satan, "Let me in."

Immediately the great doors swung open upon their hinges. For love goes down through the gates of hell and there redeems the damned.

ANONYMOUS

There is a comfort in the strength of love; t'will make a thing endurable which else would overset the brain, or break the heart.

WILLIAM WORDSWORTH

Though the place be small where love abides, ample is it above kingdoms; though it be a desert, through it runs the river of paradise, and there are the enchanted flowers. SUFI SAYING

Fathers and teachers, I ponder, "What is hell?" I maintain that it is the suffering of being unable to love. FYODOR DOSTOYEVSKI

Love is a great thing, yea, a great and thorough good; by itself it makes everything that is heavy light; and it bears evenly all that is uneven.

It carries a burden which is no burden; it will not be kept back by anything low and mean; it desires to be free from all worldly affections, and not to be entangled by any outward prosperity, or by any adversity subdued.

Love feels no burden, thinks nothing of trouble, attempts what is above its strength, pleads no excuse of imposssibility.

It is therefore able to undertake all things, and it completes many things, and warrants them to take effect, where he who does not love would faint and lie down.

Though weary, it is not tired; though pressed, it is not straitened; though alarmed, it is not confounded; but as a living flame it forces its way upward, and securely passes through all.

Love is active and sincere; courageous, patient, faithful, prudent, and manly. THOMAS À KEMPIS

Love is the only commodity that power cannot command and money cannot buy. ANONYMOUS

To renounce your individuality, to see with another's eyes, to hear with another's ears, to be two and yet but one, to so melt and mingle that you no longer know you are you or another, to constantly absorb and constantly radiate, to reduce earth, sea and sky and all that in them is to a single being so wholly that nothing whatever is withheld, to be prepared at any moment for sacrifice, to double your personality in bestowing it—that is love.

THEOPHILE GAUTIER

We have just enough religion to make us hate, but not enough to make us love one another. JONATHAN SWIFT

Let a man overcome anger by kindness, evil by good.
Victory breeds hatred, for the conquered is unhappy.
Never in the world does hatred cease by hatred; hatred ceases
    by love.

BUDDHA

Love is strong as death. Many waters cannot quench love, neither can the floods drown it; if a man would give all the substance of his house for love, it would be utterly scorned. THE BIBLE

Love, like the burning bush that Moses saw, is always burning and never consumed. JOHANNES TAULER

We can only be said to be alive in those moments when our hearts are conscious of our treasures; for our hearts are not strong enough to love every moment. THORNTON WILDER

> Ye tradeful merchants! that with weary toil,
> Do seek most precious things to make you gaine,
> And both the Indies of their treasures spoil;
> What needeth you to seek so far in vain?
> For lo! my love doth in herself contain
> All this world's riches that may far be found;
> If saphyrs, lo! her eyes be saphyrs plain;
> If rubies, lo! her lips be rubies sound;
> If pearls, her teeth be pearls, both pure and
>   round;
> If ivory, her forehead's ivory I ween;
> If gold, her locks are finest gold on ground;
> If silver, her fair hands are silver sheen;
> But that which fairest is, but few behold,
> Her mind, adorns with virtues manifold.
>
> EDMUND SPENSER

Those who love deeply never grow old. They may die of old age, but they die young. ANONYMOUS

Love does not dominate; it cultivates. JOHANN WOLFGANG VON GOETHE

The great tragedy of life is not that men perish, but that they cease to love. W. SOMERSET MAUGHAM

We like someone because. We love someone although. HENRI DE MONTHERLANT

Man

To the eye of Vulgar Logic, what is man? An omnivorous Biped that wears
Breeches.

To the eye of Pure Reason, what is he? A Soul, a Spirit, a divine Appari-
tion.

Round his mysterious Me, there lies, under all these woolrags, a Garment
of Flesh, contextured in the Loom of Heaven; whereby he is revealed to his
like, and dwells with them in Union and Division; and sees and fashions
for himself a Universe, with azure starry spaces, and long Thousands of
Years. Deep-hidden is he under that strange Garment; amid Sounds and
Colors and Forms, as it were, swathed in, and inextricably overshrouded.
Yet it is sky-woven, and worthy of a God.   THOMAS CARLYLE

What a piece of work is man! How noble in reason! How infinite in faculty!
In form and moving how express and admirable! In action, how like an angel! In apprehension how like a god! The beauty of the world! The paragon
of animals!   WILLIAM SHAKESPEARE

To feed men and not to love them is to treat them as if they were barnyard
cattle. To love them and not to respect them is to treat them as if they were
household pets.   MENCIUS

Whenever two people meet there are really six people present. There is each
man as he sees himself, each man as the other person sees him, and each
man as he really is.   WILLIAM JAMES

If man lives in slime—and there is slime always at the core of the soul—it is
nevertheless this briefly animated dust that beholds stars, writes sym-
phonies, and imagines God.   IRWIN EDMAN

Granted that man is only a more highly developed animal; that the ring-
tailed monkey is a distant relative who had gradually developed acrobatic
tendencies, and the hump-backed whale a far-off connection who in early
life took to the sea—granted that back of these he is kin to the vegetable, and

is still subject to the same laws as plants, fishes, birds, and beasts. Yet there is still this difference between man and other animals—he is the only animal whose desires increase as they are fed; the only animal that is never satisfied. The wants of every other living thing are uniform and fixed. The ox of today aspires to no more than did the ox when man first yoked him. The sea gull of the English Channel, who poises himself above the swift steamer, wants no better food or lodging than the gulls who circled round as the keels of Caesar's galleys first grated on a British beach. Of all that nature offers them, be it ever so abundant, all living things save man can take, and care for, only enough to supply wants which are definite and fixed.

HENRY GEORGE

What is man, that thou art mindful of him? And the son of man, that thou visitest him?

For thou hast made him a little lower than the angels, and hast crowned him with glory and honor.

Thou madest him to have dominion over the works of thy hands; thou hast put all things under his feet:

All sheep and oxen, yea, and the beasts of the field;

The fowl of the air, and the fish of the sea, and whatsoever passeth through the paths of the seas.

O Lord our Lord, how excellent is thy name in all the earth!

THE BIBLE

To live in the presence of great truths, to be dealing with eternal laws, to be led by permanent ideals—that is what keeps a man patient when the world ignores him, and calm and unspoiled when the world praises him.

FRANCIS GREENWOOD PEABODY

What a chimera, then, is man! What a novelty! What a monster, what a chaos, what a contradiction, what a prodigy! Judge of all things, feeble worm of the earth, depository of truth, a sink of uncertainty and error, the glory and the shame of the universe.   BLAISE PASCAL

How much lies in laughter; the cipher-key wherewith we decipher the whole man! Some men wear an everlasting barren simper; in the smile of others lies the cold glitter, as of ice; the fewest are able to laugh what can be called laughing, but only sniff and titter and sniggle from the throat outwards, or at least produce some whiffling, husky cachinnation, as if they were laughing through wool; of none such comes good. The man who cannot laugh is only fit for treasons, stratagems and spoils; but his own whole life is already a treason and a stratagem.   THOMAS CARLYLE

Like a wounded oyster, a man must mend his broken shell with pearl.

RALPH WALDO EMERSON

The most agreeable of all companions is a simple, frank man, without any high pretensions to an oppressive greatness; one who loves life, and understands the use of it; obliging, alike at all hours; above all, of a golden temper, and steadfast as an anchor. For such an one we gladly exchange the great genius, the most brilliant wit, the profoundest thinker.

GOTTHOLD EPHRAIM LESSING

> An honest man here lies at rest,
> The friend of man, the friend of truth,
> The friend of age, and guide of youth:
> Few hearts like his, with virtue warm'd,
> Few heads with knowledge so inform'd;
> If there's another world, he lives in bliss;
> If there is none, he made the best of this.
>
> ROBERT BURNS
> [From "Epitaph on a Friend"]

A man is known through his purse, pleasure and pique.   THE TALMUD

Every man regards his own life as the New Year's Eve of time.

JEAN PAUL RICHTER

The man who regards his own life and that of his fellow-creatures as meaningless, is not merely unfortunate, but almost disqualified for life.

ALBERT EINSTEIN

I decline to accept the end of man. It is easy enough to say that man is immortal simply because he will endure; that when the last ding-dong of doom has clanged and faded from the last worthless rock hanging tideless in the last red and dying evening, that even then there will still be one more sound: that of his puny inexhaustible voice, still talking.

I refuse to accept this. I believe that man will not merely endure: he will prevail. He is immortal, not because he alone among creatures has an inexhaustible voice, but because he has a soul, a spirit capable of compassion and sacrifice and endurance. The poet's, the writer's duty is to write about these things. It is his privilege to help man endure by lifting his heart, by reminding him of the courage and honor and hope and pride and compassion and pity and sacrifice which have been the glory of his past. The poet's voice need not merely be the record of man, it can be one of the props, the pillars to help him endure and prevail.   WILLIAM FAULKNER

That essence of man which is special to him can be directly known only in a living relation.   MARTIN BUBER

He that falls into sin is a man; that grieves at it may be a saint; that boasteth of it is a devil.   MARGARET FULLER

See also: ACHIEVEMENT; ADVERSITY; AFFLICTION; ASPIRATION; FEL-LOWSHIP; FRIENDSHIP; GOD; HUMANITY; MANKIND; MATURITY; PRIDE; WOMAN.

Mankind

All mankinde is of one Author, and is one volume; when one Man dies, one Chapter is not torne out of the booke, but translated into a better language; and every Chapter must be so translated; God emploies several translators; some peeces are translated by age, some by sicknesse, some by warre, some by justice; but God's hand is in every translation; and his hand shall binde up all our scattered leaves againe for that Librarie where every booke shall lie open to one another.   JOHN DONNE

Know then thyself, presume not God to scan;
The proper study of mankind is man.
Placed on this isthmus of a middle state,
A being darkly wise and rudely great:
With too much knowledge for the Sceptic side,
With too much weakness for the Stoic's pride,
He hangs between, in doubt to act or rest;
In doubt to deem himself a God or Beast;
In doubt his mind or body to prefer;
Born but to die, and reas'ning but to err.
                    ALEXANDER POPE

If men are so wicked (as we see them now) with religion, what would they be if without it?   BENJAMIN FRANKLIN

Common and vulgar people ascribe all ill that they feel, to others; people of little wisdom ascribe to themselves; people of much wisdom, to no one.

EPICTETUS

All men are ordinary men; the extraordinary men are those who know it.

GILBERT K. CHESTERTON

I have made a ceaseless effort not to ridicule, not to bewail, not to scorn human actions, but to understand them.   BARUCH SPINOZA

I will not grieve that men do not know me; I will grieve that I do not know men.   CONFUCIUS

I am a single cell in a body of three billion cells. The body is mankind. I glory in the individuality of self but my individuality does not separate me from my universal self—the oneness of man. . . .

I do not believe that humankind is an excrescence or a machine, or that the myriads of solar systems and galaxies in the universe lack order or sanction.

I may not embrace or command this universal order but I can be at one with it—for I am of it.   NORMAN COUSINS

A physician is not angry at the intemperance of a mad patient, nor does he take it ill to be railed at by a man in a fever. Just so should a wise man treat all mankind, as a physician treats a patient, and look upon them only as sick and extravagant.   SENECA

> Like the leaves in their generations, such is the
>   race of men.
> For the wind casts the leaves from their branches
>   to earthward, and again
> Others the budding greenwood each springtide brings
>   to birth,
> So do man's generations spring up and fade from
>   earth.
>
> HOMER

Great ideas, it has been said, come into the world as gently as doves. Perhaps then, if we listen attentively, we shall hear, amid the uproar of empires and nations, a faint flutter of wings, the gentle stirring of life and hope. Some will say that this hope lies in a nation; others, in a man. I believe rather that it is awakened, revived, nourished by millions of solitary individuals whose deeds and works every day negate frontiers and the crudest implications of history. As a result, there shines forth fleetingly the ever-threatened truth that each and every man, on the foundation of his own sufferings and joys, builds for all.   ALBERT CAMUS

Never be afraid to raise your voice for honesty and truth and compassion, against injustice and lying and greed. If you will do this, not as a class or classes, but as individuals, men and women, you will change the earth. In one generation all the Napoleons and Hitlers and Caesars and Mussolinis and Stalins and all the other tyrants who want power and aggrandizement, and the simple politicians and time-servers who themselves are merely baffled or ignorant or afraid, who have used, or are using, or hope to use, man's fear and greed for man's enslavement, will have vanished from the face of the earth.   WILLIAM FAULKNER

Civilization is a stream with banks. The stream is sometimes filled with blood from people killing, stealing, shouting and doing the things historians usually record, while on the banks, unnoticed, people build homes, make love, raise children, sing songs, write poetry and even whittle statues. The story of civilization is the story of what happened on the banks. Historians are pessimists because they ignore the banks for the river.   WILL DURANT

> *See also:* BEING; BROTHERHOOD; DEMOCRACY; FELLOWSHIP; HUMAN-
> ITY; INTERNATIONALISM; MAN; MATURITY; WOMAN.

Marriage

It is first in the eager love of mates that the tamest personal life quickens into a fierce ecstasy: an ecstasy whose ebbing and renewal, in the long process of marriage, is one of the perpetual miracles of life. All good things take time to develop; and marriage, the best gift to lovers, requires more time for its development and completion than any other good thing. Auguste Comte well said that a lifetime was not too long for two lovers to get acquainted in.

In time, the links multiply. In the birth of their child, the man and wife perhaps first face death together; and the woman's is the braver part; for she is the soldier of marriage, and man the civilian. In the care of their children, parents relive imaginatively their own youth, in the very act of deepening all their responsibilities as adults: honey from the body of the lion! The cares, the anxieties, the sacrifices, the tensions and tribulations of parenthood hold a couple together no less than their heady joy in each other's body, their tender feelings toward all the little insignificant things, the clear ring of a laugh, the unconscious lift of the head, or the sobriety of a reassuring hand. Marriage may hold many joys; but it is only in suffering that has been shared that the ultimate limits of love are reached and tested.

LEWIS MUMFORD

New York, Tuesday, April 12, 1832

This afternoon I enter into a matrimonial agreement with Mary Jane Robinson, a young person whose opinions on all important subjects, whose mode of thinking and feeling, coincide more intimately with my own than do those of any other individual with whom I am acquainted. . . . We have selected the simplest ceremony which the laws of this State recognize. . . . This ceremony involves not the necessity of making promises regarding that over which we have no control, the state of human affections in the distant future, nor of repeating forms which we deem offensive, inasmuch as they outrage the principles of human liberty and equality, by conferring rights and imposing duties unequally on the sexes. The ceremony consists of a simply written contract in which we agree to take each other as husband and wife according to the laws of the State of New York, our signatures being attested by those friends who are present.

Of the unjust rights which in virtue of this ceremony an iniquitous law tacitly gives me over the person and property of another, I cannot legally, but I can morally divest myself. And I hereby distinctly and emphatically declare that I consider myself, and earnestly desire to be considered by others, as utterly divested, now and during the rest of my life, of any such rights, the barbarous relics of a feudal, despotic system, soon destined, in the outward course of improvement, to be wholly swept away; and the existence of which is a tacit insult to the good sense and good feeling of this comparatively civilized age.

/S/ Robert Dale Owen

I concur in this sentiment.

/S/ Mary Jane Robinson   ROBERT DALE OWEN

Marriage resembles a pair of shears, so joined that they cannot be separated, often moving in opposite directions, yet always punishing anyone who comes between them.   SYDNEY SMITH

What is there in the vale of life
Half so delightful as a wife;

When friendship, love, and peace combine
To stamp the marriage-bond divine?
WILLIAM COWPER

God help the man who won't marry until he finds the perfect woman, and God help him still more if he finds her. BENJAMIN TILLETT

Affection can withstand very severe storms of vigor, but not a long polar frost of indifference. SIR WALTER SCOTT

Only so far as a man is happily married to himself, is he fit for married life to another, and for family life generally. NOVALIS

If a child of God marries a child of the devil, said child of God is sure to have some trouble with his father-in-law. ANONYMOUS

Caresses, expressions of one sort or another, are necessary to the life of the affections as leaves are to the life of a tree. If they are wholly restrained, love will die at the roots. NATHANIEL HAWTHORNE

What greater thing is there for two human souls than to feel that they are joined for life, to strengthen each other in all labor, to rest on each other in all sorrow, to minister to each other in all pain, to be one with each other in silent unspeakable memories at the moment of the last parting?
GEORGE ELIOT

Remember, that if thou marry for beauty, thou bindest thyself all thy life for that which perchance will neither last nor please thee one year; and when thou hast it, it will be to thee of no price at all; for the desire dieth when it is attained, and the affection perisheth when it is satisfied.
SIR WALTER RALEIGH

See also: BLESSINGS; FAMILY, THE; LOVE; MAN; WOMAN.

Maturity

Knowledge and timber shouldn't be much used till they are seasoned.
OLIVER WENDELL HOLMES, JR.

The young man who has not wept is a savage, and the old man who will not laugh is a fool.
GEORGE SANTAYANA

What you have inherited from your fathers you must earn for yourself before you can really call it yours.
JOHANN WOLFGANG VON GOETHE

I learned that assistance given to the weak makes the one who gives it strong; and that oppression of the unfortunate makes one weak.
BOOKER T. WASHINGTON

It is often easier to fight for principles than to live up to them.
ADLAI E. STEVENSON

It is dangerous to show man too clearly that he is on a level with the beasts without showing him his greatness, and it is also dangerous to show him too plainly his greatness without showing him his baseness. It is more dangerous still to leave him in ignorance of both. But it is very desirable that the one and the other should be placed before him.
BLAISE PASCAL

A mature religion will be free, knowing that growth can take place only where the human spirit is unshackled. . . .

A mature religion will be growing, constantly revising man's understanding of the universe, of himself, and of truth in the light of his growing knowledge. . . .

A mature religion will practice, not a passive tolerance with respect to its great sister faiths, but an active cooperation in good works and the appropriation and assimilation of all that is best in them into itself.

A mature religion will meet the needs of the whole man, emotional as well as intellectual, and give the feelings of the heart full scope and expression under the guidance of an alert and informed mind.

A mature religion will be concerned with society and its problems as much as with the individual, for the individual cannot be saved apart from his society but only within its context of struggle for righteousness, justice, brotherhood and peace.   DONALD SZANTHO HARRINGTON

People who fly into a rage always make a bad landing.   WILL ROGERS

The awareness of the ambiguity of one's highest achievements (as well as one's deepest failures) is a definite symptom of maturity.   PAUL TILLICH

Disciples do owe their masters only a temporary belief, and a suspension of their own judgment till they be fully instructed; and not an absolute resignation nor perpetual captivity.   SIR FRANCIS BACON

See also: AGE; BEING; CHARACTER; SELF-KNOWLEDGE; WISDOM.

Mystery

The most beautiful and most profound emotion we can experience is the sensation of the mystical. It is the dower of all true art and science. He to whom this emotion is a stranger, who can no longer pause to wonder and stand rapt in awe, is as good as dead; his eyes are closed. This insight into the mystery of life, coupled though it be with fear, also has given rise to religion. To know that what is impenetrable to us really exists, manifesting itself as the highest wisdom and the most radiant beauty which our dull faculties can comprehend only in their most primitive form—this knowledge, this feeling is at the center of true religiousness. In this sense, and in this sense only, I belong in the ranks of devoutly religious men.

ALBERT EINSTEIN

When I consider the short duration of my life, swallowed up in eternity, before and after, the little space which I fill, and even can see, engulfed in the infinite immensity of spaces which I know not and which do not know me, I am frightened, and am astonished at being here rather than there; for there is no reason why here rather than there, why now rather than then. Who has put me here? By whose order and direction have this place and time been allotted to me?   BLAISE PASCAL

The efficacy of religion lies precisely in that which is not rational, philosophic, nor external; its efficacy lies in the unforeseen, the miraculous, the extraordinary. Thus religion attracts more devotion in proportion as it demands more faith—that is to say, as it becomes more incredible to the profane mind. The philosopher aspires to explain away all mysteries, to dissolve them into light. It is mystery, on the other hand, which religious instinct demands and pursues; it is mystery which constitutes the essence of worship.

HENRI-FREDERIC AMIEL

Religion is the result of what man does with his ultimate wonder, with moments of awe, with the sense of mystery.   ABRAHAM J. HESCHEL

For My thoughts are not your thoughts,
Neither are your ways My ways, saith the Lord.
For as the heavens are higher than the earth,
So are My ways higher than your ways,
And My thoughts than your thoughts.
For as the rain cometh down, and the snow from heaven,
And returneth not thither,
But watereth the earth,
And maketh it bring forth and bud,
That it may give seed to the sower, and bread to the
        eater;
So shall My word be that goeth forth out of My mouth:
It shall not return unto Me void,
But it shall accomplish that which I please,
And it shall prosper in the thing whereto I sent it.

THE BIBLE

There are three things that only God knows: the beginning of things, the cause of things, and the end of things.   WELSH PROVERB

We are not driven from Behind, but lured from Before! Not pushed, but pulled! Magnetized from Beyond!   LLOYD C. DOUGLAS

Each interprets in his own way the music of heaven.   CHINESE PROVERB

Dreams have a poetic integrity and truth. . . . Wise and sometimes terrible hints shall in them be thrown to the man out of a quite unknown intelligence. . . . Why then should not symptoms, auguries, forebodings be, as one said, the moanings of the spirit?   RALPH WALDO EMERSON

What man, who thinks of the example of Jesus, can escape the mystery and the marvel of it, can resist its appeal? The great power of Christianity rests in that ethical and spiritual compulsion which that personality brought about. The Jewish position is as great and wondrous and appealing as is that radiant personality. That personality is not divine in any unique sense. We desire to emulate that high personality, but not to limit our emulation to and of that personality. The Jew recognizes, marvels at the radiance, the benignity of the personality of Jesus, the Nazarene Jew, but we do not class that personality by the side of God. God is One—unique, not humanly inimitable, but humanly attainable.   STEPHEN S. WISE

Let a man strive to purify his thoughts. What a man thinketh, that is he; this is the eternal mystery. Dwelling within his Self with thoughts serene, he will obtain imperishable happiness. Man becomes that of which he thinks.

                                                                    UPANISHADS

Faith and love are apt to be spasmodic in the best minds. Men live on the brink of mysteries and harmonies into which they never enter, and with their hand on the door latch they die outside.   RALPH WALDO EMERSON

The love of mystery is one of the chief achievements of the dominant religions of the western world. Those ancients who did not know Reality or God, for whom claims to know were really idolatry, nevertheless were capable of loving God and the glorious world made by Him—in all their manifold meanings and mystery. They could exult that the heavens declare the divine glory and the firmament displays the divine artistry. They could sing and dance about clouds and winds, sun and weather, even when these realities sometimes were hurtful to them. They could rejoice in that which they little knew and even less controlled. Their rejoicing had at its base a trust, a love, a hopefulness, which all the vagaries of experienced order and wildness could not destroy. The creatures of the sea and the tidal pools, the stars of the heavens, the horses, the cattle, and creeping things were not primarily objects of fear or disdain or things to be manipulated or else ignored. They were subject to man's dominion only under the law that they should be cherished and respected as part of a vast and holy symphony in which man too has many roles, some orderly, and some adventurously wild.

The greatest mystery of all is this: how is it that in spite of all men's fears, all their ingrown anxieties and hostilities, they may yet be cozened out of themselves, out of their preoccupation with security into the mood of praise? This is the primary gift of the grace of God. And in saying that, we say two things: we speak a meaning to which the evidences of mind and senses attest; and we speak a mystery toward which our spirits lean in hope.

                                                                    JOHN F. HAYWARD

The present life of man, O king, seems to me . . . like to the swift flight of a sparrow through the room wherein you sit at supper in winter. . . . Whilst the storms of rain and snow prevail abroad; the sparrow, I say, flying in at one door, and immediately out at another, whilst he is within, is safe from the wintry storm; but after a short space of fair weather, he immediately vanished out of your sight, into the dark winter from which he had emerged. So this life of man appears for a short space, but of what went before, or what is to follow, we are utterly ignorant.   THE VENERABLE BEDE

See also: ASPIRATION; BEAUTY; DEATH; DESTINY; DIVINE, THE; GOD; GRACE; IMMORTALITY; INSPIRATION; LOVE; NATURE; WONDER.

Nature

Let children walk with Nature, let them see the beautiful blendings and communions of death and life, their joyous inseparable unity, as taught in woods and meadows, . . . and they will learn that death is stingless indeed, and as beautiful as life.   JOHN MUIR

The day becomes more solemn and serene
    When noon is passed; there is a harmony
    In Autumn, and a lustre in its sky
 Which through the Summer is not heard or seen,
    As if it could not be, as if it had not been!
                    PERCY BYSSHE SHELLEY

Oh, when I am safe in my sylvan home,
    I tread on the pride of Greece and Rome;
And when I am stretched beneath the pines
    Where the evening star so holy shines,
I laugh at the lore and the pride of man,
    At the sophist schools and the learned clan;
For what are they all in their high conceit,
    When man in the bush with God may meet?
                    RALPH WALDO EMERSON

This Sequoia was a seedling in 271 B.C. Five hundred and sixteen years later, it was severely damaged by a forest fire. But Nature immediately set to work to repair the damage, and began to fold successive layers of living tissue over the gigantic scar left by the flames. This effort continued for more than a century, and by the year 350, the wounds had been completely healed. In later centuries two other fires damaged the tree badly. But when the tree was finally cut down, the scar left by the first of these fires had been completely obliterated, and the scar left by the second was in process of being covered. That last scar was a gigantic wound eighteen feet wide and thirty feet high, but had Nature been given a chance even that wound would have been entirely healed.   ANONYMOUS

[Inscription on Giant Sequoia
Tree in California]

Cement is not green yielding grass
   Nor do crows nest in brick
      To fly eerie across the sky in
          early morning. . . .
I see no liquid moon rise, no red sun. . . .
And these are things of home
In these my soul was cradled,
          succored, raised.
I see the wind in tossing lines
         of clothes,
The sunset glow in burnished window
         banks. . . .
And rain is music on the roof and eaves. . . .
But supremely—the people—
   from a lonely tower with a view
   one can feed one's soul in satiety.
Here, need knocks
    and asks
        and in the asking gives
   for God is not indeed
    in wind
      or rain
        or earthquake
but in the still small voice of
      someone's need.
         ELIZABETH STUART CALVERT

[Wife of a minister in
the East Harlem Parish in New York City]

As students of nature we are pantheists, as poets polytheists, as moral beings monotheists.   JOHANN WOLFGANG VON GOETHE

I wonder much at the boldness with which some persons endeavor to demonstrate to the unbelieving, the existence of God, from the works of nature. I would not so much wonder at this attempt, if they addressed themselves to the believing; for to them, who have a living faith in the heart, every thing that *is,* manifestly appears as the work of the God whom they adore. But it is very different with those in whom this living light is extinct and sought to be revived—those destitute of faith and grace, who, while searching with all their light, all they see in nature, which might lead them to the knowledge of God, yet find only obscurity and darkness. To say to such that they have only to behold the least of the things which surround them, and they will find God revealed therein, is at once a proof of this great and important truth; to point to the course of the moon or the planets, and profess thus to have accomplished its demonstration, is truly to afford them ground for believing that the evidences of our religion are very weak, and I am assured from reason and experience, that nothing is more fitted to inspire them with contempt of those evidences.   BLAISE PASCAL

There is a pleasure in the pathless woods,
There is a rapture on the lonely shore,
There is society where none intrudes
By the deep sea, and music in its roar:
I love not man the less but nature more
From these our interviews, in which I steal
From all I may be or have been before
To mingle with the universe and feel
What I can ne'er express, yet cannot all
    conceal.

GEORGE GORDON BYRON

See also: BEAUTY; BEING; BLESSINGS; LIFE; MYSTERY; WONDER.

Nonconformity

In this age, the mere example of nonconformity, the mere refusal to bend the knee to custom, is itself a service. Precisely because the tyranny of opinion is such as to make eccentricity a reproach, it is desirable, in order to break through that tyranny, that people should be eccentric. Eccentricity has always abounded when and where strength of character has abounded; and the amount of eccentricity in a society has generally been proportional to the amount of genius, mental vigor, and moral courage which it contained. That so few now dare to be eccentric marks the chief danger of the time.

JOHN STUART MILL

Public opinion is, in nine cases out of ten, public folly and impertinence. We are slaves to one another. We dare not take counsel of our consciences and affections, but needs suffer popular prejudices and customs to decide for us, and at their bidding are sacrificed love and friendship and all the best hopes of our lives. We do not ask, what is right and best for us, but what will the folks say of it? We have no individuality, no self-poised strength, no sense of freedom. We are conscious always of the gaze of the many-eyed tyrant. We propitiate Him with precious offerings, we burn incense perpetually to Moloch and pass through his fire the sacred first-born of our hearts. Can anythings be more pitiable than the sight of so many, who should be choosers and creators under God of their own spheres of utility and happiness, self-degraded into mere slaves of propriety and custom, their true natures undeveloped, their hearts cramped and shut up, each afraid of his neighbor, and his neighbors of him, living a life of unreality, deceiving and being deceived, and forever walking in a vain show?

JOHN GREENLEAF WHITTIER

A heretic in one generation would have been a saint if he had lived in another, and a heretic in one country would often be a hero in another.

RUFUS M. JONES

Wherever there is a creed there is a heretic round the corner or in his grave.

ALFRED NORTH WHITEHEAD

There is a time in every man's education when he arrives at the conviction that envy is ignorance, that imitation is suicide; that he must take himself for better or for worse as his portion; that though the wide universe is full of good, no kernel of nourishing corn can come to him but through his toil bestowed on that plot of ground which is given to him to till.

Whoso would be a man, must be a nonconformist. He who would gather immortal palms must not be hindered by the name of goodness, but must explore if it be goodness. Nothing is at last sacred but the integrity of your own mind.

A foolish consistency is the hobgoblin of little minds, adored by little statesmen and philosophers and divines. With consistency a great soul has simply nothing to do.   RALPH WALDO EMERSON

The only life worth living is the adventurous life. Of such a life the dominant characteristic is that it is unafraid. It is unafraid of what other people think. Like Columbus, it dares not only to assert a belief but to live it in the face of contrary opinion. It does not adapt either its pace or its objectives to the pace and objectives of its neighbors. It thinks its own thoughts, it reads its own books, it develops its own hobbies, and it is governed by its own conscience. The herd may graze where it pleases or stampede where it pleases, but he who lives the adventurous life will remain unafraid when he finds himself alone.   RAYMOND B. FOSDICK

The little mind who loves itself, will write and think with the vulgar; but the great mind will be bravely eccentric, and scorn the beaten road, from universal benevolence.   OLIVER GOLDSMITH

Fashion is a chain of the soul. It is a yoke laid by superiors on inferiors, through opinion. It disposes of our time, attention, powers. It puts the stamp of worth, dignity, happiness, on actions and conditions, and prevents us from judging for ourselves. Originating with those who are raised above natural wants, and in whom the spirit of self-sacrifice is lost in self-indulgence, it gives currency to factitious, selfish pursuits and enjoyments. Thus the mind is perverted, contracted, filled with false views, and grows mechanical, torpid, lifeless. A society is improved in proportion as individuals judge for themselves, and from their own experience and feeling, and not according to general opinion.   WILLIAM ELLERY CHANNING

See also: CHARACTER; COURAGE; DEDICATION; DEMOCRACY; DISSENT; DOUBT; EQUALITY; FREE WILL; IDEALS; INTEGRITY; LIBERTY; TRUTH.

Patience

We have need of patience with ourselves and with others; with those below and those above us, and with our own equals; with those who love and those who love us not; for the greatest things and for the least; against sudden inroads of trouble, and under our daily burdens; for disappointments as to the weather, or the breaking of the heart; in the weariness of the body, or the wearing of the soul; in our own failure of duty, or others' failure toward us; in everyday wants, or in the aching of sickness or the decay of age; in disappointment, bereavement, losses, injuries, reproaches; in heaviness of the heart or in sickness amid delayed hopes. In all these things, from childhood's little troubles to the martyr's sufferings, patience is the grace of God, whereby we endure evil for the love of God.   EDWARD B. PUSEY

The two powers which in my opinion constitute a wise man are those of bearing and forbearing.   EPICTETUS

It is not necessary for all men to be great in action. The greatest and sublimest power is often simple patience.   HORACE BUSHNELL

As a fresh wound shrinks from the hands of the surgeon, then gradually submits to and even calls for it; so, a mind under the first impression of a misfortune shuns and rejects all comfort, but at length, if touched with tenderness, calmly and willingly resigns itself.   PLINY THE YOUNGER

No school is more necessary to children than patience, because either the will must be broken in childhood or the heart in old age.
                                                      JEAN PAUL RICHTER

A young king said to a holy man: "In adversity I become half-hearted about myself and behave weakly. On the other hand, when I have a success, I am so filled with self-confidence that I become careless and make silly mistakes. Write me a book which will cure me of these faults and I will read it every day."

The holy man answered: "There is no need for a book. Give me that ring you are wearing and I will scratch on it three words which will comfort you at a time of adversity and temper you at a time of success." He scratched on the metal: "IT WILL PASS."   ANONYMOUS

How poor are they who have not patience! What wound did ever heal but by degrees?   WILLIAM SHAKESPEARE

The devil loves nothing better than the intolerance of reformers, and dreads nothing so much as their charity and patience.   JAMES RUSSELL LOWELL

Patience is power; with time and patience the mulberry leaf becomes silk.

CHINESE PROVERB

See also: ADVERSITY; AFFLICTION; AGE; BIBLE, THE; CHARACTER; CHEERFULNESS; COURAGE; DEDICATION; EXAMPLE; GRACE; MATURITY; YOUTH.

Patriotism

We will never bring disgrace to this, our nation, by any act of dishonesty or cowardice, nor ever desert our suffering comrades in the ranks.

We will fight for the ideals of the nation both alone and with others.

We will revere and respect our nation's laws, and do our best to incite a like respect and reverence in those above us who are prone to annul and set them at naught.

We will strive unceasingly to quicken the public's sense of civic duty.

Thus in all these ways we will transmit this nation not only not less but greater, better, and more beautiful than it was transmitted to us.

THE ATHENIAN OATH

Patriotism consists not in waving the flag, but in striving that our country shall be righteous as well as strong.   JAMES BRYCE

When an American says he loves his country, he means not only that he loves the New England hills, the prairies glistening in the sun, or the wide rising plains, the mountains, and the seas. He means that he loves an inner air, an inner light in which freedom lives and in which a man can draw the breath of self-respect.   ADLAI E. STEVENSON

If patriotism be a virtue indeed, it cannot mean an exclusive devotion to our country's interests, for that is only another form of devotion to personal interests, family interests, or provincial interests, all of which, if not driven past themselves, are vulgar and immoral objects. . . . I confess that I dream of a day when an English statesman shall arise with a heart too large for England; having courage in the face of his countrymen to assert of some suggested policy: "This is good for your trade; this is necessary for your domination; but it will vex a people hard by; it will hurt a people farther off; it will profit nothing to the general humanity; therefore, away with it! It is not for you or for me." When a British minister dares speak so, and when a British public applauds him speaking, then shall the nation be glorious, and her praise, instead of exploding from within, from loud civic mouths, come to her from without, as all worthy praise must, from the alliances she has fostered and the populations she has saved.

ELIZABETH BARRETT BROWNING

Lives of nations are determined, not by the count of years, but by the life-time of the human spirit. The life-time of man is three-score years and ten; a little more, a little less. The life of a nation is the fullness of the measure of its will to life. A nation, like a person, has a body—a body that must be fed and clothed and housed, invigorated and rested, in a manner that measures up to the standards of our time. A nation, like a person, has a mind—a mind that must be kept informed and alert, that must know itself, that understands the hopes and needs of its neighbors—all the other nations that live within the narrowing circle of the world. A nation, like a person, has something deeper, something more permanent, something larger than the sum of all its parts. It is that something which matters most to the future, which calls for the most sacred guarding of its present.

FRANKLIN D. ROOSEVELT

Let this nation ever remember that a people shall be saved by the power that sleeps in its own deep bosom, or by none; shall be renewed in hope, in conscience, in strength, by waters welling up from its own sweet, peren-nial springs. It shall not be saved from above, by patronage of its aristocrats; for the flower does not bear the root, but the root the flower. What some call the radicalism of our times is simply the effort of nature to release the generous energies of our people. Our people are at bottom just, virtuous, and hopeful; the roots of its being are in the soil of what is lovely, pure, and of good report. We therefore need have no fear of a radicalism that is designed to clear a way for the realization of the aspirations of a sturdy people, for that nation is best served which affords to all its citizens the amplest opportunity to give the best of themselves to its service.

WOODROW WILSON

Standing as I do, in view of God and Eternity, I realize that patriotism is not enough. I must have no hatred or bitterness for anyone.   EDITH CAVELL

Our country right or wrong. When right to be kept right. When wrong to be put right.   CARL SCHURZ

I do love
My country's good with a respect more tender,
More holy and profound, than my own life.
                              WILLIAM SHAKESPEARE

My country is the world, and my religion is to do good.   THOMAS PAINE

If patriotism is "the last refuge of a scoundrel," it is not merely because evil deeds may be performed in the *name* of patriotism, . . . but because patriotic fervor can obliterate moral distinctions altogether.   RALPH BARTON PERRY

These gentry are invariably saying all they can in dispraise of their native land; and it is my opinion, grounded upon experience, that an individual who is capable of such baseness would not hesitate at the perpetration of any villainy, for next to the love of God, the love of country is the best preventive of crime.   GEORGE BORROW

See also: AMERICA; COURAGE; DEDICATION; IDEALS; INSPIRATION; INTEGRITY; INTERNATIONALISM; JUSTICE; LIBERTY; WAR.

Peace

Only a peace between equals can last; only a peace the very principle of which is equality and a common participation in a common benefit. . . .
    The right state of mind, the right feeling between nations, is as necessary for a lasting peace as is the just settlement of questions of territory, or of racial and national allegiance.
    No peace can last, or ought to last, which does not recognize and accept the principle that governments derive all their just powers from the consent of the governed;
    And that no right anywhere exists to hand people about from sovereignty to sovereignty, as if they were property.
    The world can be at peace only if its life is stable; and there can be no stability where there is not tranquillity of spirit and a sense of justice, of freedom and of right.   WOODROW WILSON

The grim fact is that we prepare for war like precocious giants and for peace like retarded pygmies.   LESTER B. PEARSON

Today [April 13, 1945] as we move against the terrible scourge of war—as we go forward toward the greatest contribution that any generation of human beings can make in this world—the contribution of lasting peace, I ask you to keep up your faith. I measure the sound, solid achievement that can be made at this time by the straight-edge of your own confidence and your resolve. And to you, and to all Americans who dedicate themselves with us to the making of an abiding peace, I say:

The only limit to our realization of tomorrow will be our doubts of today. Let us move forward with strong and active faith.

FRANKLIN D. ROOSEVELT
[Written on the day of his death]

Our objective is not the incitement of others to violence. Our objective is not to rectify the boundaries and correct the unnatural divisions that afflict the world by force, but by the peaceful processes. Our objective is a peace consistent with decency and justice. And our prayer is that history will not say that we led a noble but a lost cause. ADLAI STEVENSON

Peace, justice and well-being are dreams as old as humanity itself. But never before in history have they been so closely within reach and so universally in demand. We must confront the unjustified pessimism of our time and the disbeliefs of so many with the vision of our hope and the courage of our will. U THANT

Five great enemies to peace inhabit with us: viz., avarice, ambition, envy, anger, and pride. If those enemies were to be banished, we should infallibly enjoy perpetual peace. PETRARCH

Wars begin in the minds of men; it is in the minds of men, therefore, that the defenses of peace must be constructed; throughout the history of mankind, ignorance of each other's ways and lives has been a common cause of that suspicion and mistrust between the peoples of the world through which their differences have all too often broken into war.

The great and terrible world wars of our times were made possible by the denial of the democratic principles of the dignity, equality, and mutual respect of men, and by the propagation, in their place, through ignorance and prejudice, of the doctrine of the inequality of men and races.

The wide diffusion of culture, and the education of humanity for justice and liberty and peace are indispensable to the dignity of man. They constitute a sacred duty which all the nations must fulfill in a spirit of mutual assistance and concern. A peace based exclusively upon the political and economic arrangements would not be able to secure the unanimous, lasting, and sincere support of the peoples of the world. To secure such support, the peace must be founded upon the intellectual and moral solidarity of mankind.

To this end, full and equal opportunities for education must be made available to all. There must be no restriction to the pursuit of objective truth. The free exchange of ideas and knowledge among people should be facilitated and all means employed for the purposes of mutual understanding and a truer and more perfect knowledge of each other's lives.

FROM UNESCO CONSTITUTION

He shall judge among many people, and rebuke strong nations afar off: and they shall beat their swords into plowshares, and their spears into pruning-hooks: nation shall not lift up a sword against nation, neither shall they learn war any more. But they shall sit every man under his vine and under his fig tree; and none shall make them afraid; for the mouth of the Lord of hosts hath spoken it.   THE BIBLE

See also: BIBLE, THE; BROTHERHOOD; CHRISTIANITY; FAITH; FELLOW-SHIP; FREEDOM; GOD; INTERNATIONALISM; LIFE; MANKIND; PEACE OF MIND; WAR.

Peace of Mind

To get peace, if you want it, make for yourselves nests of pleasant thoughts. None of us yet know, for none of us have been taught in early youth, what fairy palaces we may build of beautiful thoughts—proof against all adversity. Bright fancies, satisfied memories, noble histories, faithful sayings, treasure houses of precious and restful thoughts which care cannot disturb, nor pain make gloomy, nor poverty take away from us—houses built without hands, for our soul to live in.   JOHN RUSKIN

So long as a man quarrels and disputes about doctrines and dogmas, he has not tasted the nectar of true faith; when he has tasted it, he becomes quiet and full of peace.   RAMAKRISHNA

"Peace of mind" is no absolute good. It is quite possible to have too much of it. One can have so much peace of mind that he is utterly complacent, ceases to grow, fails to take warning at signals of real danger in his personal and social life, stops keeping his life a daring, creative adventure, retreats from a dynamic responsibility for understanding and guiding social change into a rotund respectability in support of the status quo. . . .

Peace of mind, like happiness, is not a direct goal, to be sought and cultivated in and of and for itself alone. It is rather a natural by-product of happy and harmonious living, your silent comrade when you are living fully, nobly and conscientiously in the world. . . . Peace of mind is not ease or comfort or retreat, for it follows high challenge and strenuous effort in the battle of life.

DONALD SZANTHO HARRINGTON

Great tranquillity of heart is his who cares for neither praise nor blame.

THOMAS À KEMPIS

Peace doth not dwell in outward things, but within the soul; we may preserve it in the midst of the bitterest pain, if our will remain firm and submissive. Peace in this life springs from acquiescence, not in an exemption from suffering.

FRANÇOIS FÉNELON

Be not hasty in thy spirit to be angry; for anger resteth in the bosom of fools.

THE BIBLE

Thou shalt transcend inner anxiety, recognizing thy true competence and courage. Thou shalt stand undismayed in the presence of grief. Thou shalt not deny the sadness of thy heart. Thou shalt make no detour around sorrow, but shall live through it, and by the aid of human togetherness and comradely sympathy thou shalt win dominion over sorrow.

Thou shalt eternally respect truth and tell it with kindness and also with firmness to all of thy associates, to the young child as well as to thy brother, and through truth shalt thou find healing and salvation.

Thou shalt search thy heart for the traces of immaturity and the temptations of childishness. Thou shalt reject all flight from freedom, all escape from maturity, as unworthy of thy person. Thou shalt turn away from all supine reliance upon authority, all solacing slavery to an omnipotent social father. Thou shalt seek together with thy brothers a kingdom of mature equality.

Thou shalt uproot from thy heart the false doubts and childish petulance which keep thee far from God. Thou shalt not make Him the scapegoat for thy emotional wounds and thy psychic scars. Thou shalt free thyself of the distortions which block thy way to His presence, and by that freedom thou shalt commune at last with Him, the source of truth, the giver of peace.

JOSHUA LOTH LIEBMAN

To live content with small means, to seek elegance rather than luxury, and refinement rather than fashion; to be worthy, not respectable; and wealthy, not rich; to study hard, think quietly, talk gently, act frankly; to listen to stars and birds, babes and sages, with open heart; to bear all cheerfully, do all bravely, await occasions, hurry never; in a word, to let the spiritual, unbidden and unconscious, grow up through the common. This is to be my symphony.   WILLIAM ELLERY CHANNING

Better is a handful with quietness, than both of the hands full with travail and vexation of spirit.   THE BIBLE

See also: ASPIRATION; BLESSINGS; DIVINE, THE; FAITH; GOD; GRACE; LOVE; MATURITY; PATIENCE; PERSPECTIVE; PRAYER; WORRY.

Perseverance

Unity of aim, aided by ordinary vigor of character, will generally insure perseverance, a quality not ranked among the cardinal virtues, but as essential as any of them to the proper conduct of life. Nine-tenths of the miseries and vices of mankind proceed from idleness, with men of quick minds, to whom it is especially pernicious. This habit is commonly the fruit of many disappointments, and schemes oft baffled; and men fail in their schemes, not so much from the want of strength, as the ill direction of it. The weakest living creature, by concentrating his powers on a single object, can accomplish something: the strongest, by dispersing his over many, may fail to accomplish anything. The drop, by continual falling, bores its passage through the hardest rock; the hasty torrent rushes over it with hideous uproar and leaves no trace behind.   THOMAS CARLYLE

It is not the leap at the start but the steady going on that gets there.
          JOHN WANAMAKER

Many are stubborn in pursuit of the path they have chosen, few in pursuit of the goal.   FRIEDRICH NIETZSCHE

All the performances of human art, at which we look with praise and wonder, are instances of the resistless force of perseverance.   BEN JONSON

To persevere is one's duty and to be silent is the best answer to calumny.

GEORGE WASHINGTON

Live from day to day, even from hour to hour; perseverance is one of the crowning graces of God.   BARON FRIEDRICH VON HÜGEL

When nothing seems to help, I go and look at a stonecutter hammering away at his rock perhaps a hundred times without as much as a crack showing in it. Yet at the hundred and first blow it will split in two, and I know it was not that blow that did it—but all that had gone before.   JACOB RIIS

Be always displeased with what thou art, if thou desirest to attain to what thou art not; for where thou hast pleased thyself, there thou abidest. But if thou sayest I have enough, thou perishest. Always add, always walk, always proceed. Neither stand still, nor go back, nor deviate.   SAINT AUGUSTINE

> *Lincoln's road to the White House:*
> Failed in business in 1831.
> Defeated for Legislature in 1832.
> Second failure in business in 1833.
> Suffered nervous breakdown in 1836.
> Defeated for Speaker in 1838.
> Defeated for Elector in 1840.
> Defeated for Congress in 1843.
> Defeated for Congress in 1848.
> Defeated for Senate in 1855.
> Defeated for Vice President in 1856.
> Defeated for Senate in 1858.
> Elected President in 1860.
>
> ANONYMOUS

There are but two roads that lead to an important goal and to the doing of great things: strength and perseverance. Strength is the lot of but a few privileged men; but austere perseverance, harsh and continuous, may be employed by the smallest of us and rarely fails of its purpose, for its silent power grows irresistibly greater with time.   JOHANN WOLFGANG VON GOETHE

See also: ACHIEVEMENT; AMBITION; ASPIRATION; CHARACTER; COURAGE; DEDICATION; PATIENCE; PERSPECTIVE; RELIGION; SELF-CONTROL; SELF-KNOWLEDGE; WORK.

Perspective

The illusion that times that were are better than those that are, has probably pervaded all ages.   HORACE GREELEY

All those things which are now held to be of the greatest antiquity, were at one time new; and what we today hold up by example, will rank hereafter as a precedent.   TACITUS

We are like dwarfs seated on the shoulders of giants. We see more things than the ancients and things more distant, but this is due neither to the sharpness of our own sight, nor to the greatness of our own stature, but because we are raised and borne aloft on that giant mass.

                              SAINT BERNARD OF CLAIRVAUX

Every man of us has all the centuries in him.   JOHN MORLEY

Talking is like playing on the harp; there is as much in laying the hands on the strings to stop their vibration as in the twanging them to bring out their music.   OLIVER WENDELL HOLMES, SR.

   To every thing there is a season, and a time to every purpose under the heaven:
   A time to be born, and a time to die; a time to plant, and a time to pluck up that which is planted;
   A time to kill, and a time to heal; a time to break down, and a time to build up;
   A time to weep, and a time to laugh; a time to mourn, and a time to dance;
   A time to cast away stones, and a time to gather stones together; a time to embrace, and a time to refrain from embracing;
   A time to get, and a time to lose; a time to keep, and a time to cast away;
   A time to rend, and a time to sew; a time to keep silence, and a time to speak;
   A time to love, and a time to hate; a time of war, and a time of peace.
   What profit hath he that worketh in that wherein he laboreth?
   I have seen the travail, which God hath given to the sons of men to be exercised in it.

He hath made every thing beautiful in His time: also He hath set the world in their heart, so that no man can find out the work that God maketh from the beginning to the end. THE BIBLE

There is one mind common to all individuals. Of the works of this mind history is the record. There is a relation between the hours of our life and the centuries of time.

We, as we read, must become Greeks, Romans, Turks, priest and king, martyr and executioner, must fasten these images to some reality in our secret experience, or we shall see nothing, learn nothing, keep nothing.

We must attain and maintain that lofty sight where facts yield their secret sense, and poetry and annals are alike. Time dissipates to shining ether the solid angularity of facts.

Every history should be written with a wisdom which divined the range of our affinities, and looked at facts as symbols. RALPH WALDO EMERSON

Some there are that torment themselves afresh with the memory of what is past; others, again, afflict themselves with the apprehension of evils to come; and very ridiculously both—for the one does not now concern us, and the other not yet. SENECA

Teach us that wealth is not elegance, that profusion is not magnificence, that splendor is not beauty. BENJAMIN DISRAELI

In the scale of the destinies, brawn will never weigh so much as brain. JAMES RUSSELL LOWELL

The past lives in us, not we in the past. DAVID BEN-GURION

I do not see any way of realizing our hopes about world organization in five or six days. Even the Almighty took seven. WINSTON S. CHURCHILL

Only by acceptance of the past, can you alter it. T. S. ELIOT

Better beans and bacon in peace than cakes and ale in fear. AESOP

The bow that's always bent will quickly break;
But if unstrung will serve you at your need.

So let the mind some relaxation take
To come back to its task with fresher heed.
PHAEDRUS

Do not anxiously hope for that which is not yet come; do not vainly regret what is already past. CHINESE PROVERB

See also: DIVINE, THE; MATURITY; SELF-KNOWLEDGE; VISION; WISDOM.

Prayer

Between the humble and the contrite heart and the majesty of heaven there are no barriers; the only password is prayer. HOSEA BALLOU

Keep me, O Lord, from all pettiness. Let me be large in thought and word and deed.

Let me leave off self-seeking and have done with fault-finding.

Help me put away all pretense, that I may meet my neighbor face to face, without self-pity and without prejudice.

May I never be hasty in my judgments, but generous to all and in all things.

Make me grow calm, serene, and gentle.

Teach me to put into action my better impulses and make me straightforward and unafraid.

Grant that I may realize that it is the trifling things of life that create differences, that in the higher things we are all one.

And, O Lord, God, let me not forget to be kind! MARY STUART

Pray not for lighter burdens but for stronger backs. THEODORE ROOSEVELT

More things are wrought by prayer
Than this world dreams of.
ALFRED, LORD TENNYSON

Strengthen me, O God, by the grace of Thy Holy Spirit; grant me to be strengthened with might in the inner man and put away from my heart all useless anxiety and distress.

Grant me, O Lord, heavenly wisdom, that I may learn to seek Thee above all things, and to understand all other things as they are, according to the order of Thy wisdom.

Grant me prudently to avoid the one who flatters me and patiently to bear with the one who contradicts me, for it is a mark of great wisdom not to be moved by every wind of words or to give ear to the wicked flattery of the siren. THOMAS À KEMPIS

There are few men who dare publish to the world the prayers they make to Almighty God. MONTAIGNE

O Lord, support us all the day long, until the shadows lengthen and the evening comes, and the busy world is hushed, and the fever of life is over, and our work is done. Then in Thy mercy grant us a safe lodging, and a holy rest, and peace at the last. JOHN HENRY NEWMAN

Prayer is the contemplation of the facts of life from the highest point of view. RALPH WALDO EMERSON

Prayer should be the key of the day and the lock of the night. GEORGE HERBERT

Prayer is our attachment to the utmost. Prayer takes the mind out of the narrowness of self-interest, and enables us to see the world in the mirror of the holy. Prayer clarifies our hope and intentions. It helps us discover our true aspirations, the pangs we ignore, the longings we forget. It is an act of self-purification, a quarantine for the soul. ABRAHAM JOSHUA HESCHEL

Give us strength to encounter that which is to come, that we may be brave in peril, constant in tribulation; grant us courage to endure lesser ills unshaken, and to accept death, loss and disappointment as if they were mere straws upon the tide of life. . . . May grace of courage, gaiety, and the quiet mind be ours. . . . As the clay to the potter, as the windmill to the wind, as children to their sire, we beseech of Thee this help and mercy. ROBERT LOUIS STEVENSON

I asked God for strength, that I might achieve,
I was made weak, that I might learn humbly to obey . . .

I asked for health, that I might do greater things,
I was given infirmity, that I might do better things . . .
I asked for riches, that I might be happy,
I was given poverty that I might be wise . . .
I asked for power, that I might have the praise of men,
I was given weakness, that I might feel the need of God . . .
I asked for all things, that I might enjoy life,
I was given life, that I might enjoy all things . . .
I got nothing that I asked for—but everything that I
  had hoped for.
Almost despite myself, my unspoiled prayers were answered.
I am among all men, most richly blessed.
     PRAYER OF AN UNKNOWN CONFEDERATE SOLDIER

Trouble and perplexity drive us to prayer, and prayer driveth away trouble
and perplexity.   PHILIPP MELANCHTHON

A prayer in its simplest definition is merely a wish turned Godward.
            PHILLIPS BROOKS

Sir Walter Scott records in his *Diary* that in the year 1827 he visited the
Greater and the Lesser Cumbraes, two very small islands in the Firth of
Clyde on the west coast of Scotland. On Sunday he went to the little church.
He does not record, I think, anything of the minister's sermon, but he has
preserved a sentence from his prayer: "O Lord, in thy grace and favor look
upon the people of the Greater and Lesser Cumbraes, and in thy mercy do
not forget the inhabitants of the adjacent islands of Great Britain and Ire-
land."   ROBERT J. MCCRACKEN

What men usually ask of God when they pray is that two and two not make
four.   ANONYMOUS

The day returns and brings us the petty rounds of irritating concerns and
duties. Help us to play the man, help us to perform them with laughter and
kind faces, let cheerfulness abound with industry. Give us to go blithely on
our business all the day, bring us to our resting beds weary and content and
undishonored, and grant us in the end the gift of sleep. Amen.
         ROBERT LOUIS STEVENSON

We hear in these days of scientific enlightenment a great deal of discussion about the efficacy of prayer and many reasons are given us why we should not pray, whilst others are given why we should. But in all this very little is said of the reason why we do pray. . . . The reason why we do pray is simply that we cannot help praying.   WILLIAM JAMES

Up from the world of the many
To the Over world of the One
Back to the world of the many
To fulfill the life of the One.
                    VON OGDEN VOGT

Call on God, but row away from the rocks.   INDIAN PROVERB

Any gift made in the spirit of service to mankind is indeed a prayer.
                                                                            LAO-TSE

In prayer it is better to have a heart without words, than words without a heart.   JOHN BUNYAN

Do not pray for easy lives; pray to be stronger men. Do not pray for tasks equal to your powers; pray for powers equal to your tasks. Then the doing of your work shall be no miracle, but you shall be a miracle.
                                                                    PHILLIPS BROOKS

Lord, I am no hero, I have been careless, cowardly, sometimes all but mutinous. Punishment I have deserved, I deny it not.

But a traitor I have never been; a deserter I have never been. I have tried to fight on Thy side in Thy battle against evil.

I have tried to do the duty which lay nearest me; and to leave whatever Thou didst commit to my charge a little better than I found it.

I have not been good, but at least I have tried to be good. Take the will for the deed, good Lord.   CHARLES KINGSLEY

See also: ASPIRATION; BELIEF; DIVINE, THE; GOD; GRACE; INSPIRA-
TION; MYSTERY; RELIGION; REVERENCE; SOLITUDE; WONDER; WOR-
SHIP.

Prejudice

Prejudice is a mist, which in our journey through the world often dims the brightest and obscures the best of all the good and glorious objects that meet us on our way.   LORD SHAFTESBURY

Every one is forward to complain of the prejudices that mislead other men and parties, as if he were free, and had none of his own. What now is the cure? No other but this, that every man should let alone others' prejudices and examine his own.   JOHN LOCKE

Ignorance is less remote from the truth than prejudice.   DIDEROT

Never try to reason the prejudice out of a man. It was not reasoned into him, and cannot be reasoned out.   SYDNEY SMITH

The man who never alters his opinion is like standing water, and breeds reptiles of the mind.   WILLIAM BLAKE

It is a solemn truth, not yet understood as it should be, that the worst institutions may be sustained, the worst deeds performed, the most merciless cruelties inflicted, by the conscientious and good.

Few names in history are more illustrious than Isabella of Castille. She was the model, in most respects, of a noble woman. But Isabella outstripped her age in what she thought pious zeal against heretics. Having taken lessons in her wars against the Moors, and in the extermination of the Jews, she entered fully into the spirit of the Inquisition; and by her great moral power contributed more than any other sovereign to the extension of its fearful influence; and thus the horrible tortures and murders of that infernal institution, in her ill-fated country, lie very much at her door. Of all the causes which have contributed to the ruin of Spain, the gloomy, unrelenting spirit of religious bigotry has wrought most deeply; so that the illustrious Isabella, through her zeal for religion and the salvation of her subjects, sowed the seeds of her country's ruin.   WILLIAM ELLERY CHANNING

There is no more evil thing in this present world than race prejudice, none at all! I write deliberately—it is the worst single thing in life now. It justifies and holds together more obscene cruelty and abomination than any other sort of error in the world.   H. G. WELLS

He who begins by loving Chrisitanity better than truth will proceed by loving his own sect or church better than Christianity and end in loving himself better than all.   SAMUEL TAYLOR COLERIDGE

Instead of casting away our old prejudices, we cherish them to a very considerable degree, and, more shame to ourselves, we cherish them because they are prejudices; and the longer they have lasted the more we cherish them. We are afraid to put men to live and trade each on his own private stock of reason, because we suspect that this stock in each man is small, and that the individuals would do better to avail themselves of the general bank and capital of nations and of ages.   EDMUND BURKE

When you hear a man say, "I hate," adding the name of some race, nation, religion, or social class, you are dealing with a belated mind. That man may dress like a modern, ride in an automobile, listen over the radio, but his mind is properly dated about 1000 B.C.   HARRY EMERSON FOSDICK

Prejudice is the reason of fools.   VOLTAIRE

In forming a judgment, lay your hearts void of foretaken opinions; else, whatsoever is done or said, will be measured by a wrong rule: like them who have the jaundice, to whom everything appeareth yellow.
                                                SIR PHILIP SIDNEY

He who knows only his own side of the case knows little of that.
                                                JOHN STUART MILL

See also: AMERICA; BROTHERHOOD; CHRISTIANITY; COMPASSION; DEMOCRACY; EQUALITY; LOVE; MATURITY; PRIDE; RACIAL JUSTICE; RELIGION; VISION.

Pride

I have been more and more convinced, the more I think of it, that, in general, pride is at the bottom of all great mistakes. All the other passions do occasional good; but whenever pride puts in its word, everything goes wrong; and what it might really be desirable to do, quietly and innocently, it is mortally dangerous to do proudly.   JOHN RUSKIN

If a proud man makes me keep my distance, the comfort is that he keeps his at the same time.   JONATHAN SWIFT

As Plato entertained some friends in a room where there was a couch richly ornamented, Diogenes came in very dirty, as usual, and getting upon the couch, and trampling on it, said, "I trample upon the pride of Plato." Plato mildly answered, "But with greater pride, Diogenes!"

DESIDERIUS ERASMUS

Haughtiness toward men is rebellion to God.   MOSES NAHMANIDES

Of all the causes which conspire to blind man's erring judgment and mislead the mind, what the weak head with strongest bias rules, is pride—that never-failing vice of fools.   ALEXANDER POPE

Some become proud and insolent, either by riding a good horse, wearing a feather in their hat, or by being dressed in a fine suit of clothes. . . . If there be any glory in such things, the glory belongs to the horse, the bird and the tailor; and what a meanness of heart must it be to borrow esteem from a horse, from a feather, or some ridiculous new fashion! Others value themselves for a well-trimmed bearing, for curled locks, or soft hands; or because they can dance, sing or play; but are not these effeminate men who seek to raise their reputation by so frivolous and foolish things? Others for a little learning would be honored and respected by the whole world, as if every one ought to become their pupil, and account them his masters. These are called pedants. Others strut like peacocks, contemplating their beauty and think themselves admired by every one. All this is extremely vain, foolish and impertinent; and the glory which is raised on so weak foundations is justly esteemed vain and frivolous.   SAINT FRANCIS DE SALES

It often amuses me to hear men impute all their misfortunes to fate, luck or destiny, whilst their successes or good fortune they ascribe to their own sagacity, cleverness, or penetration.　　　SAMUEL TAYLOR COLERIDGE

A man must have a good deal of vanity who believes, and a good deal of boldness who affirms, that all the doctrines he holds are true, and all he rejects are false.　　　BENJAMIN FRANKLIN

Never be haughty to the humble; never be humble to the haughty.
　　　JEFFERSON DAVIS

> Man, proud man!
> Drest in a little brief authority,
> Most ignorant of what he's most assur'd,
> His glassy essence, like an angry ape,
> Plays such fantastic tricks before high
> 　　heaven
> As make the angels weep.
> 　　　WILLIAM SHAKESPEARE

A man who bows down to nothing can never bear the burden of himself.
　　　FYODOR DOSTOYEVSKI

Pride is a vice, which pride itself inclines every man to find in others, and to overlook in himself.　　　SAMUEL JOHNSON

Pride the first peer and president of hell.　　　DANIEL DEFOE

See also: CHARACTER; GRACE; HUMILITY; INTEGRITY; MATURITY; RELIGION; SAINTLINESS; SELFISHNESS; SELFLESSNESS; SELF-CONTROL; SELF-KNOWLEDGE; SELF-RESPECT.

Purpose

As I look over the grand drama of history, I find—or seem to find—amid the apparent chaos and tragedy, evidence of law and plan and immense achievement of the human spirit in spite of disaster. I am convinced that the world is not a mere bog in which men and women trample themselves in the mire and die. Something magnificent is taking place here amid the cruelties and tragedies; and the supreme challenge to intelligence is that of making the noblest and the best in our curious heritage prevail.   CHARLES A. BEARD

To be honest, to be kind, to earn a little, and to spend a little less, to make upon the whole a family happier for his presence, to renounce when that shall be necessary and not to be embittered, to keep a few friends, but those without capitulation, above all, on the same grim conditions, to keep friends with himself—here is a task for all that man has of fortitude and delicacy.
                                              ROBERT LOUIS STEVENSON

Clay is fashioned into vessels; it is on their empty hollowness that their use depends. Doors and windows are cut out to make a dwelling, and on the empty space within, its use depends. Thus, while the existence of things may be good, it is the non-existent in them that makes them serviceable.
                                                                      LAO-TSE

A useless life is a living death.   JOHANN WOLFGANG VON GOETHE

Yet I doubt not thro' the ages one
increasing purpose runs,
And the thoughts of men are widen'd
with the process of the suns.
ALFRED, LORD TENNYSON

The best thing to give to your enemy is forgiveness; to an opponent, tolerance; to a friend, your heart; to your child, a good example; to a father, deference; to your mother, conduct that will make her proud of you; to yourself, respect; to all men, charity.   ARTHUR JAMES BALFOUR

My country is the world. My countrymen are mankind. I am in earnest, I will not equivocate, I will not excuse, I will not retreat a single step, and I will be heard.   WILLIAM LLOYD GARRISON
                                              [masthead on *The Liberator*]

This life were brutish did we not sometimes
Have intimations clear of wider scope,

Hints of occasion infinite, to keep
The soul alert with noble discontent
And onward yearnings of unstilled desire;
Fruitless, except we now and then divined
A mystery of Purpose, gleaming through
The secular confusions of the world,
Whose will we darkly accomplish, doing ours.

JAMES RUSSELL LOWELL

The pine hath a thousand years,
The rose but a day
But the pine with its thousand years
Glories not o'er the rose with its day,
If each but serves its purpose
Ere it passes away.

JAPANESE PROVERB

From the lowest depths, there is a path to the loftiest heights. The tendency to persevere, to persist in spite of hindrances, discouragements, and impossibilities—it is this in all things distinguishes the strong soul from the weak. The man without a purpose is like a ship without a rudder—a waif, a nothing, a no-man. Have a purpose in life, and, having it, throw such strength of mind and muscle into your work as God has given you.

THOMAS CARLYLE

I could almost dislike the man who refuses to plant walnut trees, because they do not bear fruit till the second generation; and so—many thanks to our ancestors, and much joy to our successors.   SIR WALTER SCOTT

The dogmas of the quiet past are inadequate to the stormy present. Let us disenthrall ourselves.   ABRAHAM LINCOLN

If you are planning for a year, plant grain. If you are planting for a decade, plant trees. If you are planning for a century, plant men.

CHINESE PROVERB

If you will it, it is no legend.   THEODOR HERZL

He who ceases to grow, becomes smaller; he who leaves off, gives up; the stationary condition is the beginning of the end.   ANONYMOUS

Racial Justice

The sin of racial pride still represents the most basic challenge to the American conscience. We cannot dodge this challenge without renouncing our highest moral pretensions. ARTHUR M. SCHLESINGER, SR.

To accept one's past, one's history, is not the same thing as drowning in it. It is learning how to use it. An inverted past can never be used. It cracks and stumbles under the pressure of life like clay in a season of drought.
JAMES BALDWIN

Minds broken in two. Hearts broken. Conscience torn from acts. A culture split in a thousand pieces. This is segregation. LILLIAN SMITH

This society is a society that suffers from the sickness of racism, a society torn by deep-seated tensions and urban rot. It won't be changed until the decent people stop talking about it and start working to create a new and better society—one in which all Americans can choose their way of life and exercise options within a democracy. WHITNEY M. YOUNG, JR.

Laws and conditions that tend to debase human personality—a God-given force—be they brought about by the State or other individuals, must be relentlessly opposed in the spirit of defiance shown by St. Peter when he said to the rulers of his day: "Shall we obey God or man?" . . .

As for myself, with a full sense of responsibility and a clear conviction, I decided to remain in the struggle for extending democratic rights and responsibilities to all sections of the South African community. I have embraced the nonviolent Passive Resistance technique in fighting for freedom because I am convinced it is the only nonrevolutionary, legitimate and humane way that could be used by people denied, as we are, effective constitutional means to further aspirations. . . .

What the future has in store for me I do not know. It might be ridicule, imprisonment, concentration camp, flogging, banishment and even death. I only pray to the Almighty to strengthen my resolve so that none of these grim possibilities may deter me from striving, for the sake of the good name of our beloved country, the Union of South Africa, to make it a true democracy and a true union in form and spirit of all the communities in the land. . . .

It is inevitable that in working for Freedom some individuals and some families must take the lead and suffer: The Road to Freedom is via the CROSS.

MAYIBUYE!

AFRIKA! AFRIKA! AFRIKA!

CHIEF ALBERT LUTHULI

The Negro problem is not only America's greatest failure but also America's incomparably great opportunity for the future. If America should follow its own deepest convictions, its well-being at home would be increased directly. At the same time America's prestige and power abroad would rise immensely. The century-old dream of American patriots, that America should give to the entire world its own freedoms and its own faith, would come true. America can demonstrate that justice, equality and cooperation are possible between white and colored persons. . . .

America is free to choose whether the Negro shall remain her liability or become her opportunity.

GUNNAR MYRDAL

Liberty cannot extend to actions which present a clear and present danger to the existence of the democratic state itself, or to the established procedures for the succession of power within that state. But within these limits, it must be liberty for all.

MAX LERNER

A young Negro student said: "If you discriminate against me because I am uncouth, I can become mannerly. If you ostracize me because I am unclean, I can cleanse myself. If you segregate me because I am ignorant, I can become educated. But if you discriminate against me because of my color, I can do nothing. God gave me my color. I have no possible protection against race prejudice but to take refuge in cynicism, bitterness, hatred, and despair."

HARRY EMERSON FOSDICK

See also: AMERICA; BROTHERHOOD; CHRISTIANITY; DEMOCRACY; EQUALITY; FELLOWSHIP; JUSTICE; LIBERTY; LOVE; PREJUDICE; RELIGION; TRUTH.

Religion

Wherein does religion consist?

In committing the least possible harm, in doing abundance of good, in the practice of pity, love, truth, and likewise purity of life.   ASOKA

The basis of all scientific work is the conviction that the world is an ordered and comprehensive entity, which is a religious sentiment. My religious feeling is a humble amazement at the order revealed in the small patch of reality to which our feeble intelligence is equal.

By furthering logical thought and a logical attitude, science can diminish the amount of superstition in the world. There is no doubt that all but the crudest scientific work is based on a firm belief—akin to religious feeling—in the rationality and comprehensibility of the world.   ALBERT EINSTEIN

There is only one religion, though there are a hundred versions of it.
                                                  GEORGE BERNARD SHAW

Compulsion in religion is distinguished peculiarly from compulsion in every other thing. I may grow rich by an art I am compelled to follow; I may recover health by medicines I am compelled to take against my own judgment; but I cannot be saved by a worship I disbelieve and abhor.
                                                          THOMAS JEFFERSON

A religious person is a person who holds God and man in one thought at one time, at all times, who suffers harm done to others, whose greatest possession is compassion, whose greatest strength is love, and defiance of despair.   ABRAHAM JOSHUA HESCHEL

Religion has two purposes: to comfort the afflicted and to afflict the comfortable.   ANONYMOUS

The foundation of all religion is one, and God's is the East and the West, and wherever ye turn, there is God's face.   THE KORAN

Men will wrangle for religion; write for it; fight for it; die for it; anything
but—*live for it.*   MONTAIGNE

Those who say that religion has nothing to do with politics, do not know what
religion means.   MOHANDAS GANDHI

I would define religion as a mysterious and mystic impulse working within
us to make us greater than we are, and the world through us better than it
is; to lift us to levels above the low ranges of physical appetite and satisfaction; to drive us to goals beyond the prudential bounds of time and sense.
Religion belongs distinctively to man not because he can think and speculate, build churches and rear altars, but rather because he can sense the
whole of life, catch a vision of the ideal in things real, and is willing to give
his life to fulfilling this vision among men. To be compelled to serve an ideal
cause by a conviction of its enduring value not merely for ourselves but for
humanity and its high destiny upon earth—this is religion.
                                                    JOHN HAYNES HOLMES

Religion, at its best, is the announcer of the supreme ideals by which men
must live and through which our finite species finds its ultimate significance.
                                                    JOSHUA LOTH LIEBMAN

Pure religion and undefiled before God and the Father is this: To visit the
fatherless and widows in their affliction, and to keep himself unspotted
from the world.   THE BIBLE

It is as difficult in our day as in the day of Jeremiah to preach "the word of
the Lord," for that runs counter to the complacency of men and of nations.
It is sharper than a "two-edged sword." It must hurt before it can heal.
                                                    REINHOLD NIEBUHR

Being religious means asking, . . . questioning the meaning of our existence.
Religion is not belief in gods or one god; not a set of activities or institutions.
Religion is concern about one's own being and about Being universally.
Religion is ultimate concern.   PAUL TILLICH

Religion is a cosmic sense. The individual feels the vanity of human desires
and aims, and the nobility and marvelous order which are revealed in nature
and in the world of thought. He feels the individual destiny as an imprison-

ment, and seeks to experience a totality of existence as a unity full of significance.   ALBERT EINSTEIN

We teach [religion] in arithmetic by accuracy. We teach it in language by
learning to say what we mean—"yea, yea" or "nay, nay." We teach it in history by humanity. We teach it in geography by breadth of mind. We teach it
in handicraft by thoroughness. We teach it in astronomy by reverence. We
teach it by good manners to one another and by truthfulness in all things.
                                                                           L. P. JACKS

Let those who call themselves Catholics, or Protestant, or Jews recall that
the function of their religion is to intensify the spiritual life of man and not to
empty the vials of bitterness into hearts, stirring up one against another.
                                                                     FULTON J. SHEEN

Religion does not say that everything is easy and comfortable, for religion is
not meant to fill our minds with illusions but fortitude.
                                                              WILLIAM LYON PHELPS

Religion, occupying herself with personal destinies and keeping thus in con-
tact with the only absolute realities which we know, must necessarily play
an eternal part in human history.   WILLIAM JAMES

Religion is the divinity within us reaching up to the divinity above.
                                                                       BAHAI SAYING

See also: ASPIRATION; BELIEF; BIBLE, THE; CHRISTIANITY; CHURCH,
THE; DIVINE, THE; FAITH; GOD; GRACE; JESUS CHRIST; LOVE; PRAYER;
REVERENCE; SAINTLINESS; SOUL; VIRTUE; WORSHIP.

Religious Freedom

It is one of the rights of man and privileges of nature that everyone should
worship according to his own convictions. One man's religion neither harms
nor helps another's. It is no part of religion to compel religion.
                                                                       TERTULLIAN

I call that mind free which protects itself against the usurpations of society, which does not cower to human opinion, which feels itself accountable to a higher tribunal than man's, which respects a higher law than fashion, which respects itself too much to be slave or tool of the many or the few. . . .

I call that mind free which resists the bondage of habit, which does not mechanically repeat itself and copy the past, which does not live on its old virtues, which does not enslave itself to precise rules, but which forgets what is behind, listens for new and higher monitions of conscience, and rejoices to pour itself forth in fresh and higher exertions.

I call that mind free which is jealous of its own freedom, which guards itself from being merged in others, which guards its empire over itself as nobler than the empire of the world.   WILLIAM ELLERY CHANNING

To be furious in religion is to be irreligiously religious.   WILLIAM PENN

I am for freedom of religion and against all maneuvers to bring about a legal ascendancy of one sect over another.   THOMAS JEFFERSON

In France I had almost always seen the spirit of religion and the spirit of freedom marching in opposite directions. But in America I found they were intimately united and they reigned in common over the same country.
                                        ALEXIS DE TOCQUEVILLE

Experience witnesseth that ecclesiastical establishments, instead of maintaining the purity and efficacy of religion, have had a contrary operation. During almost fifteen centuries has the legal establishment of Christianity been on trial. What has been its fruits? More or less, in all places, pride and indolence in the clergy; ignorance and servility in the laity; in both, superstition, bigotry and persecution.   JAMES MADISON

What our constitution indispensably protects is the freedom of each of us, be he Jew or agnostic, Christian or atheist, Buddhist or free-thinker, to believe or disbelieve, to worship or not to worship, to pray or keep silent, according to his own conscience, uncoerced and unrestrained by government.
                                        POTTER STEWART

We, Constantine and Licinius the emperors, having met in concord at Milan and having set in order everything which pertains to the common good and public security, are of the opinion that among the various things which we perceived would profit men . . . was to be found the cultivation of religion;

we should therefore give both to Christians and to all others free facility to follow the religion which each may desire.   EDICT OF MILAN

It is the will and command of God that . . . permission of the paganish, Jewish, Turkish, or anti-Christian consciences and worships be granted to all men in all nations and countries.   ROGER WILLIAMS

Broad is the carpet God has spread, and beautiful the colors He has given it. The pure man respects every form of faith.   BUDDHIST SAYING

See also: ATHEISM; BELIEF; CONSCIENCE; COURAGE; DEMOCRACY; DISSENT; DOUBT; FAITH; FREEDOM; LIBERTY; NONCONFORMITY; RELIGION.

Responsibility

Our hard entrance into the world, our miserable going out of it, our sicknesses, disturbances, and sad encounters in it, do clamorously tell us we come not into the world to run a race of delight, but to perform the sober acts and serious purposes of man; which to omit were foully to miscarry in the advantage of humanity.   SIR THOMAS BROWNE

> If you are tempted to reveal
> A tale to you someone has told
> About another, make it pass,
> Before you speak, three gates of gold.
> These narrow gates: First, "Is it true?"
> Then, "Is it needful?" In your mind
> Give truthful answer. And the next
> Is last and narrowest, "Is it kind?"
> And if to reach your lips at last
> It passes through these gateways three,
> Then you may tell the tale, nor fear
> What the result of speech may be.
>   ADMONITION FROM ARABIAN LORE

Little faithfulnesses are not only the preparation for great ones, but little faithfulnesses are in themselves the great ones. . . . The essential fidelity of the heart is the same whether it be exercised in two mites or in a regal treasury; the genuine faithfulness of the life is equally beautiful whether it be displayed in governing an empire or in writing an exercise. . . . It has been quaintly said that if God were to send two angels to earth, the one to occupy a throne, and the other to clean a road, they would each regard their employments as equally distinguished and equally happy.

FREDERICK W. FABER

God hangs the greatest weights upon the smallest wires. SIR FRANCIS BACON

> Good critics who have stamped out poet's hope,
> Good statesmen who pulled ruin on the state,
> Good patriots who for a theory risked a cause,
> Good kings who disembowelled for a tax,
> Good popes who brought all good to jeopardy,
> Good Christians who sat still in easy chairs
> And damned the general world for standing up.
> Now may the good God pardon all good men!
> ELIZABETH BARRETT BROWNING

Our grand business in life is not to see what lies dimly at a distance, but to do what clearly lies at hand. THOMAS CARLYLE

Advice after mischief is like medicine after death. DANISH PROVERB

Blessed are they who have nothing to say, and who cannot be persuaded to say it. JAMES RUSSELL LOWELL

True eloquence consists in saying all that is necessary, and nothing but what is necessary. FRANÇOIS LA ROCHEFOUCAULD

A hundred times every day I remind myself that my inner and outer life depend on the labors of other men, living and dead, and that I must exert myself in order to give in the measure as I have received and am still receiving. ALBERT EINSTEIN

Anger is never without a reason, but seldom with a good one.

BENJAMIN FRANKLIN

Thus saith the Lord: We have ordained that he who slayeth anyone shall be as though he had slain all mankind; but that he who saveth a life shall be as though he had saved all mankind alive.   THE KORAN

We are always complaining that our days are few, and acting as though there would be no end to them.   SENECA

So far as drinking is concerned, wine does of a truth "moisten the soul" and lull our griefs to sleep. But I suspect that men's bodies fare like those of plants. . . . When God gives the plant water in floods to drink, they cannot stand up straight or let the breezes blow through them; but when they drink only as much as they enjoy, they grow up straight and tall, and come to full and abundant fruitage.   SOCRATES

He who teaches his son no trade is as if he taught him to steal.
                    THE TALMUD

Now the only way to avoid this shipwreck and to provide for our posterity . . . we must be knit together in this work as one man, we must entertain each other in brotherly affection, we must be willing to abridge ourselves of our superfluities for the supply of others' necessities, we must uphold a familiar commerce together in all meekness, gentleness, patience, and liberality, we must delight in each other, make others' conditions our own, rejoice together, mourn together, labor and suffer together.   JOHN WINTHROP
[aboard the *Arbella* en route to
New England in 1630]

See also: CHARACTER; COURAGE; DEDICATION; EXAMPLE; GIVING; GOODNESS; GREATNESS; IDEALS; INTEGRITY; PERSEVERANCE; RELIGION; SELF-KNOWLEDGE.

Reverence

Fear God, and where you go men will think they walk in hallowed cathedrals.
                    RALPH WALDO EMERSON

O most high, almighty, good Lord God, to Thee belong praise, glory, honor, and all blessing!

Praised be my Lord God with all His creatures, and specially our brother the sun, who brings us the day and who brings us the light; fair is he and shines with a very great splendor: O Lord, he signifies to us Thee!

Praised be my Lord for our sister the moon, and for the stars, the which He has set clear and lovely in heaven.

Praised be my Lord for our brother the wind, and for the air and cloud, calms and all weather by the which Thou upholdest life in all creatures.

Praised be my Lord for our sister water, who is very serviceable unto us and humble and precious and clean.

Praised be my Lord for our brother fire, through whom Thou givest us light in the darkness; and he is bright and pleasant and very mighty and strong.

Praised be my Lord for our mother the earth, the which doth sustain us and keep us, and bringeth forth divers fruits and flowers of many colors, and grass. . . .

Praised be my Lord for our sister, the death of the body, from which no man escapeth. Woe to him who dieth in mortal sin! Blessed are they who are found walking by Thy most holy will, for the second death shall have no power to do them harm.

Praise ye and bless the Lord, and give thanks unto Him and serve Him with great humility.   SAINT FRANCIS OF ASSISI

With the people, and especially with the clergymen, who have Him daily upon their tongues, God becomes a phrase, a mere name, which they utter without any accompanying idea. But if they were penetrated with His greatness, they would rather be dumb, and for very reverence would not dare to name Him.   JOHANN WOLFGANG VON GOETHE

Even the hen lifteth her head toward heaven when swallowing her grain.
                    AFRICAN PROVERB

The Uncharted surrounds us on every side and we must needs have some relation to it, a relation which will depend on the general discipline of a man's mind and the bias of his whole character. As far as knowledge and conscious reason will go, we should follow resolutely their austere guidance. When they cease, as cease they must, we must use as best we can those fainter powers of apprehension and surmise and sensitiveness by which, after all, most high truth has been reached as well as most high art and poetry; careful always to seek for truth and not for our own emotional satisfaction; careful not to neglect the real needs of men and women through basing our life on dreams; and remembering above all to walk gently in a world where the lights are dim and the very stars wander.   SALLUST

The heartbeat of life is holy joy.   MARTIN BUBER

Reverence for life is more than solicitude or sensitivity for life. It is a sense of the whole, a capacity for wonder, a respect for the intricate universe of individual life. It is the supreme awareness of awareness itself. It is pride in being.   NORMAN COUSINS

The contemplation of celestial things will make a man both speak and think more sublimely and magnificently when he descends to human affairs.
                              CICERO

O my Lord! If I worship Thee from fear of hell, burn me in hell. If I worship Thee from hope of paradise, exclude me thence. But if I worship Thee for Thine own sake, then withhold not from me Thine Eternal Beauty.
                              MOSLEM PRAYER

O God, that bringest all things to pass, grant me the spirit of reverence for noble things. May I walk in the guileless paths of life, and leave behind me a fair name for my children.   PINDAR

> Now must we hymn the Master of heaven,
> The might of the Maker, the deeds of the Father,
> The thought of His heart. He, Lord everlasting,
> Established of old the source of all wonders:
> Creator all-holy, He hung the bright heaven,
> A roof high upreared, o'er the children of men;
> The King of mankind then created for mortals
> The world in its beauty, the earth spread beneath
>   them,
> He, Lord everlasting, omnipotent God.
>   CAEDMON'S HYMN

I never was without some religious principles. I never doubted, for instance, the existence of the Deity; that he made the world and govern'd it by his Providence; that the most acceptable service of God was the doing of good to men; that our souls are immortal; and that all crime will be punished, and virtue rewarded either here or hereafter. These I esteemed the essentials of every religion; and, being to be found in all the religions we had in our country, I respected them all, tho' with different degrees of respect, as I found them more or less mix'd with other articles, which, without any tendency to inspire, promote or confirm morality, serv'd principally to divide us, and make us unfriendly to one another.   BENJAMIN FRANKLIN

Lambs have the grace to kneel when nursing.   CHINESE PROVERB

See also: ASPIRATION; ATHEISM; DIVINE, THE; FAITH; GOD; GRACE; INSPIRATION; MYSTERY; PRAYER; RELIGION; WONDER; WORSHIP.

Saintliness

Saintliness was not thought to consist in specific acts, such as in excessive prayer or performance of rituals, but was an attitude bound up with all actions, concomitant with all doings, accompanying and shaping all life's activities.

Saintliness was not an excursion into spirituality. Its mark was loving-kindness.

A Saint was he who did not know how it is possible not to love, not to help, not to be sensitive to the anxiety of others.   ABRAHAM JOSHUA HESCHEL

Nothing is so strong as gentleness, nothing as gentle as real strength.
     SAINT FRANCIS DE SALES

The hero is one who kindles a great light in the world, who sets up blazing torches in the dark streets of life for men to see by. The saint is the man who walks through the dark paths of the world, himself a light.   FELIX ADLER

A saint is a person who does almost everything any other decent person does, only somewhat better and with a totally different motive.
     COVENTRY PATMORE

To make a man a saint, it must indeed be by grace; and whoever doubts this does not know what a saint is, or a man.   BLAISE PASCAL

Patient endurance of sufferings, bold resistance of power, forgiveness of injuries, hard-tried and faithful friendship, and self-sacrificing love, are seen in beautiful relief over the flat uniformity of life, or stand out in steady and bright grandeur in the midst of the dark deeds of men.

RICHARD HENRY DANA

A saint is one who makes goodness attractive.   A. E. HOUSMAN

A man can be as truly a saint in a factory as in a monastery, and there is as much need of him in the one as in the other.   ROBERT J. MC CRACKEN

It is with the saints here as with the boughs of trees in time of storm. You shall see the boughs beat one upon another as if they would beat one another to pieces, as if armies were fighting; but this is but while the wind, while the tempest lasts. Stay awhile. You shall see every bough standing in its own order and comeliness. Why? Because they are all united in one root. If any bough be rotten, the storm breaks it.   JEREMIAH BURROUGHS

See also: CHARACTER; COMPASSION; COURAGE; DIVINE, THE; FAITH; GOD; GRACE; HUMILITY; JESUS CHRIST; JUDAISM; LOVE; SELFLESS-NESS.

Self-Control

Then tell me, O Critias, how will a man choose the ruler that shall rule over him? Will he not choose a man who has first established order in himself, knowing that any decision that has its spring from anger or pride or vanity can be multiplied a thousandfold in its effects upon the citizens?

SOCRATES

He who reigns within himself and rules his passions, desires and fears is more than a king.   JOHN MILTON

He that is slow to anger is better than the mighty: and he that ruleth his spirit than he that taketh a city.   THE BIBLE

"The boneless tongue, so small and weak,
Can crush and kill," declared the Greek.

"The tongue destroys a greater horde,"
The Turk asserts, "than does the sword."

A Persian proverb wisely saith,
"A lengthy tongue—an early death,"

Or sometimes takes this form instead,
"Don't let your tongue cut off your head."

"The tongue can speak a word whose speed,"
Says the Chinese, "outstrips the steed";

While Arab sages this impart,
"The tongue's great storehouse is the heart,"

From Hebrew with the maxim sprung,
"Though feet should slip, ne'er let the tongue."

The sacred writer crowns the whole:
"Who keeps the tongue doth keep his soul."
PHILLIPS BURROWS STRONG

A man must be arched and buttressed from within, else the temple crumbles
to the dust.   MARCUS AURELIUS

O, it is excellent
To have a giant's strength; but it is tyrannous
To use it like a giant.
WILLIAM SHAKESPEARE

Every man is his own doctor of divinity, in the last resort.
ROBERT LOUIS STEVENSON

Of all forms of continence, the bridling of the tongue is the most difficult.
PYTHAGORAS

Greater is he who conquers himself than he who conquers a thousand.
BUDDHA

We can often do more for other men by correcting our own faults than by
trying to correct theirs.   FRANÇOIS FÉNELON

When angry, count ten; when very angry, a hundred.   THOMAS JEFFERSON

He is an eloquent man who can treat subjects of a humble nature with delicacy, lofty things impressively, and moderate things temperately.

CICERO

Most powerful is he who has himself in his power.   SENECA

He is a fool who cannot be angry; but he is a wise man who will not.

ENGLISH PROVERB

> Difficulties show what men are.
> Reason is not measured by size or height, but by
>   principle.
> No great thing is created suddenly, any more than
>   a bunch of grapes or a fig.
> No man is free who is not master of himself.
>
> EPICTETUS

Whatever liberates our spirit without giving us self-control is disastrous.

JOHANN WOLFGANG VON GOETHE

If you would be pungent, be brief; for it is with words as with sunbeams— the more they are condensed the deeper they burn.   ROBERT SOUTHEY

> The wind that fills my sails
> Propels; but I am helmsman.
> GEORGE MEREDITH

Govern thyself, and you will be able to govern the world.

CHINESE PROVERB

See also: CHARACTER; GRACE; INTEGRITY; MATURITY; PERSEVER-ANCE; PERSPECTIVE; PRAYER; SELF-KNOWLEDGE; SELF-RESPECT; WIS-DOM.

Selfishness

Doing nothing for others is the undoing of one's self. We must be purposely kind and generous, or we miss the best part of existence. The heart that goes out of itself, gets large and full of joy. This is the great secret of the inner life. We do ourselves the most good doing something for others.

HORACE MANN

I do not know why it is more cramping to the soul to possess things it does not need than merely desire them. It is harder to get rid of what one possesses than not to desire what one has not got; the former is like losing a limb.

SAINT AUGUSTINE

The sweetest wine, if left exposed to feed on its own sweetness, turns to sourest vinegar; so the best affections, if turned back to prey upon themselves, are changed to the bitterest hatred.

EDWARD BULWER-LYTTON

If I have faltered more or less
In my great task of happiness;
If I have moved alone among my race
And shown no glorious morning face;
If beams from happy human eyes
Have moved me not; if morning skies,
Books, my food, and summer rain
Knocked at my sullen heart in vain:—
Lord, thy most pointed pleasure take
And stab my spirit broad awake.

ROBERT LOUIS STEVENSON

There is one species of egotism which is truly disgusting: not that which leads us to communicate our feelings to others, but that which would reduce the feelings of others to an identity with our own. The atheist who exclaims "Pshaw!" when he glances his eye on the praises of Deity is an egotist; an old man when he speaks contemptuously of love-verses is an egotist; and the sleek favorites of Fortune are egotists when they condemn all "melancholy, discontented verses." Surely it would be candid not merely to ask

whether the poem pleases ourselves, but to consider whether or no there may not be others, to whom it is well calculated to give an innocent pleasure.
                                                    SAMUEL TAYLOR COLERIDGE

Selfishness is the only real atheism; aspiration, unselfishness, the only real religion.   ISRAEL ZANGWILL

If you pursue two hares, both will escape from you.   GREEK PROVERB

A man all wrapped up in himself makes a mighty small package.
                                                              ANONYMOUS

Everyone is a moon, and has a dark side which he never shows to anybody.
                                                              MARK TWAIN

Envy is uneasiness of the mind, caused by the consideration of a good we desire, obtained by one we think should not have it before us. JOHN LOCKE

The least pain in our little finger gives us more concern than the destruction of millions of our fellow men.   WILLIAM HAZLITT

The world is the glass through which we see our Maker. But what men do is this: They put the dull quicksilver of their own selfishness behind the glass, and so it becomes not the transparent medium through which God shines, but the dead opaque which reflects back themselves. So it gives back their own false feelings and nature.   FREDERICK W. ROBERTSON

Who seeks more than he needs hinders himself from enjoying what he has.
                                                        SOLOMON IBN-GABIROL

He who seeks revenge, digs two graves.   CHINESE PROVERB

See also: AMBITION; EXAMPLE; GIVING; IDEALS; INSPIRATION; INTEGRITY; LOVE; MATURITY; PRIDE; RELIGION; SELFLESSNESS; SELF-KNOWLEDGE.

Selflessness

No man can live happily who regards himself alone, who turns everything to his own advantage. Thou must live for another, if thou wishest to live for thyself. SENECA

He who comes to do good knocks at the gate; he who loves finds the door open. SIR RABINDRANATH TAGORE

> I am a blessed Thing if I
> Can but un-thing myself, forego
> All my community with things,
> My cognizance of things unknow.
>
> Man never will possess
> Perfect beautitude,
> Until what single is
> Swallows up all otherhood.
> ANGELUS SILESIUS

And so, my fellow Americans, ask not what your country can do for you; ask what you can do for your country. My fellow citizens of the world, ask not what America will do for you, but what together we can do for the freedom of man. JOHN F. KENNEDY

Even Buddha was once a carthorse, and carried the loads of others. INDIAN PROVERB

> If you sit down at set of sun
> And count the acts that you have done,
> And, counting, find
> One self-denying deed,
> That eased the heart of him who heard—
> One glance most kind,
> That fell like sunshine where it went—
> Then you may count that day well spent.
> ANONYMOUS

The tree bears not fruit for itself, nor for itself does the stream collect its waters; for the good of others does the sage appear.   SIKH SAYING

He who runs after honor, honor eludes him; he who runs from honor, honor seeks him out.   THE TALMUD

He [Theodore Parker] was willing to perish in the using. He sacrificed the future to the present, was willing to spend and be spent; felt himself to belong to the day he lived in, and had too much to do than that he should be careful for fame. He used every day, hour, and minute; he lived to the latest moment, and his character appeared in the last moments with the same firm control as in the day of strength.   RALPH WALDO EMERSON

The greatest pleasure I know is to do a good action by stealth, and to have it found out by accident.   CHARLES LAMB

See also: ASPIRATION; CHARACTER; COMPASSION; GRACE; HUMILITY; JUSTICE; KINDNESS; LOVE; PRAYER; SAINTLINESS; SELFISHNESS; VIRTUE.

Self-Knowledge

Doth a man reproach thee for being proud or ill-natured, envious or conceited, ignorant or detractive? Consider with thyself whether his reproaches are true. If they are not, consider that thou art not the person whom he reproaches, but that he reviles an imaginary being, and perhaps loves what thou really art, although he hates what thou appearest to be. If his reproaches are true, if thou art the envious, ill-natured man he takes thee for, give thyself another turn, become mild, affable and obliging, and his reproaches of thee naturally cease. His reproaches may indeed continue, but thou art no longer the person he reproaches.   EPICTETUS

One must carve one's life out of the wood one has.   GERMAN PROVERB

Not to alter one's faults is to be faulty indeed.   CONFUCIUS

No reasonable man will think more highly of himself because he has office or power in this world; he is no more than a prisoner whom the chief gaoler has set over his fellow-prisoners, until the executioner's cart comes for him, too. SIR THOMAS MORE

Folly is often more cruel in the consequence than malice can be in the intent.
GEORGE SAVILE, MARQUIS OF HALIFAX

Train up a child in the way he should go—and walk there yourself once in a while. JOSH BILLINGS

The greatest of faults, I should say, is to be conscious of none.
THOMAS CARLYLE

Let no man presume to give advice to others that has not first given good counsel to himself. SENECA

Macbeth: How does your patient, doctor?
Doctor: Not so sick, my lord,
As she is troubled with thick-coming fancies,
That keep her from her rest.
Macbeth: Cure her of that:
Canst thou not minister to a mind diseas'd;
Pluck from the memory a rooted sorrow;
Raze out the written troubles of the brain;
And with some sweet oblivious antidote
Cleanse the stuff'd bosom of that perilous stuff
Which weighs upon the heart?
Doctor: Therein the patient
Must minister to himself.
WILLIAM SHAKESPEARE

Men are four:
He who knows not, and knows not he knows not, is a fool, shun him.
He who knows not, and knows he knows not, is simple, teach him.
He who knows, and knows not he knows, is asleep, waken him.
He who knows and knows he knows, is wise, follow him.
ARAB PROVERB

To see another's fault is easy; to see one's own is hard. Men winnow the faults of others like chaff; their own they hide as a crafty gambler hides a losing throw. DHAMMAPADA

Few persons have sufficient wisdom to prefer censure (which is useful to them) to praise which deceives them.   FRANÇOIS LA ROCHEFOUCAULD

And why beholdest thou the mote that is in thy brother's eye, but considereth not the beam that is in thine own eye? Or how wilt thou say to thy brother, Let me pull out the mote out of thine eye; and, behold, a beam is in thine own eye? Thou hypocrite, first cast out the beam out of thine own eye; and then shalt thou see clearly to cast out the mote out of thy brother's eye.   THE BIBLE

He that blows the coals in quarrels he has nothing to do with has no right to complain if the sparks fly in his face.   BENJAMIN FRANKLIN

The most frequent impediment to men's turning the mind inward upon themselves is that they are afraid of what they shall find there. There is an aching hollowness in the bosom, a dark cold speck at the heart, an obscure and boding sense of something that must be kept out of sight of the conscience; some secret lodger, whom they can neither resolve to reject nor retain.   SAMUEL TAYLOR COLERIDGE

There is but one man who can believe himself free from envy, and it is he who has never examined his own heart.   CLAUDE ADRIEN HELVETIUS

> Not in the clamor of the crowded street,
>   Not in the shouts and plaudits of the throng,
> But in ourselves, are triumph and defeat.
>   HENRY WADSWORTH LONGFELLOW

A very popular error—"having the courage of one's convictions." Rather it is a matter of having the courage for an attack upon one's convictions.
    FRIEDRICH NIETZSCHE

See also: ASPIRATION; COURAGE; DOUBT; FEAR; GOD; GRACE; INTEGRITY; MATURITY; RESPONSIBILITY; TRUTH; VIRTUE; WISDOM.

Self-Respect

In the midst of winter, I finally learned there was in me an invincible summer.
ALBERT CAMUS

> Give thy thoughts no tongue,
> Nor any unproportioned thought his act.
> Be thou familiar, but by no means vulgar.
> The friends thou hast, and their adoption tried,
> Grapple them to thy soul with hooks of steel;
> But do not dull thy palm with entertainment
> Of each new-hatched, unfledged comrade.
> Beware
> Of entrance to a quarrel; but, being in,
> Bear it that the opposer may beware of thee.
> Give every man thine ear, but few thy voice.
> Take each man's censure, but reserve thy judgment.
> Costly thy habit as thy purse can buy,
> But not express'd in fancy; rich, not gaudy;
> For the apparel oft proclaims the man.
> Neither a borrower nor a lender be,
> For loan oft loses both itself and friend;
> And borrowing dulls the edge of husbandry.
> This above all: To thine own self be true;
> And it must follow, as the night the day,
> Thou canst not then be false to any man.
WILLIAM SHAKESPEARE

Watch what people are cynical about, and one can often discover what they lack, and subconsciously, beneath their touchy condescension, deeply wish they had.
HARRY EMERSON FOSDICK

The whole worth of a benevolent deed lies in the love that inspires it.
THE TALMUD

The first and best victory is to conquer self; to be conquered by self is of all things the most shameful and vile.
PLATO

He who gains a victory over other men is strong; but he who gains a victory over himself is all powerful.   LAO-TSE

> O reputation! dearer far than life,
> Thou precious balsam, lovely, sweet of smell,
> Whose cordial drops once spilt by some rash hand,
> Not all the owner's care, nor the repenting toil
> Of the rude spiller, ever can collect
> To its first purity and native sweetness.
>   SIR WALTER RALEIGH

May I be no man's enemy, and may I be the friend of that which is eternal and abides. May I never quarrel with those nearest me; and if I do, may I be reconciled quickly. May I never devise evil against any man; if any devise evil against me, may I esaape uninjured and without the need of hurting him. May I love, seek, and attain only that which is good. May I wish for all men's happiness and envy none. May I never rejoice in the ill-fortune of one who has wronged me. When I have done or said what is wrong, may I never wait for the rebuke of others, but always rebuke myself until I make amends. . . . May I win no victory that harms either me or my opponent. . . . May I reconcile friends who are wroth with one another. May I, to the extent of my power, give all needful help to my friends and to all who are in want. May I never fail a friend in danger. When visiting those in grief may I be able by gentle and healing words to soften their pain. . . . May I respect myself. . . . May I always keep tame that which rages within me. . . . May I accustom myself to be gentle, and never be angry with people because of circumstances. May I never discuss who is wicked and what wicked things he has done, but know good men and follow in their footsteps.   EUSEBIUS

There are three marks of a superior man: being virtuous, he is free from anxiety; being wise, he is free from perplexity; being brave, he is free from fear.   CONFUCIUS

When thou art obliged to speak, be sure to speak the truth; for equivocation is halfway to lying, and lying is the whole way to Hell.   WILLIAM PENN

See also: ACHIEVEMENT; BELIEF; CHARACTER; CONSCIENCE; COURAGE; GRACE; INTEGRITY; JUSTICE; SELF-CONTROL; SELF-KNOWLEDGE; TRUTH; WISDOM.

Solitude

Solitary we must be in life's great hours of moral decisions; solitary in pain and sorrow; solitary in old age and in our going forth at death. Fortunate the man who has learned what to do in solitude and brought himself to see what companionship he may discover in it, what fortitude, what content.

WILLIAM L. SULLIVAN

But little do men perceive what solitude is, and how far it extendeth. For a crowd is not company; and faces are but a gallery of pictures; and talk but a tinkling cymbal, where there is no love.   SIR FRANCIS BACON

Come now, little man! Flee for a while from your tasks, hide yourself for a little space from the turmoil of your thoughts. Come, cast aside your burdensome cares, and put aside your laborious pursuits. For a little while give your time to God, and rest in Him for a little while. Enter into the inner chamber of your mind, shut out all things save God and whatever may aid you in seeking God; and having barred the door of your chamber, seek Him.

SAINT ANSELM

I never found the companion that was so companionable as solitude.

HENRY DAVID THOREAU

> By all means use some time to be alone.
> Salute thyself: see what thy soul doth wear.
> Dare to look in thy chest; for 'tis thine own:
> And tumble up and down what thou findest there.
> Who cannot rest till he good fellows find,
> He breaks up house, turns out of doors his mind.
>
> GEORGE HERBERT

When you have shut your doors, and darkened your room, remember never to say that you are alone; for God is within, and your genius is within, and what need have they of light to see what you are doing?   EPICTETUS

I am never less at leisure than when at leisure, nor less alone than when I
am alone.   SCIPIO AFRICANUS

What I must do is all that concerns me, not what the people think. This rule,
equally arduous in actual and intellectual life, may serve for the whole distinction between greatness and meanness. It is the harder because you will
always find those who think they know what is your duty better than you
know it. It is easy in the world to live after the world's opinion; it is easy in
solitude to live after your own; but the great man is he who in the midst of
the crowd keeps with perfect sweetness the independence of solitude.
                                                  RALPH WALDO EMERSON

Letter-writing is the only device for combining solitude and good company.
                                                  GEORGE GORDON BYRON

See also: BEING; GOD; MYSTERY; PRAYER; SELF-KNOWLEDGE; VISION.

Soul

Men seek out retreats for themselves, cottages in the country, lonely sea-
shores and mountains. Thou art disposed to hanker greatly after such things:
and yet all this is the very commonest stupidity; for it is in thy power, whenever thou wilt, to retire into thyself. Nowhere is there any place whereto a
man may retire quieter and more free from cares than his own soul; above
all if he have within him thoughts such as he need only regard attentively
to be at perfect ease: and that ease is nothing else than a well-ordered mind.
Constantly then use this retreat, and renew thyself therein. And be thy principles brief and elementary, which, as soon as ever thou recur to them, will
suffice to wash thy soul entirely clean, and send thee back without vexation
to whatsoever awaiteth thee.   MARCUS AURELIUS

> Great truths are portions of the soul of man;
> Great souls are portions of Eternity.
> > JAMES RUSSELL LOWELL

> O Lord, who can comprehend Thy power?
> For Thou hast created for the splendour of Thy glory a
>   pure radiance

"Hewn from the rock of rocks and digged from the bottom
    of the pit."
Thou hast imparted to it the spirit of wisdom
And called it the Soul.
And of flames of intellectual fire hast Thou wrought its
    form,
And like a burning fire hast Thou wafted it,
And sent it to the body to serve and guard it,
And it is as fire in the midst thereof yet doth not consume
    it,
For it is from the fire of the soul that the body hath been
    created,
And goeth from Nothingness to Being,
"Because the Lord descended on him in fire."
                          SOLOMON IBN-GABIROL

Our venture is a glorious one! The soul with her proper jewels—which are justice and courage and nobility and truth—in these arrayed she is ready to go on her journey when her time comes.   SOCRATES

The cultivation of the mind is a kind of food supplied for the soul of man.
                          CICERO

In every feast remember that there are two guests to be entertained, the body and the soul; and that what you give the body you presently lose; but what you give the soul remains forever.   EPICTETUS

If thou hast two loaves of bread, sell one and buy white hyacinths for thy soul.   ISLAMIC SAYING

Dust thou art, to dust returnest,
Was not spoken of the soul.
HENRY WADSWORTH LONGFELLOW

See also: ASPIRATION; BEING; BELIEF; COMPASSION; DIVINE, THE; GOD; GRACE; INSPIRATION; MYSTERY; PRAYER; SELF-KNOWLEDGE; WORSHIP.

Suffering

Let us be thankful that our sorrow lives in us as an indestructible force, only changing in form, as forces do, and passing from pain to sympathy. To have suffered much is like knowing many languages. Thou hast learned to understand all.   GEORGE ELIOT

To have suffered, nay, to suffer, sets a keen edge on what remains of the agreeable. This is a great truth and has to be learned in the fire.

Granted that life is tragic to the marrow, it seems the proper function of religion to make us accept and serve in that tragedy.

Noble disappointment, noble self-denial are not to be admired, not even to be pardoned, if they bring bitterness.

Gentleness and cheerfulness, these come before all morality; they are the perfect duties.

To do our best is one part, but to wash our hands smilingly of the consequence is the next part of any sensible virtue.

Man is indeed marked for failure in his efforts to do right. But where the best consistently miscarry, how tenfold more remarkable that under every circumstance of failure, without hope, without help, without thanks, all should continue to strive.

This is not alone their privilege and glory, but their doom; they are condemned to some nobility.

Let it be enough for faith, that the whole creation groans in mortal frailty, strives with unconquerable constancy; surely not all in vain.

To believe in immortality is one thing, but it is first needful to believe in life.   ROBERT LOUIS STEVENSON

> Thou art God, and all things formed are Thy servants
>   and worshippers.
> Yet is not Thy glory diminished by reason of those
>   that worship aught beside Thee,
> For the yearning of them all is to draw nigh to Thee.
> But they are like the blind,
> Setting their faces forward on the King's highway,
> Yet still wandering from the path,
> One sinketh into the well of a pit
> And another falleth into a snare,
> But all imagine they have reached their desire,
> Albeit they have suffered in vain.
>
> SOLOMON IBN-GABIROL

Of all the griefs that harass the distress'd,
Sure the most bitter is a scornful jest;
Fate never wounds more deep the generous
heart,
Than when a blockhead's insult points the dart.
SAMUEL JOHNSON

The best prayers have often more groans than words.   JOHN BUNYAN

The gem cannot be polished without friction, nor man perfected without trials.   CONFUCIUS

You've never wept while tasting bread?
Nor lain awake for agonizing nights,
Tossed, tormented, on your bed?
You know them not, these Heavenly Powers!
JOHANN WOLFGANG VON GOETHE

Man is neither angel nor brute, and his misery is that he who would act the angel acts the brute.   BLAISE PASCAL

See also: ADVERSITY; AFFLICTION; CHARACTER; COURAGE; DEATH; FAILURE; FEAR; GRACE; GRIEF; PATIENCE; PERSEVERANCE; PERSPECTIVE.

Truth

God offers to every mind its choice between truth and repose. Take which you please. You can never have both. Between these, as a pendulum, man oscillates. He in whom the love of repose predominates will accept the first creed, the first philosophy, the first political party he meets, most likely his father's. He gets rest, commodity and reputation; but he shuts the door of truth. He in whom the love of truth predominates will keep himself aloof from all moorings, and afloat. He will abstain from dogmatism, and recognize all the opposite negations between which, as walls, his being is swung. He submits to the inconvenience of suspense and imperfect opinion, but he is a candidate for truth, as the other is not, and respects the highest law of his being.   RALPH WALDO EMERSON

Truth is not only violated by falsehood; it may be equally outraged by silence.
                                            HENRI-FREDERIC AMIEL

Falsehood is cowardice, truth is courage.   HOSEA BALLOU

As scarce as truth is, the supply has always been in excess of the demand.
                                            JOSH BILLINGS

Man with his burning soul has but an hour of breath to build a ship of truth
in which his soul may sail—sail on the sea of death, for death takes toll of
beauty, courage, youth, of all but truth.   JOHN MASEFIELD

> Truth, crushed to earth, shall rise again;
> Th' eternal years of God are hers;
> But Error, wounded, writhes in pain,
> And dies among his worshippers.
>   WILLIAM CULLEN BRYANT

A man protesting against error is on the way toward uniting himself with all
men that believe in truth.   THOMAS CARLYLE

The broadminded see the truth in different religions; the narrowminded see
only the differences.   CHINESE PROVERB

I wish to regard myself as belonging not to a sect, but to the community of
free minds, of lovers of truth. I desire to escape the narrow walls of a particular church and to live under the open sky, in the broad light, looking far
and wide, seeing with my own eyes, hearing with my own ears and following truth meekly but resolutely, however arduous and solitary be the pass in
which she leads. I am then no organ of a sect, but speak for myself alone;
and I thank God that I live at a time, and under circumstances, which make
it my duty to lay open my whole mind with freedom and simplicity.
                                            WILLIAM ELLERY CHANNING

The grave of one who dies for truth is holy ground.   GERMAN PROVERB

Once to every man and nation comes the moment to decide,
In the strife of Truth with Falsehood, for the good or evil
  side. . . .
Truth forever on the scaffold, Wrong forever on the throne. . . .
Then to side with Truth is noble when we share her wretched
  crust,
Ere her cause bring fame and profit, and 'tis prosperous to
  be just;
Then it is the brave man chooses, while the coward stands
  aside. . . .

JAMES RUSSELL LOWELL

Truth is strong next to the Almighty.
She needs no policies, no stratagems, to make her victorious.
These are the shifts and the defenses that error uses against her power.
Give her but room, and do not bind her when she sleeps.
  So Truth be in the field, we do injuriously, but suppressing and prohibiting,
to misdoubt her strength.
  Let Truth and Falsehood grapple; whoever knew Truth put to the worse in
a free and open encounter!

JOHN MILTON

Great men's errors are to be venerated as more fruitful than little men's
truths.

FRIEDRICH NIETZSCHE

Truth never yet fell dead in the streets; it has such affinity with the soul of
man, the seed however broadcast will catch somewhere and produce its
hundredfold.

THEODORE PARKER

Truth often suffers more by the heat of its defenders, than from the arguments of its opposers.

WILLIAM PENN

He who tells a lie is not sensible how great a task he undertakes; for he
must be forced to invent twenty more to maintain that one.

ALEXANDER POPE

Search for truth is the noblest occupation of man, its publication a duty.

MADAME GERMAINE DE STAËL

If you shut your door to all errors truth will be shut out.

SIR RABINDRANATH TAGORE

One must not promise to give something to a child, and not give it to him, because thereby he is taught to lie. THE TALMUD

It takes two to speak the truth—one to speak, and another to hear.

HENRY DAVID THOREAU

> *See also:* ASPIRATION; CHARACTER; CONSCIENCE; DIVINE, THE; GRACE; IDEALS; INTEGRITY; LOVE; PROVIDENCE; RELIGION; SELF-KNOWL-EDGE; WISDOM.

Virtue

When one subdues men by force, they do not submit to him in heart, but because they are not strong enough to resist. When one subdues men by virtue, they are pleased to the heart's core, and sincerely submit.　MENCIUS

Better do a good deed near home, than travel a thousand miles to burn incense. CHINESE PROVERB

A man without virtue cannot long abide in adversity, nor can he long abide in happiness. CONFUCIUS

Hypocrisy is the homage which vice renders to virtue.

FRANCOIS LA ROCHEFOUCAULD

One on God's side is a majority. WENDELL PHILLIPS

Mankind can hardly be too often reminded, that there was once a man named Socrates, between whom and the legal authorities and public opinion of his time, there took place a memorable collision. Born in an age and country abounding in individual greatness, this man has been handed down to us by those who best knew both him and the age, as the most virtuous man in it; while *we* know him as the head and prototype of all subsequent teachers of virtue, the source equally of the lofty inspiration of Plato and the judicious utilitarianism of Aristotle, the two headsprings of ethical, as of all other, philosophy. This acknowledged master of all the eminent thinkers who have since lived—whose fame, still growing after more than two thousand years, all but outweighs the whole remainder of the names which make his native city illustrious—was put to death by his countrymen, after a judicial conviction, for impiety and immorality. Impiety, in denying the gods recognized by the State; indeed his accusers asserted (see the *Apologia)* that he believed in no gods at all. Immorality, in being, by his doctrines and instructions, a "corrupter of youth." Of these charges the tribunal, there is every ground for believing, honestly found him guilty, and condemned the man, who probably of all then born had deserved best of mankind, to be put to death as a criminal. JOHN STUART MILL

Any government is free to the people under it (whatever be the frame) where the laws rule, and the people are a party to those laws, and more than this is tyranny, oligarchy, or confusion. But lastly, when all is said, there is hardly one frame of government in the world so ill designed by its first founders that, in good hands, would not do well enough.

. . . Governments, like clocks, go from motion men give them; and as governments are made and moved by men, so by them they are ruined too. Wherefore governments rather depend upon men, than men upon governments. Let men be good, and the government cannot be bad; if it be ill, they will cure it. But if men be bad, let the government be never so good, they will endeavour to warp and spoil it to their turn. WILLIAM PENN

I have a contempt for a fugitive and cloistered virtue, unexercised and unbreathed, that never sallies out and sees her adversary, but slinks out of the race where that immortal garland is to be run for, not without dust and heat.
JOHN MILTON

The path of virtue is closed to no one, it lies open to all; it admits and invites all, whether they be free-born men, slaves or freedmen, kings or exiles; it requires no qualifications of family or property; it is satisfied with a mere man. SENECA

I am no herald to inquire into men's pedigree; it sufficeth me if I know their virtues. SIR PHILIP SIDNEY

See also: BEAUTY; BIBLE, THE; BLESSINGS; CHRISTIANITY; CONSCIENCE; DIVINE, THE; GOD; GRACE; IDEALS; INTEGRITY; JUDAISM; TRUTH.

Vision

The vision of things to be done may come a long time before the way of doing them appears clear. But woe to him who distrusts the vision.

JENKIN LLOYD JONES

The farther backward you can look, the farther forward you are likely to see.   WINSTON S. CHURCHILL

The Vision of God is the greatest happiness to which man can attain. Our imprisonment in bodies of clay and water and entanglement in the things of sense constitute a veil which hides the Vision of God from us.

AL-GHAZZALI

No one regards what is before his feet; we all gaze at the stars.

QUINTUS ENNIUS

Vision looks inward and becomes duty. Vision looks outward and becomes aspiration. Vision looks upward and becomes faith.   STEPHEN S. WISE

We travel together, passengers on a little spaceship, dependent upon its vulnerable reserves of air and soil; all committed for our safety to its security and peace; preserved from annihilation only by the care, the work, and —I will say—the love we give our fragile craft. We cannot maintain it—half fortunate, half miserable; half confident, half despairing; half slave to the ancient enemies of man, half free in a liberation of resources undreamed of until this day. No craft, no crew can travel safely with such vast contradictions. On their resolution depends the survival of us all.

ADLAI E. STEVENSON
[Recorded minutes before his death]

Your old men shall dream dreams, and your young men shall see visions.

THE BIBLE

The prophet and the martyr do not see the hooting throng. Their eyes are fixed on the eternities.   BENJAMIN N. CARDOZO

I have lived in the pursuit of a vision, both personal and social. Personal: to care for what is noble, for what is beautiful, for what is gentle; to allow moments of insight to give wisdom at more mundane times. Social: to see in imagination the society that is to be created, where individuals grow freely, and where hate and greed and envy die because there is nothing to nourish them.   BERTRAND RUSSELL

You can put two men to sleep in the same bed, but you can't make them dream the same dream.   CHINESE PROVERB

"The road is always better than the inn." These words by the great Spanish writer Cervantes mean a way of living. In my younger days, I often aimed too hard to reach some goal, finish some job. "When this is done," I'd say, "I shall find real satisfaction and reward."

But later I came to realize that each achievement, like each inn, is only a point along the road. The real goodness of living comes with the journey itself, with the striving and desire to keep moving. Now I find that I can look back on my 84 years [as of 1946] with pleasure and, what is even more important to me, that I can still look to the future with hope and desire. I have learned to take each inn along the way with a traveler's stride—not as a stopping point, but a starting point for some new and better endeavor.

                                    MAURICE MAETERLINCK

See also: ASPIRATION; BELIEF; BIBLE, THE; DIVINE, THE; GENIUS; GOD; GRACE; IDEALS; INSPIRATION; MYSTERY; PRAYER; RELIGION.

War

War some day will be abolished by the will of man. This assertion does not in any way invalidate the truth that war is fundamentally caused by impersonal, political, economic and social forces. But it is the destiny of man to master and control such force, even as it is his destiny to harness rivers, chain the lightning and ride the storm. It is human will, operating under social forces, that has abolished slavery, infanticide, duelling, and a score of other social enormities. Why should it not do the same for war?

                                    JOHN HAYNES HOLMES

There has never been a kingdom given to so many civil wars as that of Christ.   MONTESQUIEU

As never before, the essence of war is fire, famine and pestilence. They contribute to its outbreak; they are among its weapons; they become its consequences. When people speak to you about a preventive war, you tell them to go and fight it. After my experience, I have come to hate war. War settles nothing.   DWIGHT D. EISENHOWER

One of the most remarkable things about war, as Thucydides has remarked, is that it takes away your freedom and puts you in a region of necessity. You may choose whether or not to fight, but once fighting, your power of choice is gone.   GILBERT MURRAY

What we now need to discover in the social realm is the moral equivalent of war: something heroic that will speak to men as universally as war does, and yet will be as compatible with their spiritual selves as war has proved itself to be incompatible.   WILLIAM JAMES

Oh, Lord Our Father, our young patriots, idols of our hearts, go forth to battle. Be Thou near them! With them—in spirit—we also go from the sweet peace of our beloved firesides to smite the foe.

Oh, Lord our God, help us to tear their soldiers to bloody shreds with our shells; help us to cover their smiling fields with the pale forms of their patriot dead; help us to drown the thunder of the guns with the wounded, writhing in pain; help us to lay waste their humble homes with the hurricane of fire; help us to wring the hearts of their unoffending widows with unavailing grief; help us to turn them out roofless with their little children to wander unfriended over wastes of their desolated land in rags and hunger and thirst, sport of the sun-flames of summer and the icy winds of winter, broken in spirit, worn with travail, imploring Thee for the refuge of the grave and denied it—for our sakes, who adore Thee, Lord, blast their hopes, blight their lives, protract their bitter pilgrimage, make heavy their steps, water their way with their tears, stain the white snow with the blood of their wounded feet! We ask of One who is the spirit of Love and Who is the ever-faithful refuge and friend of all that are sore beset, and seek His aid with humble and contrite hearts. Grant our prayer, Oh Lord, and thine shall be the praise and honor and glory, now and forever, Amen.   MARK TWAIN

All the talk of history is of nothing almost but fighting and killing, and the honor and renown which are bestowed on conquerors, who, for the most part, are mere butchers of mankind, mislead growing youth, who, by these means, come to think slaughter the most laudable business of mankind, and the most heroic of virtues.　　　　　　　　　　　　　　　　　JOHN LOCKE

War is a profession by which a man cannot live honorably; an employment by which the soldier, if he would reap any profit, is obliged to be false, rapacious, and cruel!　　　　　　　　　　　　NICCOLO MACHIAVELLI

The tragedy of war is that it uses man's best to do man's worst.
　　　　　　　　　　　　　　　　　　HARRY EMERSON FOSDICK

More than an end of war, we want an end to the beginnings of all wars—yes, an end to this brutal, inhuman and thoroughly impractical method of settling the differences between governments.　　　FRANKLIN D. ROOSEVELT

Break Thou the spell of enchantments that make the nations drunk with the lust of battle and draw them on as willing tools of death. Grant us a quiet and steadfast mind when our own nation clamors for vengeance and aggression. O Thou strong Father of all nations, draw all Thy great family together with an increasing sense of our common blood and destiny, that peace may come on earth at last, and Thy sun may shed its light rejoicing on a holy brotherhood of peoples.　　　　　　　　WALTER RAUSCHENBUSCH

I join with you most cordially in rejoicing at the return of peace [1783]. I hope it will be lasting, and that mankind will at length, as they call themselves reasonable creatures, have reason enough to settle their differences without cutting throats; for, in my opinion, there never was a good war or a bad peace. What vast additions to the conveniences and comforts of life might mankind have acquired, if the money spent in wars had been employed in works of utility! What an extension of agriculture, even to the tops of the mountains; what rivers rendered navigable, or joined by canals; what bridges, aqueducts, new roads, and other public works, edifices and improvements, rendering England a complete paradise, might not have been obtained by spending those millions in doing good, which in the last war have been spent in doing mischief—in bringing misery into thousands of families, and destroying the lives of so many working people, who might have performed the useful labors.　　　　　　　BENJAMIN FRANKLIN

See also: ADVERSITY; AFFLICTION; AMBITION; DEATH; DEMOCRACY; DISSENT; INTERNATIONALISM; LIBERTY; PEACE; RACIAL JUSTICE.

Wealth

Lay not up for yourselves treasures upon earth, where moth and rust doth corrupt, and where thieves break through and steal:

But lay up for yourselves treasures in heaven, where neither moth nor rust doth corrupt, and where thieves do not break through nor steal:

For where your treasure is, there will your heart be also.

The light of the body is the eye: if therefore thine eye be single, thy whole body shall be full of light.

But if thine eye be evil, thy whole body shall be full of darkness. If therefore the light that is in thee be darkness, how great is that darkness!

No man can serve two masters: for either he will hate the one, and love the other; or else he will hold to the one, and despise the other. Ye cannot serve God and mammon. THE BIBLE

Money may buy the husk of things, but not the kernel. It brings you food but not appetite, medicine but not health, acquaintances but not friends, servants but not faithfulness, days of joy but not peace of happiness.

HENRIK IBSEN

Poverty is the load of some, and wealth the load of others, perhaps the greater load of the two. It may weigh them to perdition. Bear the load of thy neighbor's poverty, and let him bear with thee the load of thy wealth. Thou lightenest thy load by lightening his. SAINT AUGUSTINE

Nothing is more fallacious than wealth. Today it is for thee, tomorrow it is against thee. It arms the eyes of the envious everywhere. It is a hostile comrade, a domestic enemy. SAINT JOHN CHRYSOSTOM

Look to your health; and if you have it, praise God, and value it next to a good conscience; for health is the second blessing that we mortals are capable of; a blessing that money cannot buy. IZAAK WALTON

Of two good men, the better is not the richer in property, any more than of two good pilots you will call him better who owns the finer ship. SENECA

The devil comes where money is; where it is not he comes twice.

SWEDISH PROVERB

He who loves gold is a fool; he who fears it, is a slave; he who adores it, an idolater; he who hoards it up, a dunce; he who uses it, is the wise man.

OLD FARMER'S ALMANAC

Few of us can stand prosperity. Another man's, I mean.   MARK TWAIN

> I care for riches to make gifts
> To friends, or lead a sick man back to health
> With ease and plenty. Else small aid is wealth
> For daily gladness; once a man be done
> With hunger, rich and poor are all as one.
>
> EURIPIDES

See also: ACHIEVEMENT; AMBITION; BLESSINGS; GIVING; WORK.

Wisdom

To make no mistakes is not in the power of man; but from their errors and mistakes the wise and good learn wisdom for the future.   PLUTARCH

The arts are the servants of life: wisdom its master.   SENECA

> The wise man could ask no more of Fate
> Than to be simple, modest, manly, true,
> Safe from the Many, honored by the Few;
> To count as naught in World, or Church, or State;
> But inwardly in secret to be great.
>
> JAMES RUSSELL LOWELL

A knife of the keenest steel requires the whetstone and the wisest man needs advice.   ZOROASTER

When anger rises, think of the consequences.   CONFUCIUS

Happy is the man that findeth wisdom, and the man that getteth understanding.   SOLOMON

Man is but a reed—the weakest thing in nature—but he is a reed that thinks.
It is not necessary that the whole universe should arm itself to crush him. A
vapor, a drop of water, is enough to kill him. But if the universe should crush
him, man would still be nobler than that which slays him, for he knows that
he dies; but of the advantage which it has over him the universe knows
nothing. Our dignity consists, then, wholly in thought. Our elevation must
come from this, not from space and time, which we cannot fill. Let us, then,
labor to think well: that is the fundamental principle of morals.

                                                            BLAISE PASCAL

A man should never be ashamed to own he has been in the wrong, which
is but saying in other words that he is wiser today than he was yesterday.

                                                            ALEXANDER POPE

The first key to wisdom is assiduous and frequent questioning. For by
doubting we come to inquiry, and by inquiry we arrive at truth.

                                                            PETER ABELARD

Common sense in an uncommon degree is what the world calls wisdom.
                                                    SAMUEL TAYLOR COLERIDGE

Wisdom is the principal thing; therefore, get wisdom: and with all thy getting get understanding.   THE BIBLE

When the wise is angry, he is wise no longer.   THE TALMUD

The whole secret of remaining young in spite of years, and even of gray
hairs, is to cherish enthusiasm in oneself, by poetry, by contemplation, by
charity—that is, in fewer words, by the maintenance of harmony in the soul.
When everything is in its right place within us, we ourselves are in equilib-
rium with the whole work of God. Deep and grave enthusiasm for the
eternal beauty and the eternal order, reason touched with emotion and a
serene tenderness of heart—these surely are the foundations of wisdom.

                                                    HENRI-FREDERIC AMIEL

God, give us grace to accept with serenity the things that cannot be changed, courage to change the things that should be changed, and the wisdom to distinguish the one from the other. REINHOLD NIEBUHR

All that we are is the result of what we have thought; it is founded on our thoughts, it is made up of our thoughts. If a man speaks or acts with an evil thought, pain follows him, as the wheel follows the foot of him who draws the carriage. BUDDHA

See also: AGE; ASPIRATION; BIBLE, THE; BOOKS; DIVINE, THE; EDUCATION; GENIUS; GRACE; INSPIRATION; KNOWLEDGE; RELIGION; TRUTH.

Woman

I am a full and firm believer in the revelation that it is through woman that the race is to be redeemed. And it is because of this faith that I ask [in 1875] for her immediate and unconditional emancipation from all political, industrial, social and religious subjection.

Ralph Waldo Emerson says, "Men are what their mothers made them." But I say, to hold mothers responsible for the character of their sons while you deny them any control over the surroundings of their lives, is worse than mockery, it is cruelty! Responsibilities grow out of rights and powers. Therefore, before mothers can be held responsible for the vices and crimes, the wholesale demoralization of men, they must possess all possible rights and powers to control the conditions and circumstances of their own and their children's lives. SUSAN B. ANTHONY

The universal social pressure upon women to be all alike, and do all the same things, and to be content with identical restrictions, has resulted not only in terrrible suffering in the lives of exceptional women, but also in the loss of unmeasured feminine values in special gifts. The Drama of the Woman of Genius has been too often a tragedy of misshapen and perverted power. Col. [Thomas Wentworth] Higginson said that one of the great histories yet to be written is that of the intellectual life of women. When that is accomplished, those truly great women whose initiative was choked by false ideals of feminine excellence, whose natures were turned awry for want of "space to burgeon out their powers," whose very purpose to "aggrandize the human mind by cultivating their own" was made a cross for their crucifixion, will be given just honor. ANNA GARLIN SPENCER

Recent studies in heredity, including the work on Mendel's law, seem to me to show conclusively that boys and girls inherit equally from both mothers and fathers in mathematical proportion, that a woman's place in the inheritance and transmission of physical and mental and moral qualities is precisely the same as a man's, that she is discriminated against in no way.

M. CAREY THOMAS

> God in her harmony has equal ends
> For cedar that resists and reed that bends;
> For good it is a woman sometimes rules,
> Holds in her hand the power, and manners, schools,
> And laws, and mind; succeeding master proud,
> With gentle voice and smiles she leads the crowd,
> The somber human troop.

VICTOR HUGO

I long to hear that you have declared an independency [by legislation in the first Continental Congress]. And in the new code of laws which I suppose it will be necessary for you to make, I desire you would remember the ladies, and be more generous and favorable to them than your ancestors. . . . If particular care and attention is not paid to the ladies, we are determined to foment a rebellion and will not hold ourselves bound by any laws in which we have no voice or representation.

ABIGAIL ADAMS
[In letter to her husband, John Adams]

It is the duty of a government to do all in its power to promote the present and future prosperity of the nation over which it is placed. This prosperity will depend on the character of its citizens. The characters of these will be formed by their mothers; and it is through the mothers that the government can control the characters of its future citizens, to form them such as will ensure their country's prosperity. If this is the case, then it is the duty of our present legislators to begin now, to form the characters of the next generation, by controlling that of the females, who are to be their mothers, while it is yet with them a season of improvement.

EMMA HART WILLARD

I would have woman lay aside all thought, such as she habitually cherishes, of being taught and led by men. I would have her free from compromise, from complaisance, from helplessness, because I would have her good enough and strong enough to love one and all beings, from the fullness, not the poverty of being.

MARGARET FULLER

A hundred men can build an encampment, but it takes a woman to make a home.   CHINESE PROVERB

There is no worse evil than a bad woman; and nothing has ever been produced better than a good one.   EURIPIDES

We seek a new fusion of spirit and body that can bring upon man's humanization all the powers which he has won through his world-transcending *élan*. Our model is neither that of the romanticized primitive jungle, nor the modern technological wasteland. Rather it expresses itself in a new command to learn to cultivate the garden, for the cultivation of the garden is where the powers of the rational consciousness come together with the harmonies of nature in partnership. . . .

The revolution of the feminine revolts against the denatured Babel of concrete and steel that obliterates the living soil. But it does not merely reject the spirit-child born from the earth, but seeks to reclaim spirit for body and body for spirit in a messianic epiphany of the Body of God.

ROSEMARY RUETHER

O Woman! in our hours of ease
Uncertain, coy, and hard to please,
And variable as the shade
By the light quivering aspen made;
When pain and anguish wring the brow,
A ministering angel thou!

SIR WALTER SCOTT

The buckling on of a knight's armor by his lady's hand was not a mere caprice of romantic fashion. It is the type of an eternal truth that the soul's armor is never well set to the heart unless a woman's hand has braced it, and it is only when she braces it loosely that the honor of manhood fails.

JOHN RUSKIN

Men make the roads; but it is the women who teach children how to walk in them.   FRENCH PROVERB

See also: BEAUTY; BEING; BLESSINGS; CHURCH, THE; FAMILY; GOD; LIFE; LOVE; MAN; MARRIAGE; MYSTERY; SOUL.

Wonder

Two things fill the mind with ever new and increasing admiration and awe, the oftener and more steadily we reflect on them: the starry heavens above and the moral law within. I have not to search for them and conjecture them as though they were veiled in darkness or were in the transcendent region beyond my horizon; I see them before me and connect them directly with the consciousness of my existence.   IMMANUEL KANT

When we observe the needle of the mariner, without visible organ, or sense of faculty, pointing with a trembling and pious fidelity to the unseen pole, and guiding, no one favored people only, but all nations, at all times, across a wilderness of waters, so that a ship sails forth from one shore and strikes the narrowest inlet or bay on the other side of the globe, why ought we not to be filled with awe as reverential and as religious as though we had seen the pillar of cloud by day, and of fire by night, which led the children of Israel in their journey through the wilderness?   HORACE MANN

The greatest insights happen to us in moments of awe.

ABRAHAM JOSHUA HESCHEL

Standing at the masthead of my ship during a sunrise that crimsoned sky and sea, I once saw a large herd of whales in the east, all heading towards the sun, and for a moment vibrating in concert with peaked flukes.

As it seemed to me at the time, such a grand embodiment of adoration of the gods was never beheld, even in Persia, the home of the fire worshippers.

As Ptolemy Philopator testified of the African elephant, I then testified of the whale, pronouncing him the most devout of all beings. For according to King John, the military elephants of antiquity often hailed the morning with their trunks uplifted in the profoundest silence.   HERMAN MELVILLE

The man who cannot wonder is but a pair of spectacles behind which there is no eye.   THOMAS CARLYLE

Consider this bee: five eyes—three simple ones on top of the head, two compound ones with thousands of lenses; five thousand nostrils—enough to smell an apple tree half a mile away; two sets of wings—which can be hooked together in flight, so that they flap as one: 16,000 times each moment, twenty miles an hour, seven miles, nonstop.

No matter how zigzag the dizzy dance, always that beeline straight home to the all-important hive and the next big job to be done there. Acting as street cleaners, water carriers, nurses, sentries, masons, engineers, air conditioners, electric fans—often fanning twelve hours at a stretch, indoors; on top of twelve hours of gathering honey, outdoors. All that dipping into dandelions and blossoms in obedience to God's holy ordinance that "while the earth remaineth, seedtime and harvest shall not cease." This is a beautiful business, expertly done.

A mere mortal feels almost a heartbreak, however, over the discovery that to make one pound of honey one bee would need to travel 50,000 miles, more than twice the distance round the globe. And, actually, a single teaspoon of honey in six weeks is a bee's entire life quota. But his buzz is not a grumble, merely his motor working overtime.   MARGARET T. APPLEGARTH

[The scientist's] religious feeling takes the form of a rapturous amazement at the harmony of natural law, which reveals an intelligence of such superiority that, compared with it, all the systematic thinking and acting of human beings is an utterly insignificant reflection. This feeling is the guiding principle of his life and work, insofar as he succeeds in keeping himself from the shackles of selfish desire. It is beyond question closely akin to that which has possessed the religious geniuses of all ages.   ALBERT EINSTEIN

We have loved the stars too fondly to be fearful of the night.
INSCRIPTION IN CRYPT OF ALLEGHENY
OBSERVATORY, UNIVERSITY OF PITTSBURGH

The world will never starve for want of wonders.   GILBERT K. CHESTERTON

Who can number the sand of the sea, and the drops of rain, and the days of eternity?   THE APROCRYPHA

See also: BEAUTY; GOD; MYSTERY; PRAYER.

Work

The work an unknown good man has done is like a vein of water flowing hidden underground, secretly making the ground green.   THOMAS CARLYLE

Excellence is never granted to man, but as the reward of labor. It argues, indeed, no small strength of mind to persevere in the habits of industry, without the pleasure of perceiving those advantages which, like the hands of a clock, whilst they make hourly approaches to their point, yet proceed so slowly as to escape observation.   SIR JOSHUA REYNOLDS

The man who rolls up his shirt sleeves is rarely in danger of losing his shirt.
                                                                                                                    ANONYMOUS

But before virtue the immortal gods have put the sweat of man's brow.
                                                                                                                    HESIOD

If you want knowledge, you must toil for it; if food, you must toil for it; and if pleasure, you must toil for it. Toil is the law. Pleasure comes through toil, and not by self-indulgence and indolence. When one gets to love work, his life is a happy one.   JOHN RUSKIN

Light is the task where many share the toil.   HOMER

Thank God every morning when you get up that you have something to do which must be done, whether you like it or not. Being forced to work, and forced to do your best, will breed in you temperance and self-control, diligence and strength of will, cheerfulness and content, and a hundred virtues which the idle never know.   CHARLES KINGSLEY

The gods sell all things at the price of toil.   ANCIENT GREEK PROVERB

Nothing is so fatiguing as the eternal hanging on of an uncompleted task.
                                                                                                                    WILLIAM JAMES

Genius may conceive, but patient labor must consummate.   HORACE MANN

See also: ACHIEVEMENT; AMBITION; ASPIRATION; CHARACTER; RESPONSIBILITY; WEALTH.

Worry

It is not work that kills men; it is worry. Work is healthy; you can hardly put more upon a man than he can bear. Worry is rust upon the blade. It is not the revolution that destroys the machinery, but the friction. Fear secretes acids; but love and trust are sweet juices. HENRY WARD BEECHER

To carry care to bed is to sleep with a pack on your back.

THOMAS C. HALIBURTON

Worry is an old man with bended head,
Carrying a load of feathers
Which he thinks are lead.

ANONYMOUS

Worry often gives a small thing a big shadow. SWEDISH PROVERB

Each day has its care, but each care has its day. ANCIENT PROVERB

To believe a business impossible, is the way to make it so. How many feasible projects have miscarried through despondency and been strangled in the birth by a cowardly imagination. JEREMY COLLIER

Never bear more than one trouble at a time. Some people bear three kinds—all they have ever had, all they have now, and all they expect to have.

EDWARD EVERETT HALE

Little minds have little worries, big minds have no time for worries.

RALPH WALDO EMERSON

See also: ADVERSITY; AFFLICTION; AGE; DOUBT; FEAR; PRAYER; WISDOM.

Worship

The gods we worship write their names on our faces, be sure of that. And a man will worship something—have no doubt about that, either. He may think that his tribute is paid in secret in the dark recesses of his heart—but it will out. That which dominates will determine his life and character. Therefore, it behooves us to be careful what we worship, for what we are worshipping we are becoming.   RALPH WALDO EMERSON

Without a poignant consciousness of the goods of life, in all their freshness and intensity, without some daily glimpse of beauty, some expression of tenderness and stir of passion, some release in gaiety and laughter, some quickening of rhythm and music, our very humanity is not safe. To summon up the courage to go through our daily tasks, above all in a Time of Troubles, where no goals can be reached without sacrifice, we must remind ourselves, by conscious daily dedication, of the goods we desire and value. This dedication is perhaps the psychological core of prayer; and every concrete expression of the good, in a song or symphony, a poem or a loving embrace, has some of the quality of prayer.   LEWIS MUMFORD

O, Lord, grant us to love Thee; grant that we may love those that love Thee; grant that we may do the deeds that win Thy love. Make the love of Thee be dearer to us than ourselves, than our families, than wealth and even than cool water.   MOHAMMED

O God, if I worship Thee from fear of Hell, burn me in Hell, and if I worship Thee from hope of Paradise, shut me out of Paradise; but if I worship Thee for Thine own sake, then withhold not Thine everlasting beauty.   RABIAH

The camel always kneels when drinking from the streams of Allah, and kneels also to receive his burden for the day.   ARAB PROVERB

Give us the unchanging bravery of the pine, that we too may face the storms of life unconquered and unafraid. Give us the courage of the plum to flower gloriously in the midst of bleak adversity. And give to us throughout the years the straight, tough fiber and resilience of the green bamboo. *Amen.*
                     JAPANESE PRAYER

Evening after evening in the summer, I have gone to see the white clover fall asleep in the meadow.

Kneeling and looking very closely, one sees the two lower leaves on each stalk gently approach one another like little hands that were going to clap but thought better of it, and at last lie folded quietly as though for prayer.

Then the upper leaf droops, as a child's face might, until it rests on the others.

Everywhere in the dusk the white clover leaves are sleeping in a attitude of worship. MARY WEBB

If you are too busy to pray, you are too busy. ANONYMOUS

Glory be to God for dappled things—
        For skies of couple-color as a brindled cow;
                For rose-moles all in stipple upon trout that swim;
Fresh-firecoal chestnut-falls; finches' wings;
        Landscape plotted and pieced-fold, fallow, and plough;
                And all trades, their gear and tackle and trim.

All things counter, original, spare, strange;
        Whatever is fickle, freckled (who knows how?)
                With swift, slow, sweet, sour—adazzle, dim;
He fathers-forth whose beauty is past change:
        Praise Him.

GERARD MANLEY HOPKINS

See also: ASPIRATION; BELIEF; BIBLE, THE; DIVINE, THE; FAITH; GOD; GRACE; MYSTERY; PRAYER; RELIGION; REVERENCE; SOLITUDE.

Youth

Youth, though it may lack knowledge, is certainly not devoid of intelligence; it sees through shams with sharp and terrible eyes. H. L. MENCKEN

Youths will never live to age unless they keep themselves in breath by exercise, and in heart by joyfulness. Too much thinking doth consume the spirits; and oft it falls out, that while one thinks too much of doing, he fails to do the effect of his thinking. SIR PHILIP SIDNEY

Denunciation of the young is a necessary part of the hygiene of older people and greatly assists in the circulation of their blood.   LOGAN PEARSALL SMITH

Remember now thy Creator in the days of thy youth, while the evil days come not, nor the years draw nigh, when thou shalt say, I have no pleasure in them;

While the sun, or the light, or the moon, or the stars, be not darkened, nor the clouds return after the rain:

In the day when the keepers of the house shall tremble, and the strong men shall bow themselves, and the grinders cease because they are few, and those that look out of the windows be darkened,

And the doors shall be shut in the streets, when the sound of the grinding is low, and he shall rise up at the voice of the bird, and all the daughters of music shall be brought low;

Also when they shall be afraid of that which is high, and fears shall be in the way, and the almond tree shall flourish, and the grasshopper shall be a burden, and desire shall fail: because man goeth to his long home, and the mourners go about the streets:

Or ever the silver cord be loosed, or the golden bowl be broken, or the pitcher be broken at the fountain, or the wheel broken at the cistern.

Then shall the dust return to the earth as it was: and the spirit shall return unto God who gave it.   THE BIBLE

It is as natural and as right for a young man to be imprudent and exaggerated, to live in swoops and circles, and beat about his cage like any other wild thing newly captured, as it is for old men to turn grey, or mothers to love their offspring, or heroes to die for something worthier than their lives.
                                        ROBERT LOUIS STEVENSON

A conservative young man has wound up his life before it was unreeled. We expect old men to be conservative; but when a nation's young men are so, its funeral bell is already rung.   HENRY WARD BEECHER

When I shall be divorced, some ten years hence,
From this poor present self which I am now;
When youth has done its tedious vain expense
Of passions that forever ebb and flow;
Shall I not joy youth's heats are left behind,
And breathe more happy in an even clime?
Ah no! for then I shall begin to find

A thousand virtues in this hated time.
Then I shall wish its agitations back,
And all its thwarting currents of desire;
Then I shall praise the heat which then I lack,
And call this hurrying fever, generous fire,
And sigh that one thing only has been lent
To youth and age in common—discontent.

MATTHEW ARNOLD

You need repent none of your youthful vagaries. They may have been over the score on one side, just as those of age are probably over the score on the other. But they had a point; they not only befitted your age and expressed its attitude and passions, but they had a relation to what was outside of you, and implied criticisms on the existing state of things, which you need not allow to have been undeserved, because you now see that they were partial. All error, not merely verbal, is a strong way of stating that the current truth is incomplete. Their most antisocial acts indicate the defects of our society. When the torrent sweeps the man against a boulder, you must expect him to scream, and you need not be surprised if the scream is sometimes a theory. Shelley, chafing at the Church of England, discovered the cure of all evils in universal atheism. Generous lads, irritated at the injustices of society, see nothing for it but the abolishment of everything and Kingdom Come of anarchy. Shelley was a young fool; so are these cocksparrow revolutionaries. But it is better to be a fool than to be dead. It is better to emit a scream in the shape of a theory than to be entirely insensible to the jars and incongruities of life and take everything as it comes in a forlorn stupidity. Some people swallow the universe like a pill; they travel on through the world, like smiling images pushed from behind. For God's sake give me the young man who has brains enough to make a fool of himself!

ROBERT LOUIS STEVENSON

Bestow thy youth so that thou mayest have comfort to remember it when it hath forsaken thee, and not sigh and grieve at the account thereof. While thou art young thou wilt think it will never have an end; but the longest day hath its evening, and thou shalt enjoy it but once; it never turns again; use it therefore as the spring-time, which soon departeth, and wherein thou oughtest to plant and sow all provisions for a long and happy life.

SIR WALTER RALEIGH

Youth is the period of building up in habits, and hopes, and faiths. Not an hour but is trembling with destinies; not a moment, once passed, of which the appointed work can ever be done again, or the neglected blow struck on the cold iron.   JOHN RUSKIN

Youth is a wonderful thing. What a crime to waste it on children.

GEORGE BERNARD SHAW

Young men are as apt to think themselves wise enough, as drunken men are to think themselves sober enough. They look upon spirit to be a much better thing than experience, which they call coldness. They are but half mistaken; for though spirit without experience is dangerous, experience without spirit is languid and ineffective.

EARL OF CHESTERFIELD

See also: AGE; CHARACTER; DOUBT; EDUCATION; FAITH; HAPPINESS; INSPIRATION; MATURITY; NONCONFORMITY; PERSPECTIVE; SELF-KNOWLEDGE; VISION.

INDEX OF AUTHORS

Pha

a